LONG BEACH and LOS ANGELES

This aerial of both harbors, San Pedro and Port of Los Angeles on the left, Long Beach and Long Beach Harbor on the right, was taken in 1983. Courtesy, Long Beach Harbor Department

LONG BEACH and LOS ANGELES

A Tale of Two Ports

CHARLES F. QUEENAN

Partners in Progress by Stephen T. Sato

Produced in cooperation with the Marine Exchange of Los Angeles/Long Beach Harbor

Windsor Publications, Inc.
Northridge, CA

To
The Port of Long Beach
on the occasion of its
75th anniversary

Windsor Publications, Inc.—History Book Division

Publisher: John M. Phillips
Editorial Director: Teri Davis Greenberg
Design Director: Alexander D'Anca

Staff for *Long Beach and Los Angeles: A Tale of Two Ports*
Senior Editor: Michelle Hudun
Director, Corporate Biographies: Karen Story
Assistant Director, Corporate Biographies: Phyllis Gray
Editor, Corporate Biographies: Judith Hunter
Editorial Assistants: Kathy M. Brown, Laura Cordova, Marcie Goldstein, Marilyn Horn, Pat Pittman, Sharon Volz
Designer: Christina McKibbin
Layout Artist, Text: Ellen Ifrah
Layout Artist, Corporate Biographies: Mari Catherine Preimesberger
Sales Representatives, Corporate Biographies: Jacquie Carroll, Sandy Israel, Elaine Weiler, Mary Beth West

Published 1986
Printed in the United States of America
First Edition

Library of Congress Cataloging-in-Publication Data

Queenan, Charles F.
Long Beach and Los Angeles.

Bibliography: p.
Includes index.
1. Harbors—California—Long Beach—History. 2. Port of Long Beach—History. 3. Harbors—California—Los Angeles—History. I. Title.
HE554.L6Q44 1986 387.1'09794'93 86-5644
ISBN 0-89781-178-X

Endpapers
Depicted is a circa 1910 view across the main channel at Nob Hill, which was later leveled to make way for commercial development. At right is one of the Terminal Island canneries. Courtesy, Historical Society of Long Beach

CONTENTS

PREFACE

To the true history buff who considers recorded events and people who inhabited the real world fully as interesting and absorbing as any fiction, the story of the growth of the two world-class ports on the Bay of San Pedro is a fascinating one.

The first—and older by a couple of centuries—was pressured into expansion by the demands of a swelling population center which it served, despite serious navigational shortcomings such as water less than two feet deep and a network of shifting sandbars.

The other was fully content to operate as a seaside resort and let the port across the bay serve them as well, until the dynamics of municipal growth and the vision of its leaders dictated that Long Beach should have a harbor of its own.

From the most diverse of origins, both survived near-disastrous events to emerge as side-by-side competitors for the lion's share of the multi-billion-dollar West Coast maritime trade, each completely independent of the other in ownership and operation, even though the two ports form one continuous harbor around the crest of the bay.

The research for this book was a history lover's delight, transporting one back easily and effortlessly to the halcyon days of the great ranchos and the missions, and the gala fiestas that marked that colorful era of Spanish and Mexican occupancy before California became part of the Union.

A number of people made that research easier by their assistance and cooperation, and I would like to express my thanks to them here for their help on this project. A genial gentleman named Ray Berbower, recently retired as assistant chief harbor engineer for the Port of Long Beach and one of its leading in-house historians for years, was especially generous of his time and vivid in his recollections of the post-World War II period in that port.

Elmar Baxter, a longtime veteran in the Public Affairs Department at the Port of Long Beach and an author in his own right, expended a great deal of time and effort in providing background information and many of the historic photographs in this book. Zona Gale Forbes, archivist at the Long Beach Historical Society, spent many hours resurrecting, dating, and giving information on old photographs from her own vast storehouse of knowledge about Long Beach's early history. The society will be fortunate indeed if it ever finds anyone with Mrs. Forbes' dedication and enthusiasm to succeed her in the years to come.

My good friend, Ernest Marquez, another author whose ancestors once owned part of the original rancho that borders on the Santa Monica shore, was most generous with advice and additional photographs from his personal collection. Lee Zitko and Glenn Hughes of the Los Angeles Harbor Department were also very helpful, as was another old friend, Bill Oleson of San Pedro.

And last but far from least, my deepest gratitude to my dear wife Beverly for her patience and understanding during the countless warm, sunny weekends when she could have found many better things to do than sit and watch me bending over a typewriter.

Charles F. Queenan
Huntington Beach, California
May 1986

The Vincent Thomas Bridge is pictured in the early 1960s. Courtesy, Los Angeles Harbor Department

The Pilgrim, *of* Two Years Before the Mast *fame, was a 180-ton brig owned by Bryant & Sturgis that sailed from Boston in 1834 under Captain Francis A. Thompson. Richard Henry Dana spent a year with the* Pilgrim *crew before he was sickened by Thompson's brutal flogging of two seamen while the ship was anchored off San Pedro and had himself transferred to another Bryant & Sturgis ship, the* Alert. Pilgrim *was later destroyed by fire off the coast of North Carolina. Courtesy, Security Pacific National Bank Photograph Collection/Los Angeles Public Library*

C H A P T E R I

DISCOVERY

That suffocating, primeval fear of what might lie beyond the horizon had been conquered. Indeed, it was the greatest era of discovery and enlightenment in recorded history, when men of uncommon courage and vision were steadily adding astonishing new dimensions to the outer limits of the known world.

Christopher Columbus had already completed his monumental passage to the North American continent, and now, fifty years later and more than 3,000 wilderness miles away, another intrepid explorer sailed north along the other side of that enormous landmass on still another voyage of search and conquest for Spain.

This was the Portuguese navigator Juan Rodriguez Cabrillo, sent by Don Antonio de Mendoza, first Viceroy for New Spain, to locate the Northwest Passage to fabled Cathay, a route eagerly sought by France and England, as well as Spain. Cabrillo set sail on June 27, 1542, from Puerto de Navidad on Mexico's west coast, with his flagship *El Salvador,* which he owned, and *La Vittoria,* which had been built in Navidad.

Centuries would pass before his journey would be recognized as one of the most remarkable and productive for its duration in the annals of world exploration.

Cabrillo's small, hand-hewn caravels were poorly equipped to cope with the powerful ocean elements. After three months of bitter struggle against unrelenting head winds and high seas, the battered little ships and their exhausted crews finally sighted land. On September 28, 1542, Cabrillo and his men stepped ashore in an excellent natural harbor which he called San Miguel and a later Spanish expedition would rename San Diego. His log wasted no words: "A good port. Well enclosed."

After claiming possession under the Royal Standard of Spain, Cabrillo again sailed north, still battling those remorseless northwest winds every mile of the way. Less than a week later, *El Salvador* and *La Vittoria* sighted a pair of islands, which the commander promptly named after his gallant little vessels. Today, they are called San Clemente and Santa Catalina. Cabrillo and his men were greeted by a large band of friendly Indians, who welcomed them ashore.

The massive, irregular outline of what appeared to be another island loomed, mysterious and inviting, a scant twenty miles or so to the east, and a day later—October 8, 1542—Cabrillo's ships set sail for that distant shore. The ship's log records the events of that fateful day:

The Sunday following . . . they came to the

mainland in a large bay, which they named "Bahia de los Fumos" on account of the many smokes they saw there. Here they engaged in intercourse with some Indians they captured in a canoe. The bay is thirty-five degrees latitude; it is an excellent harbor and the country is good with many plains and groves of trees.

This entry bears explanation. The "smokes" came from fires which the Indians regularly used to drive small game into the open. "Captured" was scarcely the appropriate word to describe Cabrillo's non-violent contact with the gentle, childlike natives. Finally, Cabrillo had good reason to call this an "excellent" harbor. He saw immediately the exceptional natural protection afforded by the lofty peninsula on the north side of the crescent-shaped bay and the shelter it provided from the northwest gales that had made his own progress such a brutal ordeal.

This was the shallow mud flat that one day would be transformed into not one, but two of the busiest, most important and most profitable international ports in North America, sharing the same vast, continuous waterfront in direct competition with each other.

Cabrillo lingered only a day in the Bay of Smokes before hauling anchor and heading north, leaving the Indians to ponder and puzzle for the next sixty years over the visit of these strange, hirsute creatures with their beards and unusual clothes, and the huge, grotesque vessels that had brought them and carried them away.

Cabrillo's brilliant voyage of discovery was soon to end in tragedy, however. About two months later he broke his arm near the shoulder in a shipboard fall at San Miguel Island in the Santa Barbara Channel. Despite the pain he must have endured, he continued his explorations above present-day San Francisco before returning to San Miguel. With no effective medical treatment available, gangrene set in and the valiant seafarer died in agony on January 3, 1543.

Although the exact location of his grave is unknown, Cabrillo almost certainly was buried in San Miguel. In those times and in that environment, a man was interred where he fell—and quickly. The log of his voyage was found in Madrid centuries after his death, and only then did the significance of his extraordinary achievement become fully known.

The natives' next encounter with the white man in Bahia de los Fumos came on November 26, 1602, with the arrival of another Spanish expedition from Acapulco under the command of Sebastian Vizcaino, sailing for the Viceroy of Spain. Ferdinand Magellan had discovered the Philippines by then, and Vizcaino had orders to establish ports of refuge for the treasure-laden Spanish galleons returning from Manila to Panama.

Vizcaino's log called the bay "a very good *ensenada* with shelter from the northwest, west and southwest winds . . . ." With no known record of Cabrillo's earlier voyage at the time, Vizcaino named it *Ensenada de San Andres,* in the belief that November 26 was the feast day of that revered saint.

He was wrong, but the name remained in the official records for another 132 years, before the renowned Spanish pilot Cabrera Buena gave the bay its present name of San Pedro in honor of Saint Peter, the archbishop of Alexandria, who was martyred in A.D. 311.

The local Indians, who would later be commonly known as the Gabrielenos because they eventually came under the jurisdiction of the San Gabriel Mission, remained almost completely undisturbed during those centuries.

At the time of Cabrillo's arrival, a half-dozen or more Indian villages were scattered along the inner shore of the bay and the cliffs around Point Fermin, with others a little farther inland. Each was formed from related families comprising a single large clan, or groups of smaller clans who had banded together.

One of the largest and most important of

nearly a dozen villages on the north side of the bay was Suangna, located on a hillside above present-day Anaheim Street, and near the junction of several major Indian trails. The spot is now known as the Five Corners intersection of Gaffey and Anaheim streets, Vermont Avenue and Palos Verdes Drive North.

Farther south, around the sweeping curve of the bay, on the grounds of the present Rancho Los Alamitos, was the sacred Indian settlement of *Puvunga,* one of the holiest of the native "holy" villages in the area. This was where *Chungichnish,* the Indians' principal god, was born, according to Gabrieleno religious belief.

Not much is known of the Gabrieleno culture, but those few early observers whose journals were passed down seem to agree that they were small in stature, but muscular and well built. Records of those first visitors variously referred to the natives as handsome, friendly, highly intelligent, and among the most culturally advanced of all primitive American groups.

Although usually peaceful, the Gabrieleno would occasionally wage savage, all-out war, with one group of villages assaulting another group over some real or imagined transgression. More often they settled their disputes with nonviolent verbal exchanges, in which the opponents would vent their anger by singing insulting or obscene songs at each other.

However primitive, elements of the Gabrieleno lifestyle today are part of modern society. They took daily baths, slept on raised platforms instead of the ground, loved to socialize, gamble, and gossip, and exhibited exceptional skill in the creation of basketry, cooking implements, ceremonial items, hunting gear, paintings, and carvings. Like the neighboring Chumash tribe to the north, they were superb seamen and offshore fishermen, and had mastered the intricate construction of the planked skiff, as opposed to the rudimentary dugout and reed raft commonly used by other early North Americans.

In addition to the ocean fish that provided the main staple of diet, their swift, highly maneuverable boats enabled the Indians to travel easily along the coast and to the offshore islands, where they quarried soapstone to make their fine cooking pots, beads, ceremonial bowls, and exquisitely-carved miniatures of fish, seals, and whales.

It was a tranquil, idyllic existence for one of the more advanced and—until the Europeans came—fortunate of early American natives. The weather was eternally mild and beneficial; no glacial northern winters here. The dry desert climate would have made agriculture difficult, but the Gabrielenos' skill as hunter-gatherers, especially of seafood and the acorn, more than provided for their needs. Land was endless and forever, more than anyone could want, so there was no cause for dispute there. There was also ample time to meditate and contemplate the mysteries of religion, the universe, and the hereafter.

The fragile edifice of this simple pagan culture was never designed to withstand the intrusion of a driving, materialistic civilization whose values were completely incomprehensible to the aboriginal mind. The collapse and eventual degradation and extermination of that culture took place over a period of years, but its doom was sealed the moment Cabrillo set foot on Alta California. For the Spaniards it was a bright, promising beginning; for the Indians, a tragic, inevitable end.

As time passed it became obvious that Spain had better reaffirm and reinforce its claims to Alta California and the offshore islands if it intended to retain control of that territory. Francis Drake and his legendary *Golden Hinde* had landed on the upper California coast as early as 1579. Now the English were prowling the vast expanse of the Pacific Ocean, ever eager to add new trophies and outposts to their growing global empire. The Russians had crossed the north Pacific and were probing farther and farther down the coast.

Above
The south facade of the San Gabriel Mission, founded in 1771 as the fourth in the mission chain begun by Fra Junípero Serra, is pictured in the late 1880s with the small town that grew up around it. The San Gabriel fathers were the first traders in the Bay of San Pedro. Courtesy, Security Pacific National Bank Photograph Collection/Los Angeles Public Library

Opposite page
Pictured are the ruins of one of the first buildings in San Pedro – possibly the original hide house that was built circa 1818 by the San Gabriel Mission fathers and later acquired by Abel Stearns. Richard Henry Dana described it in detail in Two Years Before the Mast. *Courtesy, Los Angeles Harbor Department*

Accordingly, the Spanish launched their first overland expedition to colonize Alta California in 1769, headed by Gaspar de Portolá, then Governor of the Californias. One of his principal assignments was to take possession of what Vizcaino had considered the finest harbor north of San Diego. Vizcaino had named it El Puerto de Monte Rey for the Viceroy of New Spain, whose title was the Conde de Monterey.

Another purpose of the expedition on a more spiritual level was to establish a chain of missions along the coast of Alta California and bring Spain's own version of godliness and civilization to the natives, whether they wanted it or not. Charged with this formidable responsibility with the Portolá party was Junípero Serra, a tiny, fifty-six-year-old Franciscan priest from the Mediterranean island of Majorca. Barely five feet tall, lame, and in frail health, Serra's physical limitations never dampened an enormous dedication to his spiritual calling and a lion-hearted determination to spread the word of God among the resident pagan population.

Serra dedicated Mission San Diego de Alcala, the first in the chain in mid-1769. San Gabriel, the fourth one, was founded in 1771, and San Juan Capistrano became the sixth in the series in 1776. For the monks and priests, life at the missions was hard, the amenities non-existent, and their early years in Spain a distant and wistful memory.

To sustain these faraway outposts, supply ships sailed up from San Blas twice a year with a cargo of goods for the missions and military garrisons. For the return trip, they took on a load of hides and tallow, which the missions were producing in increasing quantities.

The shallow inlet called San Pedro was the designated point of exchange, and the mission *padres* from San Gabriel and San Juan Capistrano became the first traders in that historic bay.

As Father Serra and his hardy band of spiritual pioneers pushed the mission chain northward, Spain renewed its efforts to solidify its presence in the territory. Eleven families from the provinces of Sonora and Sinaloa made the seemingly endless, seven-month trek to a place near the Indian village of *Yang-na,* about twenty miles inland from San Pedro.

There the Spaniards built a cluster of huts as a primitive village, which they called *El Pueblo de Nuestra Señora La Reina de Los Angeles de Porciuncula* on September 4, 1781. Two centuries later, the tiny settlement would become the nucleus of the second largest concentration of population, employment, business, industry, and finance in the richest country in the world.

In 1784 three aging veterans of the Portolá expedition of 1769 were given huge land grants by Governor Pedro Fages for their devoted service to the Spanish crown. On sixty-five-year-old bachelor Juan José Domínguez, Fages conferred a grant of 74,000 acres. It was called Rancho San Pedro and included present-day Palos Verdes, Palos Verdes Estates, San Pedro, Torrance, Gardena, Compton, Redondo Beach, Wilmington, Lomita, Harbor City, and Carson.

Another vast expanse went to José María Verdugo, covering an area that is now Glendale

and parts of Burbank. By far the largest grant was given to Manuel Pérez Nieto, a 300,000-acre section adjoining Rancho San Pedro. It ran south around the bay and extended for miles inland and down the coast. Today that land is occupied by the City of Long Beach and a dozen surrounding communities.

These were the first of the great California ranchos, which became the focal point of one of the most colorful and exciting chapters in the early history of the region.

In the meantime the dusty little *pueblo* of Los Angeles continued to struggle along at a painfully slow rate. Three of its original founders had been ejected for being worthless during its first few years, and the other eight were given title to their land on the town's fifth anniversary. They and the *rancheros* with their gigantic land grants became the first landholders in California.

Livestock and agriculture, the latter thanks to the *padres'* skill at irrigating arid soil, became the principal activities at the ranchos and missions. Both soon became highly productive operations, with abundant crops and steadily increasing herds of cattle, horses, and sheep.

While beef and grain were put to immediate use, the ranchos and missions soon began to accumulate a tremendous stockpile of hides and tallow that they had no use for. Another unexpected native resource that soon became a valuable commodity was the soft, rich pelt of the sea otter, which inhabited the nearby kelp

Above
José Dolores Sepúlveda, a young Spanish officer who switched sides and fought for Mexico in the revolution, was given permission to graze his cattle on Rancho San Pedro in 1822. When ordered to remove them, he instead laid claim to a huge section of the rancho, calling it Rancho Los Palos Verdes. Two years later he was killed in an Indian uprising at Mission de la Purisima Concepcion at present-day Lompoc. Courtesy, Domínguez Family Archives

Top, right
Manuel Domínguez was only twenty-two when his father, Cristóbal, died and he became owner of the vast Rancho San Pedro. He made it more productive than ever and became one of the great cattle owners of California and one of the state's foremost citizens. Courtesy, The Henry E. Huntington Library

beds by the hundreds of thousands. Millions of the defenseless little creatures were slaughtered before belated legislation barely saved them from extinction.

Isolated and entirely dependent on the supply ships from the House of Trades, the *rancheros* and mission fathers became increasingly dissatisfied with the poor choice of goods being shipped up from Mexico. To compound the problem, foreign ships that probably were carrying supplies they dearly wanted were sternly prohibited from stopping at Spanish ports unless in dire need of water or repairs.

Thus the stage was set and the pressure almost irresistible for the furtive birth of unauthorized trade—smuggling, if you will. The time was ripe, the classic forces of supply and demand overpowering, and the location—the Bay of San Pedro—couldn't have been more advantageous for such stealthy business if a master smuggler had laid out the site on a drawing board himself.

The first record of trade in San Pedro was in 1805, when Captain William Shaler guided the *Lelia Byrd* into the bay. After his harrowing experience in San Diego, Shaler must have been filled with delight at the conditions he found in San Pedro. A year or two earlier Shaler had tried to slip out of San Diego with a quantity of confiscated otter skins when gunners in the old fort overlooking the harbor entrance opened fire. Several shots hit the vessel before the *Lelia Byrd* mercifully drifted out of range.

By contrast the shore in San Pedro was completely open and unguarded. The military detachment and revenue officers all were headquartered in Los Angeles, and the rugged terrain discouraged them from making the hard day's march to the port unless there was very good reason for it. When there was, news of the violation reached the authorities long after the deed was done.

According to some reports, the pious but eminently practical *padres* from San Gabriel were involved in the first illicit transaction in San Pedro when they exchanged cloth, sugar, and household goods from the *Lelia Byrd* for otter pelts, hides and shipboard provisions. The resourceful Shaler soon had a thriving business going, operating from the safety of Catalina Island and making frequent trips across the channel with silks, shawls, ready-made shoes, and other amenities for the luxury-starved settlers.

Smuggling in San Pedro continued to escalate for well over the next decade or more, until the independent government of Mexico seized control of that country from Spain, and with it control of Alta California, in 1822. Two years later, the ban against foreign ships visiting California ports was lifted, and San Pedro got its first full taste of free trade.

During that time, the status quo at the two big ranchos adjacent to the Bay of San Pedro had changed considerably.

Juan José Domínguez died, blind and ninety years old, in 1809, leaving his sprawling Rancho San Pedro to his nephew Cristóbal, commander of the military detachment at Mission San Juan Capistrano. Manuel Gutiérrez, the old man's lifelong friend and executor of his will, had been given a life estate in the rancho by Domínguez and stayed on to operate the vast spread.

That arrangement worked well until José Dolores Sepúlveda, a young Spanish officer who had switched sides and fought for Mexico in the revolution, arrived as commander of the garrison in Los Angeles in 1822. Sepúlveda acquired some livestock, ingratiated himself with Gutiérrez, and got permission from him to graze his horses and cattle on Rancho San Pedro property.

When he learned of it, Cristóbal angrily demanded that Sepúlveda remove his livestock from the Domínguez rancho at once. Apparently acting on the theory that the best defense is an offense, Sepúlveda not only refused to move his stock, but stunned Domínguez by suddenly laying claim to a large segment of Rancho San Pedro, which he called Rancho Los Palos Verdes.

Neither man lived long enough to see the dispute settled. In 1824, while Domínguez was trying to figure out how to recover his land, Sepúlveda rode to Monterey, the colonial capital of Alta California, to restate his claim to Governor Pio Pico. While returning, he was captured and killed by Indians during an uprising at Mission de la Purisima Concepcion above Santa Barbara. Three years after his death, the governor gave Sepúlveda's five small children a provisional grant to Rancho Los Palos Verdes.

Cristóbal Domínguez died only a year after Sepúlveda's demise. His son Manuel, then only twenty-two years old, took full control of Rancho San Pedro and made it more productive and successful than ever. He later became one of the most prominent cattlemen of California, and a leading judicial, military, and political figure of that day.

To the south, Manuel Pérez Nieto had plenty of problems of his own with his vast tract of land grant real estate, including a bitter squabble with his neighbor, Domínguez, over thousands of head of cattle that wandered back and forth between the two ranchos. More grief came when the missionaries claimed Nieto's stock was grazing on Indian-owned land and he was forced to give up a huge chunk of property in San Gabriel Valley.

Nieto died in 1804 and his widow and children remained on the rancho, which by then had been reduced by almost half of its original size to approximately 170,000 acres. The old soldier's heirs eventually petitioned for a division of the property. In 1833, in a plan reportedly engineered by Nieto's eldest son Juan José, the land was divided into five separate ranchos—Los Cerritos and Los Alamitos, where the City of Long Beach and five smaller cities are located; Los Bolsas; Los Coyotes; and Santa Gertrudes. Juan José kept Los Alamitos and Los Coyotes for himself.

The advent of unrestricted trade gave further impetus to San Pedro as the leading hide-trading center on the coast, and Los Angeles grew accordingly into a rough, tough, wide-open frontier town in the time-honored western tradition. Hide production continued to increase, and the burgeoning New England leather industry was sending more and more of its stately sailing ships on the tortuous, months-long voyage around Cape Horn to bring back all of that precious commodity they could carry.

Despite its growing commercial reputation, conditions both onshore and in the Bay of San Pedro were as rudimentary and difficult as they could be for merchantmen attempting to trade there. Virtually nothing about it had changed since Cabrillo first saw it nearly three centuries earlier. The bay was still just a series of tidal flats formed by deposits of several rivers running into it, with marshes and small lakes extending well inland. A long, slender sand spit ran into the bay. It was a favorite basking spot for snakes washed down into the harbor, and soon became known as Rattlesnake Island.

An even more sinister appellation was given the "small island" in the middle of the bay, which Vizcaino had described in his log. Looming like a fortress above the water, the rocky outcropping became the burial place for a number of early casualties of life in frontier San Pedro and earned its baleful title of Deadman's Island. It became a fearsome presence to superstitious seamen when the rum was flowing freely, and an infuriating disaster to the many unwary sailors who crashed into its jagged sides in heavy fog or utter darkness. It remained a major nautical headache to generations of mariners until it was finally removed in 1928.

A much more insoluble navigational impediment to movement through the bay was the depth of the water—actually, the almost total lack of it. Much of it was shallow enough for an average man to wade across with water no higher than his waist. Other parts could be traversed on his hands and knees without getting his head wet.

Shallowest of all was the half-mile stretch of water between the western shore of the bay and Deadman's Island, which eventually became the main entrance to the Port of Los Angeles. Across that stretch, lurking just below the surface like some unkind aberration of nature, was a long strand of rock and sand that brought the depth to under two feet at low tide.

Ships had no choice but to anchor well offshore, and few small boats carrying goods to and from shore could pass that rock-and-sand obstacle without one or more of their occupants having to hop into the water and push or pull the craft across. The struggle over that barrier was only part of it. Incoming cargo then had to be hauled up a steep cliff for exchange at a small adobe structure called the "hide house," originally built by the San Gabriel fathers and considered by most historians to be the first building in San Pedro. The cured hides then had to be thrown, shoved, or pulled down to the beach for transfer to the waiting vessels.

It was back-breaking work, and visiting crews hated the ordeal that awaited them whenever they came to San Pedro. The difficult conditions in San Pedro, as well as the harsh realities of shipboard life in the early 1880s, were an arcane business of little or no interest to the young American nation on the eastern seaboard until a well-born young Bostonian named Richard Henry Dana dropped out of Harvard University, shipped aboard the brig *Pilgrim,* and first arrived in San Pedro in 1835.

Dana's account of his experiences became one of the acknowledged classics of American literature, *Two Years Before the Mast.* His description of the grim existence of the ordinary seaman shocked the American public and led to humane reforms that markedly improved the treatment of sailors at sea. His withering references to San Pedro made it clear that he and his shipmates detested the place and could not wait to leave:

There was no sign of a town . . . what brought us into such a place we could not conceive . . . we lay exposed to every wind that could blow, except from the northwest . . . . I also learned to my surprise that the desolate-looking place we were in was the best place on the whole coast for hides. It was the only port for a distance of eighty miles and about thirty miles in the interior was a fine plane country, filled with herds of cattle, the center of which was the pueblo of Los Angeles—the largest town in California—and several of the wealthiest missions: to all of which San Pedro was the seaport. Two days had brought us to San Pedro and two days more, to our no small joy, gave us our last view of that place which was universally called the hell of California and seemed in every way designed for wear and tear on sailors.

Not all of the Americans who sailed or otherwise drifted into California shared Dana's antipathy toward the place. Conversely, a number of more imaginative and enterprising outsiders found it laden with golden opportunities and set about acquiring property and power by whatever methods it required.

Two of the most successful of these colorful carpetbaggers, both natives of Massachusetts, were John Temple and Abel Sterns, who followed remarkably similar paths to eventually rank among the richest and most influential landowners in the state.

Temple opened the first general merchandise store in Los Angeles in 1828, and went on to become one of the leading businessmen and political figures in the city. No less an opportunist was Stearns, who dealt in wine, a little discreet smuggling on the side, and became a powerful operator in the lucrative hide business when he purchased the adobe "hide house" from the San Gabriel fathers in the mid-1830s.

Both Temple and Stearns had become Catholics and Mexican citizens to enhance an already intimate rapport with the colonial authorities and, like hawks of a feather, each later married into a well-known Mexican family to further bind the ties and open new doors of opportunity.

Temple's marriage to Dona Rafaela Cota automatically made him a relative of Manuela Nieto de Cota, the heiress to Rancho Los Cerritos. Some years later, Stearns chose a bride from the renowned Bandini family, and he did not have an easy time of it. In fact, what is usually a rather happy occasion for most men turned into an embarrassing ordeal for the Yankee-born entrepreneur. Homely enough to be nicknamed *Cara de Caballo* (Horseface) and pushing middle age, Stearns provoked widespread glee and irreverent comment when it was announced that he would marry the beautiful, fourteen-year-old Dona Arcadia Bandini.

The similarity in the careers of these two

American promoters became even more pronounced when they assumed ownership of the land that is the present City of Long Beach. A year after his 1841 marriage, Stearns purchased Rancho Los Alamitos, including the old Nieto home, for approximately $6,000. He eventually acquired enough additional property to become the biggest landowner in California.

In 1843 John Temple became Stearns' neighbor when he bought the adjacent Rancho Los Cerritos, which had belonged to the second cousin of Temple's wife, for slightly over $3,000. The boundary between the two ranchos is now Alamitos Avenue in Long Beach. The two men remained close friends for years, and each was able to help the other when land authorities and former heirs suddenly surfaced to seriously challenge their titles to the ranchos.

Mexico's tenuous hold on its faraway territory had been deteriorating for some time. An influx of aggressive, ambitious Americans followed the trading vessels in and were putting increasing pressure for change on Alta California's basic institutions—the missions and the ranchos—as well as its colonial government.

The mission system had been effectively dissolved in 1833, when Mexican liberals pushed through the Secularization Act, allegedly liberating the Indians from mission control and returning their lands to them. In reality it served to hasten the complete dislocation and downfall of the natives, who first had been forced to abandon their own culture and now were cast loose into a world they could never understand.

Where land was once available for the asking, a growing number of predatory outsiders were acquiring large tracts, much of it the property of disenfranchised Indians, who had no one to defend them and their rights. This shameless exploitation extended to the Californios, who lost much of their initiative when they discovered that the lowly, rootless Indian could be hired for a pittance to do the work as little more than slave labor.

Mexico's position was further weakened by a

steady decline in coordination and cooperation between the colonial government in Monterey and their Mexican masters thousands of miles away. The provincial staff resented the lukewarm interest and support they were receiving from home, and their loyalties were severely tested by the intriguing American presence and influence, which many officials frankly preferred over their own archaic systems and traditions. On the American side, the government was in the process of settling the West, and sentiment in Washington was that California was part of its natural birthright—even if it took military action to make it so.

What followed was virtually inevitable under the circumstances, and it turned out to be one of the strangest wars the United States has ever been involved in. Much of it was more operetta than armed conflict.

The purported "enemy" really didn't want to fight at all. The Californios would have cheerfully capitulated on the spot if they hadn't been provoked by the highhanded behavior of the Americans—perhaps the forerunners of

Opposite page
John Temple was one of the first and most successful of the Yankee entrepreneurs who found fame and fortune in California. He opened the first general merchandise store in Los Angeles in 1828, the first general store in San Pedro in 1848, and the first harbor-to-city shipping line with cart and oxen. He later became the owner of Rancho Los Cerritos, part of it the site of present-day Long Beach. Courtesy, The Henry E. Huntington Library

Right
Abel Stearns was another of the most successful of the New England adventurers, whose career closely paralleled that of John Temple. Nicknamed "Horseface," he caused widespread merriment when, at the age of forty-three, he married the beautiful fourteen-year-old daughter of the prestigious Bandini family. Stearns was an important figure in harbor trade as the onetime owner of the hide house in San Pedro and later the owner of Rancho Los Alamitos, which became much of Long Beach. Courtesy, The Henry E. Huntington Library

Below
Los Angeles remained a tiny, sparsely settled hamlet for many years, as evidenced by this lithograph. It was made in 1853 by an artist with the first government party sent west to make a survey for a possible transcontinental railroad route on orders of Secretary of War Jefferson Davis. Several decades later its population had skyrocketed to over 50,000. From the Ernest Marquez Collection

that "ugly" breed that has misbehaved on foreign soil over the years.

Except for a battle or two, there was little of the ebb and flow of textbook military warfare, as the war was waged in a "combat" zone that was full of people going about their own business and paying little or no attention to the occasional skirmish that erupted among them. Most of it was erratically planned, badly executed, and generally lacking in coordination.

Communication was especially poor. The United States declared war on May 13, 1846, and no one in California, including the Mexican officials, were even aware of it until July 2, when a flotilla of American warships casually sailed into Monterey harbor and took over the provincial capital without resistance.

Fully occupied with its hide-trading business and other pursuits, San Pedro was startled to suddenly find itself designated as a military base of operations, as the American War Office decided that the capture of Los Angeles was a target of highest priority. After camping on the edge of the bay, Commodore Robert R. Stockton led a force of marines in an assault on the city.

The residents greeted the American forces more as liberators than invaders, even going so far as to bury their only serviceable weapon of any size, a four-pound cannon, to avoid any possible unpleasantness. It was turning out to be a bloodless war until Stockton made the serious mistake of putting an impetuous young lieutenant named Archibald Gillespie in charge of a small force to maintain the peace in the city.

The worst possible choice for such duty, Gillespie was openly contemptuous of the Mexicans who refused to fight. His belligerence and obnoxious behavior offended even the patient, friendly Angelenos. They finally dug up their old cannon and pinned down Gillespie and his fifty-man force, which soon found itself running short of food and water. The beaten Americans were driven back to San Pedro, where their guns were spiked and thrown into the bay, and they were ordered to leave on the first available ship that would take them.

As the Gillespie party prepared to depart in disgrace, Stockton returned with reinforcements aboard the frigate *Savannah.* The Battle of Dominguez Ranch soon developed on Rancho San Pedro, where the Californios used their old four-pounder with telling effect. Some historians report of a clever ploy the Mexicans used to confuse the Americans by running a large number of horses back and forth at a distance to make their forces appear much stronger than they were. Six United States marines were killed in the battle and buried on Deadman's Island.

Another scenario with musical comedy overtones was played out earlier when the sloop of war *Cyane* was sent south to secure San Diego before the attack on Los Angeles. On board were Kit Carson and John Fremont with his 150-man Battalion of California Volunteers. The *Cyane* caused no commotion when it arrived, nor did the flag-raising before a small group of disinterested bystanders.

Juan Bandini himself gave Fremont one of his best horses and a saddle to make his ride north to Los Angeles as comfortable as possible. Commodore Stockton was put in charge and, after a brief misunderstanding, Mexican hospitality was lavish. Bandini's daughters personally made a new American flag to replace one hauled down by dissenters. Casa de Bandini became Stockton's military headquarters. Presidio Hill was rechristened Fort Stockton and the frigate's band played nightly in the main plaza.

The war dragged on for several months, and the Californios did give General Kearney's highly-regarded Army of the West a sound drubbing at San Pascual just to make it clear that they could fight as well as anyone when they wanted to. Yet they had proved their point and they knew that even if they had wanted to continue, they could never muster the support or manpower to resist the growing American strength that was increasing by the week.

The conflict finally ground to a halt with the surrender of General Andrés Pico at Cahuenga Pass in January 1847, and Mexico officially ceded California to the United States on February 2, 1848.

Like most wars, this one could easily have been avoided if it had not been for the brash approach of the Americans and the total lack of communication between the two sides. Had the protagonists been wise enough to hark back to the old Gabrieleno safety-valve subterfuge of just singing obscene or insulting songs at each other, there would not have been any bloodshed at all.

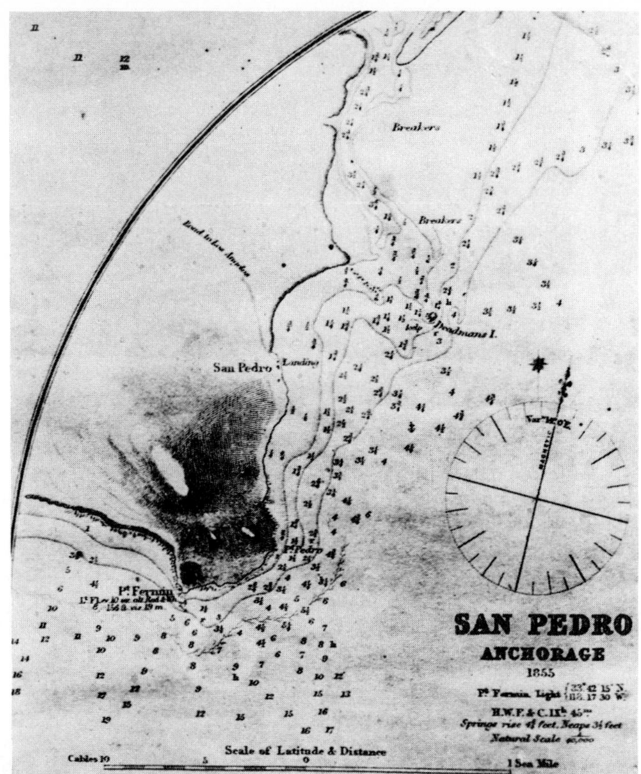

Above
Pictured is a sketch of one of the final battles of the war with Mexico, the Battle of the Plains of Mesa on January 9, 1847. The sketch's description reads: "The American forces commanded by R.R. Stockton in hollow square charged by Genl Floras on 4 sides." The war ended with the surrender of Mexican forces at Cahuenga Pass later that same month. Courtesy, Domínguez Family Archives

Top
The extreme shallowness of San Pedro waters is apparent in this 1855 navigational map, with water depths recorded as low as one-fourth of a foot. The main channel was first dredged to a depth of minus ten feet in 1871. Courtesy, Security Pacific National Bank Photograph Collection/ Los Angeles Public Library

Jotham Bixby, who served as manager and half-owner of Rancho Los Cerritos for many years, moved with his family to more comfortable quarters in 1881, but always returned to oversee the annual harvest at the rancho in later years. Courtesy, Rancho Los Cerritos Museum

CHAPTER II

GROWING PAINS

The abortive Mexican War, the United States acquisition of California, and the discovery of gold in 1848 unleashed a new swarm of strangers into San Pedro and Los Angeles—the typical motley, ragtag collection of adventurers, dreamers, con men, psychopaths, fugitives, and desperadoes that roamed the frontier in those days. Nearly all were armed; many were dangerous. It was an explosive mix, and violence erupted often.

No one had previously seen much need for, or indeed even cared about, the permanent development of San Pedro. Traders completed their business at the hide house or on the beach and usually returned to their ships or to the ranchos or the city. Despite its thriving commercial activity, the bay remained almost entirely uninhabited. By 1830, when San Pedro was known far and wide as the leading hide center on the West Coast, the nearest home—the casa of Juan Sepúlveda—was three miles from the bay.

Over the next two decades San Pedro gradually acquired a small squatter population, and the volume of materials being shipped through to Los Angeles was increasing by the week. The profit potential there was not lost on the entrepreneurial instincts of John Temple, the respected owner of Rancho Los Cerritos, which ran south for several miles along the shoreline.

Temple saw the opportunity to establish a lucrative business close to home and joined Juan Alexander in the purchase of nearly two acres of Rancho Los Palos Verdes waterfront in 1848. A year later the two partners had opened the first general store in San Pedro and were operating the first organized shipping company between San Pedro and the city, using carts and oxen.

The main San Pedro-Los Angeles road followed an old Indian trail, leaving the bay and proceeding along what is now Gaffey Street, and moving roughly east, along the path of the present Harbor Freeway. In between lay twenty miles of dangerous terrain, pitch-black by night and frequented by large numbers of thugs and bandits who preyed at will on the usually defenseless travelers. Only sporadic vigilante action held down the mounting toll of murders and robberies along that road.

Temple and Alexander's lumbering equipment proved adequate for commercial shipments into the city, but something more civilized had to be devised to transport the growing number of passengers arriving by ship. Diego Sepúlveda found a way when he established the first stagecoach line over that route.

As part of the service, Sepúlveda also built a primitive wharf—the first on record in San Pedro—a storehouse on the beach, and a building on the bluff near the original hide house to shelter passengers awaiting arrival of the stages.

Among the army of drifters who stopped in and around the bay in the immediate postwar period, most went on through to the northern California goldfields. Some stayed and a few had a considerable impact on the waterfront.

One who did was an eccentric German named Augustus W. Timms, first mate on a trading vessel who jumped ship when it stopped in San Pedro, and immediately headed north to seek his fortune. Even among the hodgepodge of foreigners of every origin and tongue, Timms' Prussian speech and manner won him few friends and less gold. He surfaced again in San Pedro after arranging to represent several San Francisco shipping firms in the harbor.

Below
Los Angeles resembles a dusty little Mexican pueblo of single-story stucco buildings in this painting of about 1843. Courtesy, Security Pacific National Bank Photograph Collection/Los Angeles Public Library

The lack of housing around the bay proved no obstacle to the resourceful Timms. When the *Mary Jane* sank and was abandoned in 1852, Timms towed part of the hull and deck-houses to a point alongside Sepúlveda's Landing. Then the army transport *Abraham Lincoln* conveniently ran ashore during a storm practi-

Opposite page
This 1870 lithograph of Timms & Company, one of the first shipping operations in San Pedro, shows a small boat being loaded from a primitive wharf, with Deadman's Island in the distance at the left. Augustus Timms was one of the harbor's many colorful characters during its early days. Courtesy, Los Angeles Harbor Department

cally on Timms' doorstep, and he further enlarged his ramshackle abode with more wreckage. Sand and silt gradually built up around the architectural monstrosity and considerably expanded the land there, which became known as Timms Point.

The main reason for San Pedro's arrested development was the complete absence of a single individual or group of citizens dedicated or interested enough to improve the shabby little port. Just when it appeared this paralysis would be permanent, the much-needed messiah arrived in the person of a big, hulking, twenty-one-year-old named Phineas Banning aboard a clipper ship from Delaware in 1851. A giant for that period, over six feet tall and powerfully built, Banning had the initiative, ambition, and energy to match his size. He soon emerged as the most dynamic and dominant leader of harbor development in the entire history of the bay, a visionary with the intellectual capacity to recognize the harbor's unlimited potential and the temperament to back up his opinions with force, if necessary.

In the meantime, with thousands of newcomers streaming into California, it was inevitable that large landholders like John Temple and Abel Stearns would come under increasing pressure from various groups who could see no reason why so much land should be owned by so few. Furthermore, they argued, the rancho system had been introduced by the Spaniards and perpetuated by the Mexicans, but this was American soil now and America's generous land distribution laws should replace the old ones.

The Land Act of 1851 was a direct consequence of this pressure. It was intended to verify ownership of Spanish and Mexican land grants, and the once all-powerful *rancheros* suddenly found their claims under intense scrutiny and themselves in grave danger of losing their huge holdings. As the area's largest landowners, Stearns and Temple were among the most vulnerable, and the pair went through a years-long struggle in and out of court to keep their property.

The old institutions and systems on which they had built their power and influence were mostly gone, and Stearns, the wealthiest landholder in Southern California, came perilously close to losing everything. Only the timely collaboration of his loyal friend Temple and a healthy payoff to a particularly clamorous

would-be heir saved his title to Rancho Los Alamitos.

Back on the waterfront Phineas Banning had not been idle. As soon as he found lodgings, he rented a boat and sold fresh water by the keg to ships in the bay. He then got a job as a stagecoach driver and mail rider. He must have done it well. One early historian described him as "a bold and daring rider who carried the mail from Los Angeles to Fort Tejon through very dangerous country." Next, he bought out Temple's share of Temple and Alexander, upgraded its rolling stock to wagons and stages, and steadily expanded the business.

San Pedro-to-Los Angeles transportation went from nonexistent to fiercely competitive within a few years. Timms started his own line, and a hard-bitten operator named John J. Tomlinson joined the field when he took over Sepúlveda's stage line. Tomlinson and Banning took an immediate dislike toward each other. Tomlinson and Timms both went out of their way to make life miserable for Banning in a number of disputes, many of which ended up in the courtroom. Banning, who had worked in his brother's law office in Baltimore, usually handled his own case.

As much as he relished a good scrap, Banning eventually tired of the battle and, when a storm wrecked his small San Pedro wharf in 1857, he made a drastic move. Three years earlier he and two partners had purchased 2,400 acres of Rancho San Pedro waterfront five miles up the channel, and now he shifted his entire shipping operation there.

The site was largely one big mud flat—"Banning's Hog-waller," the local wags called it—and it took hard work with scows and hand pumps to cut a channel, siphon off most of the water, and reclaim the land. Banning first called it New San Pedro, then renamed it Wilmington after his home town in Delaware. The water was even shallower far up in the bay, but Banning built his own fleet of flat-bottomed barges and shallow-draft steamers to reach his wharf. With his extraordinary organizational skill, he was soon monopolizing most of the commercial and passenger traffic moving through San Pedro.

The big ranchers continued to struggle for survival. It was either feast or famine, as natural and man-made events combined in a cruel conspiracy to keep them in a constant state of siege and upheaval. Fortune smiled for a time when cattle, previously valued only for their hide and fat, suddenly became an urgently

Opposite page
This ship chandlery was part of Phineas Banning's well-organized Wilmington operations that drew most of the harbor traffic away from San Pedro in the decade preceding the Civil War. Courtesy, Historical Society of Long Beach

Above
The Los Angeles & San Pedro Railroad ran close to the Domínguez ranchhouse, in the upper left on Rancho San Pedro in this lithograph probably commissioned by the Domínguez family in the mid-1870s. Courtesy, Domínguez Family Archives

Top
Phineas Banning's wharf in Wilmington was the ocean end of the twenty-one-mile Los Angeles & San Pedro Railroad, the first railroad in Southern California. A train carrying lumber and passengers is pictured leaving for Los Angeles, while a sidewheel tugboat departs from the dock at the left. Photo by Godfrey. From the Ernest Marquez Collection

needed commodity to feed the northern miners, and prices soared many times over their normal level. On the other hand, the labor market was decimated when some of the best cowboys left to pursue the legendary mother lode.

Profits from the beef bonanza continued to roll in until supply abruptly overtook demand, the market plummeted, and a number of ranchers were forced into bankruptcy—but not those two canny old Yankee survivors, John Temple and Abel Stearns. Both came through that crisis richer than ever, but the storm clouds were gathering. A shattering earthquake in 1857 was the forerunner of a series of natural disasters over which they had no control.

For Southern California ranchers the early 1860s were a prolonged nightmare of misery and misfortune, with only brief intervals of relief and hope before another, even worse tragedy engulfed them. An economic skid led off the decade. Then came a grasshopper plague that ravaged both crops and pasturage. What appeared to be providential winter rains arrived early, but then seemed as though they would never stop. It poured incessantly for nearly forty-five days straight, drowning hundreds of thousands of cattle, wrecking farms, and taking a heavy toll of human lives.

Above
Recalcitrant soldiers who broke the rules were incarcerated in this old stockade at Fort Drum in Wilmington, which was abandoned along with about twenty other buildings when the Army left Fort Drum in 1866. Wilson College, a small Methodist school, was housed in two of the abandoned buildings, and a large warehouse was dismantled and used to build a huge barn at Rancho Los Alamitos, ten miles away. Courtesy, Historical Society of Long Beach

Opposite page
Phineas Banning is pictured in his early forties, at the peak of his career as the transportation king of Southern California. Courtesy, Banning Museum

The malevolent weather appeared to atone, at least in part, for the desolation it had wrought by producing the finest pasturage within memory in the summer of 1862, but then the winter rains did not arrive at all, nor did they fall in any beneficial quantity for the next three years. Heat and a withering drought gripped the once rich grasslands. Crops and pastures dried up and died, along with tens of thousands of cattle. Even the previously indestructible Stearns and Temple could not withstand such massive devastation, and their days were clearly numbered.

Waterfront operators were not nearly as susceptible to the vagaries of freakish weather as the stricken landholders, and Banning's burgeoning empire continued to flourish and grow. His reputation grew steadily from that of daring driver of six-horse stages to respected business tycoon, and the dynamo that drove him never seemed to run down.

While the embattled California ranchers fought desperately to stay afloat, combat of a more serious and savage nature was about to erupt several thousand miles away, where the issue of slavery had driven a deep emotional wedge between the North and South. With a groundswell of pro-Southern sentiment manifesting itself in the Los Angeles area, the Army decided in 1859 that a garrison in that region would serve the dual purpose of keeping Southern sympathizers in line and serving as a convenient base for action against the more

intractable Indian tribes in the Southwest.

Captain Phil Sheridan arrived in 1861 to set up a military post in the harbor, and the ubiquitous Banning and his partner promptly donated sixty acres of land in Wilmington to the cause. The Army rewarded their generosity with a contract to build more than twenty buildings on the new base, which was called Fort Drum for Adjutant General Richard Coulter Drum, commander of the Army's Department of the West.

An outspoken Union supporter, Banning became the Army's indispensable right arm during the war years. He was instrumental in establishing the harbor area's first telegraph for the military in 1861, as well as the community's first post office and first newspaper. His shipping companies moved many tons of vital supplies across thousands of miles of desert to remote outposts in Arizona, New Mexico, and Texas.

The assignment of thousands of soldiers, many with families, to Fort Drum nearly inundated tiny Wilmington, which was suddenly engulfed in a tidal wave of prosperity. Euphoric businessmen invested recklessly, a half-dozen schools were built, and the entire village bathed in the warm glow of a bright but suspiciously metallic wartime economy. The crash came when the war ended and the Army decided to abandon Fort Drum in 1866. Banning tried valiantly to help, but Wilmington never really recovered.

Distance spared the Bay of San Pedro from the terrible loss of life and property on the battlefields of the Civil War. Its only serious disaster during that period was the explosion of the shallow-draft steamer *Ada Hancock* in 1863, in which twenty-six passengers were killed and another twenty-six injured, including Banning and his wife Rebecca, who were aboard at the time. In terms of loss of life, it was the worst maritime accident in harbor history.

The end of the war also marked the closing of the long, eventful reign of John Temple and Abel Stearns as two of California's most illustrious land barons. Crushing financial obligations had forced Stearns to mortgage Rancho Los Alamitos for $20,000 to San Francisco businessman Michael Reese in 1861. When he defaulted five years later, Reese took over the ranch.

Stearns' old compatriot fared no better. Desperate for cash and with nowhere to turn, Temple sold his 27,000-acre Rancho Los Cerritos for the giveaway price of about seventy-five cents per acre in 1866. Temple died suddenly in San Francisco not long afterward. Although in failing health, the aging Stearns was gamely trying to stage a comeback with his remaining property when he also died in 1871.

A few miles to the north, the indefatigable Banning had launched a one-man campaign for progress in the harbor. He became a state senator and immediately set out to improve transportation between the bay and the city, which had become progressively inadequate. He introduced the first railroad bill in the State Legislature, and pushed through a Los Angeles bond issue to finance the first railroad in Southern California.

The entire project was a Phineas Banning production from inception to completion. His company began construction on the line in 1868 and completed it a year later. It was called the Los Angeles & San Pedro Railroad, with Banning as one of its principal owners. Despite its name, the twenty-one-mile railroad never got to San Pedro; it ended at Banning's wharf in Wilmington.

Traffic in the bay picked up sharply after the war due to increased coastal trade and a steady acceleration in the growth of Los Angeles and the surrounding area. It took wood to build cities, and the dry, arid Southern California landscape could provide little of that. Lumber began arriving in ever increasing quantities from the Pacific Northwest and would soon become the Bay of San Pedro's biggest import—or next to it—in terms of volume for most of the next century.

The emerging importance of Los Angeles could not long be ignored, and the United States Army Corps of Engineers finally consented to make its first feasibility study of the harbor. Almost predictably, Phineas Banning led the move to submit blueprints for the harbor's first breakwater to Congress. Next to come under federal scrutiny was that intolerable sandbar that lowered the water depth to less than two feet at low tide and effectively barred all but the smallest, shallow-draft vessels from even entering the commercial side of the bay.

No harbor of any importance could function with such a handicap, and it was an historic step forward when the first federal dredging project was approved and $200,000 appropriated to remove the sandbar and deepen the lower end of the channel to a depth of ten feet. That was 1871, when work also began on a 6,700-foot jetty—the harbor's first—between Deadman's Island and Rattlesnake Island, and harbor traffic rose to an unprecedented 50,000 tons per year. After centuries of aimless inertia, it was a dazzling year of progress for the little bay.

Along the east side of the bay, the colorful Temple-Stearns era was now history, and a new family dynasty was beginning, this one without benefit of the land grant largesse lavished so openhandedly on the Domínguezes, Sepúlvedas, and Nietos.

The Flint-Bixby clan from Maine was a nobler strain than the majority of carpetbaggers who came to the new territory, greedily grabbed anything they could by whatever means necessary, and never let scruples or ethics stand in their way.

Benjamin Flint came to California first in 1849, followed in 1851 by brother Thomas and cousin Lewellyn Bixby, and Jotham and Marcellus Bixby in 1852. Instead of looking for gold, they sold beef and other services to the miners and saved their money. In 1853 the Flint brothers and Lewellyn Bixby made the long trip back East for a quick visit with their Maine kinfold before heading west to Illinois.

There they formed Flint, Bixby & Company and gathered a herd of 1,880 sheep. On May 8, 1853, they set out for California on an epic journey of courage and human endurance. The three cousins and a few teamsters drove the herd straight across the prairie, through the Rocky Mountains, and down the Fremont Trail to San Gabriel, arriving in the Mormon colony of San Bernardino after eight months of constant struggle against searing heat, flooding rivers, marauding Indians, and other hazards of the frontier wilderness.

They wintered at Rancho San Pasqual on the site of the present city of Pasadena, then drove the herd north. By the summer of 1855 they reached Monterey County, where they purchased Rancho San Justo. This became family headquarters for years, while the clan prospered as sheep ranchers. All of the early arrivals had passed close to the rich, rolling ranchland just east of San Pedro on their way north during the Gold Rush days, and they never lost their interest in owning property around that bay to the south. The opportunity came in 1866.

Lewellyn Bixby had always remembered that beautiful, lush grassland running down to the wide beach near San Pedro, and when financially-strapped John Temple offered to sell his 27,000-acre Rancho Los Cerritos for a ridiculously low $20,000, Flint, Bixby & Company of San Francisco quickly purchased it. Jotham Bixby was installed as manager of Los Cerritos and made half-owner with his own company, J. Bixby & Company. Jotham began raising sheep instead of cattle and the rancho soon became a profitable operation after years of staggering losses.

The decision to sink artesian wells that provided precious water, effective breeding with superior imported stock, and the natural tendency of the hardier sheep to handle extremes in weather better than cattle all contributed to that success. Even so, that dramatic renaissance did not continue for long. Within a half-dozen years, the same crippling drought that had destroyed John Temple and Abel Stearns would be back, trying to ruin the Bixbys as well.

In the meantime Jotham Bixby's cousin, John Bixby, had arrived from New England to work on Rancho Los Cerritos in 1870. The adjacent Rancho Los Alamitos was still in the hands of Michael Reese, who had acquired it from Abel Stearns, and John Bixby soon developed an overpowering desire to own that choice property on the other side of the line. He was to realize that dream within a decade, leasing Los Alamitos from the Reese estate in 1878, and then joining J. Bixby & Company and Los Angeles banker I.W. Hellman in purchasing the coveted rancho for $125,000 a few years later.

It made the Bixby family the largest landowners of waterfront property on the Bay of San Pedro and stewards of nearly all the land that would one day become the city of Long Beach.

Among those who chanced to view the broad, empty beaches lining the eastern end of the bay was English-born visionary William E. Willmore. The young man had disembarked in Wilmington in 1870 and set out on foot for the Anaheim Settlement, as it was called in those days.

Diego Sepúlveda became the most active of José Dolores Sepúlveda's five children. He started the first stagecoach line between the harbor and the city and built the first primitive wharf in San Pedro. Sepúlveda later donated three acres of blufftop land for the site of the Point Fermin lighthouse, one of San Pedro's most picturesque landmarks. Courtesy, The Henry E. Huntington Library

The path paralleled the shoreline, and when he paused after several miles to rest and gaze out over the bucolic tableau before him, a surge of inspiration fired his imagination and an overpowering fantasy began to take shape in his mind. The thought filled him with excitement.

"Some day, a great city will arise here, and at the waterfront will load and unload ships bearing cargoes to and from the seven seas," Willmore later recalled thinking at the time. As preposterous as it must have seemed then, that grandiose prediction did indeed come true—but not at all as the prescient Englishman would have had it happen.

As it turned out, Willmore himself would be the principal casualty in the long and convoluted birthing of the city that eventually would be called Long Beach. Oddly enough, it would be the San Francisco Chamber of Commerce which would begin turning Willmore's whimsical dream into reality.

Transportation rapidly became one of the most pressing national problems after the Civil War, as a tidal wave of expansion and population completely inundated the old horse-and-wagon and stagecoach system that had served its purpose during the young nation's adolescent years of tentative movement and sometime progress.

There was no other way to go then anyway, but the old system was primitive, haphazard, severely limited in capacity and, with the exception of companies like the stage lines and Phineas Banning's operation, almost totally disorganized.

Worse yet, it was utterly incapable of handling the skyrocketing volume of goods and people moving constantly across the country. Towns and villages had been springing up like wildfire throughout the new territories and with them came the more venturesome souls who left the East Coast in droves to populate them.

Relief from the transportation crunch came not a moment too soon in the form of the railroads, which virtually overnight rendered many millions of dollars worth of horseflesh and rolling stock obsolete. It was clearly the end of an era, because not the strongest teams of horses nor the largest wagons could compete with the speed, safety, efficiency, and carrying capacity of the newest transportation vehicle.

As the only game in town, the railroads soon discovered that they could wield tremendous power and influence if they chose to do so, and some of them used and abused that power in the most outrageous way. The more power-hungry railroad magnates made their own rules as they went along, corrupting politicians, forcing through or simply paying for favorable legislation, and trampling roughshod on the rights of anyone who had the temerity to question their tactics or attempt to resist them.

A fascinating case in point—and one that had a profound impact on the city of Los Angeles and its citizens and especially on the Bay of San Pedro and its future—was the Southern Pacific Railroad.

The Southern Pacific was operated by four men who got their start selling picks, shovels, and similar hardware to miners in Sacramento during the gold-rush years and eventually ranked among the most renowned names in the state's history—Collis P. Huntington, Leland Stanford, Mark Hopkins, and Charles Crocker.

Widespread elation at the advent of the railroad and the vast improvement it brought to transportation in California was soon tempered by the Southern Pacific's preemptory behavior as it extended its line south from San Francisco. The railroad's cold-blooded approach earned it the nickname of "The Octopus." Its tactics became familiar as it neared each town on the proposed route.

Southern Pacific officials would meet with the town fathers and bluntly state their terms as a thinly-veiled ultimatum: a large sum of money (usually much more than the town could afford), a wide right-of-way, and a large piece of property in the center for its depot. If

Right
John W. Bixby was a young Maine schoolteacher who came to California to work for his cousin, Jotham Bixby, at Rancho Los Cerritos in 1870. He leased the adjacent Rancho Los Alamitos in 1878, then joined a partnership to purchase Los Alamitos in 1881. He died six years later of a ruptured appendix at the age of thirty-nine. Courtesy, Rancho Los Cerritos Museum

Below
Jotham Bixby looks every inch the patriarch of one of Long Beach's pioneer families, which he was, in this portrait taken about 1915. He was made manager of Rancho Los Cerritos after Flint, Bixby and Company had purchased it from John Temple and made half owner of the rancho, where he raised sheep instead of cattle. For years he was one of Long Beach's most influential citizens and a leader in municipal development. Courtesy, Rancho Los Cerritos Museum

a town refused the railroad simply rerouted its tracks to bypass the community and let it die on the vine.

Los Angeles was the ripest plum of all and especially vulnerable to the Southern Pacific's coercive methods because everyone knew the fast-growing city desperately needed outside railroad connections.

As the SP construction crew approached Los Angeles, the tracks began to veer alarmingly southeast toward Yuma and their eventual destination in Texas. The railroad innocuously stated it had not planned to pass through Los Angeles, then let city leaders agonize over the consequences of being isolated from the vital national rail network.

Predictably, SP negotiators did not have long to wait before anxious city officials were ready to listen. The railroad's demands were formidable: $600,000 in cash, the usual wide right-of-way property, sixty acres of choice downtown land for its depot, and, most significant of all, possession of the Los Angeles & San Pedro Railroad, by then the crucial link with the harbor.

It was outright blackmail, giving the Southern Pacific a total monopoly over all commercial shipping in and out of Los Angeles. The public angrily opposed the proposal, and it was a bitter choice for Phineas Banning, part owner of the little rail line who had sold it the Wilmington land for its depot for $39,000 and had laid the track for $19,000 per mile. Nevertheless Los Angeles had to have rail connections to the rest of the county at all costs, and the city grudgingly accepted the Southern Pacific offer in 1872 after a year of tumultuous wrangling and debate.

The Southern Pacific immediately set out to punish the local business community for the audacity of its opposition. With the iron-willed Collis Huntington in dictatorial control, the railroad steadily raised shipping rates higher and higher, remorselessly destroying dozens of businesses in the process. There was no way a merchant could challenge "The Octopus" and survive.

The Los Angeles & Independence Railroad wharf, completed in 1875, was 1,740 feet long and 80 feet wide. Senator John P. Jones of Nevada sank a fortune into the railroad and was finally forced to sell it to the Southern Pacific Railroad for one-quarter of its original investment. From the Ernest Marquez Collection

CHAPTER III

BATTLE FOR SURVIVAL

With the completion of the transcontinental railroad in 1869, the myriad hardships of long-distance overland travel were over, and the nation finally had safe, reliable coast-to-coast mobility for the first time. Civic and business leaders in California were then giving considerable thought to devising a means of attracting a more substantial type of citizen than the rough, often violent itinerants who were responsible for the rampant lawlessness up and down the state.

With the quantum leap forward in transportation that the railroads provided, the aggressive San Francisco Chamber of Commerce came up with the idea of enticing a more desirable element to settle in California by offering land at very low prices. Much of this property was available in the southern end of the state, where the major landholders were still suffering severely from drought and probably would be receptive to any reasonable offer that would end their ordeal.

A California Immigrant Union (CIU) was formed in 1870 to organize and coordinate this campaign, with the task financed by an annual subscription of $36,000 from its members. The effort had the wholehearted support of most of the state's leading citizens, who were acutely aware of the urgent need for a more stable, law-abiding population to provide the impetus for growth and progress.

A familiar name from California's recent past entered the picture when young John Temple, nephew of the late land baron, became a CIU subscriber and director. Temple worked hard to promote the Union, and when someone was needed to manage the CIU's southern operation, the board accepted Temple's recommendation of William E. Willmore, the same young man who had paused six years earlier and envisioned a future metropolis on a deserted section of the east side of San Pedro Bay.

Willmore had carried that dream with him when he left to work in the Pacific Northwest, and now he was back and ready to make that vision a reality. In 1880 he was able to persuade Jotham Bixby, another ardent CIU supporter, to subdivide a section of Rancho Los Cerritos shoreline property and offer if for sale through the California Immigrant Union.

This was precisely what the young Englishman had spent years hoping for, and he already had most of the details of his "dream" city worked out and down on paper. His so-called "American Colony" would be made up chiefly of farms ranging in size from five to forty acres and covering approximately 10,000 acres—although the original plan covered nearly three times that area.

Rhode Island-born Robert S. Baker was another of the New England carpetbaggers who came to California and made a fortune in sheep and cattle. He later married the widow of Abel Stearns and acquired valuable property along the Santa Monica waterfront that was later acquired by the Southern Pacific Railroad. From the Ernest Marquez Collection

Farming would be the principal activity, but Willmore also envisioned a small town with wide streets, parks, schools, churches, a city hall, hotels overlooking the ocean, a boardwalk, beaches that would be open to the public, and possibly a college.

Local newspapers gave the new colony many columns of favorable publicity and a saturation advertising campaign heralded its existence in publications all over the country, but public response was no better than lukewarm. Disappointed, Willmore traveled back East and personally rounded up several dozen interested citizens and escorted them to the site of his would-be city. Many publicly endorsed in glowing terms the seaside location, the fine quality of the soil, and the bargain price of just twenty-five dollars per acre.

The American Colony came to be known more commonly as Willmore City during that period. Whatever its name, the embryonic community still seemed to be going nowhere. The lack of any tangible sign of progress caused widespread disappointment, and support of the project steadily diminished, even among those who had been most enthusiastic about the concept from the beginning. In mid-1882 the California Immigrant Union dealt Willmore a crushing setback when it withdrew its backing of the American Colony.

Frantic at the thought that his dream was going up in smoke, Willmore immediately organized the American Land, Water and Town Association and contracted with J. Bixby & Company for an option to purchase 4,000 acres for twenty-five dollars per acre. Willmore estimated that he could resell the land for fifty dollars an acre to make his payments, but the terms were completely unrealistic for an investor with no capital of his own to begin with.

Almost before he could catch his breath, Willmore was faced with a large payment to J. Bixby & Company in less than four months. He decided that his only hope for a quick, substantial financial fix was a property auction, and he feverishly set about making arrangements with a target date of October 1882. With little available cash, he was forced to begin using choice land to pay for the services needed to make Willmore City both accessible and presentable for the forthcoming auction.

In order to attract as many potential purchasers as possible from Los Angeles, Willmore needed a way to transport visitors to the auction from Wilmington, which they would reach on the Los Angeles & San Pedro Railroad. His first contract was for a makeshift rail line that would cover the three miles to the site.

With a vigor born of desperation, Willmore plunged ahead in his campaign to build a city. Captain Charles T. Healey, the state's first licensed surveyor, arrived to help improve Willmore's original city layout. Healey's revised design covered 4,000 acres, bounded by four streets—California, Tenth, Magnolia, and Ocean. The main north-south and east-west thoroughfares were the present Long Beach Boulevard and Ocean Park Avenue.

There were also the first encouraging signs of progress. Early visitors who had inspected the property and gone home now returned and purchased land to build on. Others set up housekeeping in temporary quarters. Construction began on the Bay View Hotel, the city's first. In 1882 more families arrived to share a company house, and J.R. Cook built the first real home in the new town.

Nevertheless, Willmore was still struggling to meet the impossible terms of his original contract to buy the land. He was forced to surrender more valuable property to pay for new improvements to put the city in shape for the auction. Even then, Willmore City had little to offer except the rosy prospects of a bright and flourishing future. It took a special kind of faith, and not many people shared Willmore's obsessive devotion to the cause.

The property auction took place as scheduled on October 31, 1882, and for a brief interval, it appeared that Willmore might pull it off after all. A trainload of visitors from Los Angeles swarmed over the property and several dozen lots were sold at prices ranging from $125 near the beach to $25 further inland. Yet it was no use. Willmore had been fighting a losing battle from the start, and even with the auction sales and a boost from the local press, those ruinous contract payments were simply too much for him to handle.

Willmore's fortunes went from bad to worse. Plans for activities that would have brought both people and money into the tiny town fell through and the weather, the curse and ruination of so many other businessmen in Southern California, brought an end to his own private dream. A series of heavy rainstorms wrecked the temporary railroad that connected Wilmington to Willmore City, and the defeated visionary finally gave up. Released from his contract with J. Bixby & Company, Willmore drifted out of his dream city, which had only twelve homes when he departed.

There was little or no solace in the $8,000 Willmore was paid for the town's water system by the Long Beach Water & Land Company, which bought up Willmore's option with J. Bixby & Company shortly after he relinquished it. Nor did anyone take the time to lament the demise of Willmore City, and even his name disappeared from the local consciousness in short order.

Within a few weeks of Willmore's departure, someone with no imagination whatsoever took a long, hard look at the place, focused on the six-mile stretch of the town's most obvious feature, and blandly rechristened it "Long Beach." Many preferred "Crescent City" in a close vote.

In Los Angeles the Southern Pacific's oppressive monopoly over transportation continued to dominate commerce in the city. The first glimmer of hope appeared in 1874 when Senator John P. Jones of Nevada, one of the Comstock Lode millionaires, decided to build a railroad from central Los Angeles to a new sea-

Left
Senator John P. Jones of Nevada was a Comstock Lode millionaire who tried to challenge the Los Angeles shipping monopoly of the Southern Pacific Railroad by building his own rail line from Los Angeles to Santa Monica. Collis P. Huntington and his powerful Southern Pacific machine quickly drove Jones out of business, and the senator later became a political ally of the Southern Pacific. From the Ernest Marquez Collection

Below
Santa Monica Canyon was a popular spot for swimmers, campers, and picnickers until Senator Jones decided to build his ill-fated railroad. Visitors traveled the 18.5 miles from Los Angeles by stagecoach. Tent saloons were set up as early as the 1860s during the summer months. From the Ernest Marquez Collection

side community that would be called Santa Monica. The senator also declared that he would make his new town not only the preferred port-of-entry for Los Angeles over San Pedro/Wilmington, but also the most important city in Southern California.

Jones should have known better than to pontificate so recklessly in view of the Southern Pacific's well-known propensity for swift and ruthless retaliation against even the hint of competition. SP spokesmen had no comment, as Jones proceeded to build his railroad from the city to the shore and a 1,740-foot wharf into the sea. Its dockside depth was twenty-four feet, which could accommodate the largest vessels of that period.

The Los Angeles & Independence Railroad was officially completed on November 31, 1875, with considerable fanfare. On that same day the Southern Pacific suddenly reduced its grossly-inflated Los Angeles-San Pedro shipping rates by half. The next day, when the new railroad opened for business, the SP slashed its rates even more.

Jones was taken aback, but not unduly disturbed. His railroad almost immediately drew crowds of beachgoers from the city to Santa Monica, and the devious senator had a formidable ace up his sleeve to protect his personal investment. He was fully determined to use his position as a member of the powerful Senate Commerce Committee to kill any proposal for funds to improve San Pedro Harbor and instead press for construction of a breakwater in Santa Monica.

It was a blatant conflict-of-interest situation, but quite common in those days among legislators and others in power who did not hesitate to use their elected offices to expand their interests and enrich themselves. It was just such reprehensible conduct by people like Jones and businesses like the Southern Pacific that ultimately led to a congressional code of ethics and regulatory legislation to control the runaway power of utilities like the railroads.

Jones never got the chance to put his unethical plan to use. The Southern Pacific's rock-bottom rates and Huntington's blunt warning that shippers had better keep using his line if they wanted their goods to go beyond Los Angeles quickly decimated the Los Angeles & Independence's business. A panic in Comstock securities further eroded Jones' financial reserves and he found himself in deep trouble.

The harried senator finally decided to sell, but could find no takers. Los Angeles County officials refused to listen, fearful of provoking the Southern Pacific. Jones also attempted to sell the line to the Union Pacific Railroad, but Huntington had a word with his Union Pacific friends and that proposal went nowhere. Jones was then allowed to twist slowly in the wind until Huntington agreed to take the Los Angeles & Independence off Jones' hands for one-quarter of the senator's investment.

It was an old tactic Huntington had used before to his advantage. In addition to acquiring a railroad for a fraction of its worth, the wily SP boss won the undying gratitude of still another in the legion of legislators and decision-makers who could be called upon to promote and protect the railroad's interests. Jones would prove very useful later on.

Once Jones' railroad was in hand, the Southern Pacific immediately reverted to its villainous old role. Shipping rates climbed higher than ever before. Curiously, instead of using its new acquisition to expand Southern Pacific operations, service on the Los Angeles & Independence was sharply curtailed and its wharf abandoned and eventually dismantled. With that convenient city-to-beach transportation cut, Santa Monica slipped into a steady but temporary decline.

During the short-lived and predictable battle of the railroads, business through Wilmington was increasing by the month. With Phineas Banning's highly efficient operation handling the bulk of harbor traffic and the SP-owned Los Angeles & San Pedro Railroad moving

Opposite page, top
The Los Angeles & Independence train pauses with passengers and crew at the Los Angeles depot before making the 18.5-mile run to Santa Monica. The railroad drew crowds of beachgoers from the city, but soon succumbed to the power of the ruthless Southern Pacific. From the Ernest Marquez Collection

Opposite page, bottom
Passengers have just disembarked from the steamship to the right on the Los Angeles & Independence wharf and are purchasing tickets at the depot for the train ride into Los Angeles. From the Ernest Marquez Collection

Below
Santa Monica had few buildings when this photograph of the coastline was taken from the Los Angeles & Independence wharf, with the roofs of railroad cars in the foreground. The large building with four chimneys on top of the bluff at the left is the Santa Monica Hotel, which was built in 1875 and burned to the ground in 1889. On the beach below is the bathhouse. From the Ernest Marquez Collection

goods effectively to and through Los Angeles, San Pedro had lost much of its earlier trade.

Yet recent harbor improvements, especially removal of the bothersome sandbar and deepening of the main channel, bolstered San Pedro's prospects considerably. New wharfage could now handle larger vessels along the deepened channel. A vital navigational aid was added with construction of the Point Fermin lighthouse in 1874. Delayed by the Civil War after Congress had approved $4,000 to build it in 1858, the handsome gingerbread structure still stands as one of the area's best preserved historical landmarks.

The Southern Pacific's despotic behavior grew even more insufferable. Its men would barge into a company, demand to see the books, and establish rates that would barely permit the firm to continue short of bankruptcy. Protesters were ruthlessly wiped out by im-

Above
Collis P. Huntington was a transplanted New Englander who first sold hardware to miners during the Gold Rush years and became one of the most powerful, feared, and hated men of his time as the mastermind behind the growth of the Southern Pacific Railroad. From the Ernest Marquez Collection

Opposite page, top
Only a stub was left and used as a fishing pier when the Southern Pacific took over the Los Angeles & Independence Railroad and tore down its wharf in Santa Monica. The remnant was still standing as late as 1909, when a new cement pier was built in the same location. From the Ernest Marquez Collection

Opposite page, bottom
Lumber was already clogging the waterfront in this 1883 photograph of San Pedro Harbor and Deadman's Island. That longtime navigational hazard was blasted away in 1928 to widen the entrance channel, and the debris was used to add sixty-two acres of new landfill to Terminal Island. Courtesy, Historical Society of Long Beach

possible rates. Unbelievable as it sounds, rail rates became so inflated that it actually cost more to ship goods from Los Angeles to San Pedro than from San Pedro to Hong Kong! Public outrage and demands for state and federal legislation to control the SP's incredible power availed nothing. Huntington's influential friends saw to that.

While the Southern Pacific carelessly discarded the Los Angeles & Independence as of no further use, the Huntington braintrust took a renewed interest in the much-improved maritime picture in San Pedro. Probably alerted through legislative sources that the main channel would be dredged another five feet to a depth of fifteen feet in 1881, the railroad reacted quickly. By whatever means, it had purchased from the heirs of Rancho Los Palos Verdes a 200-foot right-of-way across the marshes from Wilmington and down the west side of the channel to the bluffs overlooking the ocean in San Pedro.

It gave the Southern Pacific almost total control over the business side of the channel, and when the SP extended the Los Angeles & San Pedro tracks across the marshes and down to the bluffs in 1882, Wilmington was finished as a viable port for all time.

The SP's shift to San Pedro as the harbor terminus also dealt a severe blow to Wilmington's founder, Phineas Banning, whose long and brilliant career as the "transportation king" of the Southwest and a leading political and civic figure in the state had been on the wane in recent years.

Time, progress, and the overpowering intrusion of the Southern Pacific Railroad all combined to erode Banning's thirty-year reign as the unchallenged leader of harbor business and progress, and one of the area's most colorful and influential personalities.

Ironically, he crusaded tirelessly in the name of progress for developments that ultimately ruined his own business interests. He campaigned hard for the railroads, which quickly

rendered his farflung wagon and stagecoach properties obsolete. As a partner in the Los Angeles & San Pedro Railroad, its takeover by the Southern Pacific was another damaging loss.

Banning used all of his energies and influence to press for the dredging of the harbor, after he had solved the recurrent problem of shallow water by building his own fleet of shallow-draft steamers. The harbor deepening that he championed so fervently automatically made his steamer fleet unnecessary.

Phineas Banning is pictured in his early fifties, shortly before his death at the age of fifty-five from injuries suffered in a fall from a cable car in San Francisco in 1885. Banning was generally acclaimed as the "Father of Los Angeles Harbor." Courtesy, Banning Museum

Banning had long been a legendary figure on the waterfront by then. He was immensely popular with most, disliked and feared by some who had felt the sting of his fiery temper, but respected by all. He lived in baronial style, entertained royally at his palatial home in Wilmington, and his stature was such that he became the target of an occasional challenge by some inebriated stranger in a local saloon. A fighter by instinct, he invariably strapped on his guns and headed downtown for a High Noon-style shootout, only to find his detractor had long since taken flight.

Now, with his once thriving business empire disintegrating beyond recovery, the aging entrepreneur refused to accept defeat. Undaunted, he acquired a number of harbor vessels from the Southern Pacific Railroad and formed the Wilmington Transportation Company, the oldest continuous business operation in the harbor today.

The Banning saga came to an abrupt and tragic end in San Francisco, where he was visiting on business. He fell from a cable car and was struck by a passing wagon, and never really recovered from his injuries. He died on March 8, 1885, at the age of fifty-five, and his passing shocked the little community where, as one harbor historian put it, "For many years, Banning's powerful figure, hearty manner, and red suspenders loomed large on the San Pedro and Wilmington waterfronts."

He was one of a kind, a rare man of extraordinary talents and enormous energy who saw the seeds of greatness in the shabby little marshland and the city it supported, and made prodigious efforts to make it become a reality. Phineas Banning has been generally acclaimed as the "Father of Los Angeles Harbor," and no one has ever challenged him for the title.

While one end of the harbor was adjusting to the loss of its most distinguished citizen, the fledgling community on the other side of the bay was taking palpable steps toward permanence and beginning to develop its own local institutions, for better or for worse.

One of the first local favorites was the rickety little 2.5-mile railroad that had been feverishly assembled out of available odds and ends in time for Willmore's futile land auction in 1882. Jam-packed with visitors, it overturned on its first trip, but no one was hurt and the passengers dutifully lifted it back on the tracks and pushed it the rest of the way into town.

Henceforth it was lovingly referred to as the GOP (Get Out and Push) Railroad, and even though it broke down all the time and the engine caught fire regularly, it did cut the cost of shipping grain by a dollar a bushel. A lot of citizens were sorry to see their funny little railroad acquired in 1888 by the Southern Pacific, which had no sense of humor at all.

The action in Long Beach really started to pick up in 1884. Colonel W.W. Lowe opened the city's first general merchandise store, which also became the first post office, with mail brought from Wilmington by stagecoach. That was the year Long Beach got its name, thanks to Belle Lowe's tireless campaign, and Judge R.M. Widney, mastermind of the popular GOP Railroad, had the first wharf built.

Construction also began in 1884 on the city's first major building, the Long Beach Hotel, a splendid, five-story, $50,000 structure that featured such rare luxuries as bells to signal the front desk in every room and telephone connections with Los Angeles. Unfortunately it also was sometimes called the Willmore Hotel, which probably had nothing to do with the fact that it burned to the ground in 1888, talk of evil spirits to the contrary.

A year later the first newspaper, the *Long Beach Journal,* was founded, and culture began to rear its unaccustomed head in the shabby little village when the ubiquitous Belle Lowe and Llewelyn Bixby raised enough money to pay sixteen-year-old Grace Bush twenty-five dollars per month to teach nine students in a tent classroom, the first school. Early photos indicate Bush was a determined young woman who stood for no nonsense.

Long Beach took on a new look in 1885, and a very sedate one it was in the context of the raucous, wide-open nature of most California towns of that day because the impetus came from religion.

The Methodists decided to make the city by the sea their camp meeting headquarters. Through the new land development firm, the Alamitos Land Company, they acquired an entire square block in the middle of the town—bounded by what is now Long Beach Boulevard, Locust Avenue, and Third and Fourth streets—as the site for their tabernacle, which soon became a popular community gathering place.

Long Beach still needed more people, and as if by divine intercession, the Southern Pacific and Santa Fe railroads became engaged in a cutthroat price war that eventually slashed fares from mid-America from $125 to a paltry one dollar and brought swarms of visitors to Southern California. The timing was perfect, and even though the land speculators among them threw land values completely out of kilter for awhile, others were impressed by Long Beach and took up residence there.

The lack of a permanent and stable business community was another problem that plagued the young city. Local commerce was still largely in the hands of fly-by-night entrepreneurs and tiny, one-man operations that opened one day and disappeared a day or a week later. That, too, began to change in 1886 when Richard Loynes opened a large brick-making plant that employed sixteen men, and others soon followed suit.

A year later the newly organized Long Beach Development Company paid $250,000 for the remaining unsold property of the Long Beach Land and Water Company and its water system, as well as the inimitable GOP Railroad.

To inflate the package, Long Beach Land and Water threw in an 800-acre section of marshland, which was regarded as something of a sly joke on the purchasers because no one could conceive of any use ever being made of that swamp. Later, others with more foresight did; they dredged it and it became Long Beach Harbor.

The year 1888 marked a milestone in the brief annals of Long Beach. On January 10, residents voted, 106 to 3, to incorporate, and a month later the County Board of Supervisors issued a proclamation incorporating Long Beach as a new city of the sixth class, based on population. With a constituency weighted heavily by the Methodists, it came as no surprise that the first official action of the new municipal government was to adopt an ordinance prohibiting saloons and gambling within the city limits. The first tax was imposed on the owners of dogs.

The ban on liquor soon became the most explosive and controversial issue in the early history of Long Beach. Trying to promote itself as a popular resort without spirits seemed an anomaly on the face of it. Tempers heated up as the "wets" and the "drys" quickly took sides. The debate was shrill and intense and overshadowed all other municipal affairs. Dyed-in-the-wool Methodists considered drink the source of nearly every evil that had ever befallen mankind. The opposition considered a stiff libation or two the proper ending to a hard day's work or, better still, the ideal fuel to keep the engine going to complete that work. A third group, which sided with the latter, simply did not want the decision made for them.

San Pedro and Wilmington citizens watched with detached bemusement as the battle raged, and saloon-keepers in both towns delightedly welcomed the thirsty crowds that regularly traveled around the bay in search of more convivial entertainment. The GOP Railroad must have lost many a homeward bound reveler as its open-air cars swayed through the darkness on the late-night run, but the ground was not hard nor the walk home very long.

The brouhaha over liquor continued between a simmer and a full boil for many years. Ordinances pertaining to it were alternately tightened and relaxed according to the preferences of the city councilmen, who were elected or rejected on that basis alone. The initial ordinance banning spirits altogether was modified a year later to permit hotels with fifteen or more rooms to serve wine to dinner guests, but only if they were staying there. It was liberalized even further in 1890, when retail liquor sales were permitted, but with several restrictions.

No sooner had Dennis McCarthy opened the only legal saloon in the city than the drys again managed to seize the majority vote on the council and outlaw the retail sale of liquor. With the honeymoon of legal spirits cruelly cut short, the wets seethed in frustration for the next half-dozen years. Finally, by recruiting a faction angry over high taxes, the anti-prohibitionists were able to muster enough strength to petition for an election to disincorporate. On July 27, 1896, the vote to disincorporate was passed by a narrow margin.

Despite its preoccupation with the liquor dilemma, Long Beach made tangible strides forward during those years. Another struggle, nearly as vehement as that over spirits, erupted in 1891 when the city council granted the Los Angeles Terminal Railroad Company the right to connect Long Beach by rail with Los Angeles, via its line to San Pedro. It had significant advantages—namely, fine passenger and freight connections—but the right-of-way along Ocean Avenue, the city's showcase thoroughfare overlooking the beach, drew outrage from environmentalists and ecologists.

A Long Beach Board of Trade, predecessor to the Chamber of Commerce, was also established in 1891. The first pier was built on the ocean front and the Baptists erected their first church in the city in 1893, followed by construction of the First Baptist Church the fol-

lowing year. A primary school had been opened in 1888, and now came the first high school in 1895. A volunteer fire department was organized at about the same time. Wealthy landowner Jotham Bixby became president of the First Bank of Long Beach.

In the meantime the wets were exhilarated by the success of their campaign to disincorporate, even though various court actions would delay its official enforcement for another eleven months. The fruits of victory, however, rapidly turned rancid when the populace discovered it was neither fish nor fowl, under neither city nor county jurisdiction, with no responsible authority to maintain the town.

When potholes developed in the streets, they stayed there. The wharf was neglected and parks were unkempt. When streetlights went out no one replaced them. Mail was not delivered. Everything was going downhill when desperate city fathers called on the county to help. The citizens were promptly hit with the highest tax rate in the state to pay off the city's mounting debts.

Disincorporation finally became official in June 1897. By then the people of Long Beach had been watching their city steadily falling apart for nearly a year, and they had had more than enough. Another election was arranged, and the electorate could hardly wait to get to the polls and vote for reincorporation by a landslide. The vote was 237 to 27.

Above
Pine Avenue, Long Beach's principal thoroughfare, is shown around the turn of the century. Courtesy, Long Beach Historical Society

Top
Around the turn of the century, the original Pine Avenue Pier was the most popular place in Long Beach for a Sunday stroll. Oldtimers recall that whenever a crowd of any size gathered, one could always count on Kimble's Tamale stand to be there, open and ready for business. Courtesy, Historical Society of Long Beach

Senator Stephen M. White became the widely-acclaimed hero of the Free Harbor Fight when he defeated Collis Huntington and his Southern Pacific machine in a dramatic showdown on the floor of the United States Senate, thereby saving the future of the Bay of San Pedro. The hard-fought battle affected White's health and he died in 1901 at forty-nine. From the Ernest Marquez Collection

C H A P T E R I V

TAMING THE OCTOPUS

One of the most fascinating episodes in the history of this area, which took place a century ago, is largely unknown to all save historians and possibly some octogenarians. It involved a ferocious political struggle during which Santa Monica very nearly became the official port-of-entry for Los Angeles. A Santa Monica victory would have reduced the Bay of San Pedro—today the site of two of the nation's foremost international ports—to second-class status, along with the cities along its crescent-shaped shore. Only the last-minute heroics of a young senator from Los Angeles foiled the Machiavellian design of an iron-willed railroad tycoon and saved the bay from oblivion. It all began innocuously enough, or so it seemed.

When the Southern Pacific Railroad extended its Los Angeles & San Pedro tracks down the west side of the San Pedro channel in 1882, it also quietly began acquiring coastal land in and around Santa Monica for no apparent reason—except that Collis Huntington rarely did anything without a purpose. What he had in mind, which did not become known until sharpening competition forced him to act nearly a decade later, was so mindboggling by its sheer audacity that no one could have imagined that even the egomaniacal transportation magnate would attempt to pull off such a scheme.

The competition that compelled Huntington to show his hand began to appear in 1885, at a time when Los Angeles shippers had despaired of ever shaking loose of the cruel clutches of the Southern Pacific monopoly.

The Atchison, Topeka & Santa Fe Railroad had been steadily working its way west, and as it curved through Southern California toward its San Diego destination, it ran a branch off its main line to a site that is now Marina del Rey. The plan was to create its own seaport, called Port Ballona. Coincidentally, another new port began to take shape a few miles down the coast at Redondo in 1889. The newly-organized Redondo Railroad Company built a narrow-gauge line from Los Angeles to Redondo and a wharf on the beach to serve as its ocean terminus.

Redondo's capabilities were further strengthened shortly afterward when the trial balloon that was Port Ballona failed, and the Santa Fe built an extension south to Redondo, where it also installed a new pier. Suddenly, the little beachfront village was in the port business in a big way.

While extremely shallow water restricted most waterborne traffic along the coast—notably in San Pedro—Redondo had what appeared to be a major advantage over most of the oth-

ers. A broad underwater canyon faced the shore, and by building on the canyon's subsurface ridges it required a relatively short wharf to reach water deep enough for large vessels to unload directly at its docks. Ironically, that same underwater configuration eventually prevented Redondo from ever becoming a seaport of consequence because it made it impossible to build the protective breakwater that every safe harbor must have.

Nevertheless, with its deep-water wharves and location a full half-day's less sailing time on the coastal route from San Francisco, Redondo soon began to flourish. Long-suffering shippers gladly shifted their business away from the Southern Pacific. In 1892 Redondo's wharves accommodated more than 250 vessels and handled 62 percent of all waterborne commerce to and from Los Angeles, except for lumber and coal, which the Southern Pacific continued to bring in through San Pedro.

A much more serious threat loomed in 1891 when a group of St. Louis businessmen organized the Los Angeles Terminal Railway and immediately challenged The Octopus in its own territory. The St. Louis cartel purchased Rattlesnake Island from the Domínguez family for $250,000 and promptly changed its macabre name to the more prosaic Terminal Island.

The new company ran its tracks from the city down the east side of the Los Angeles River and across the water on trestles to Terminal Island, where they built a depot on the west end that they called East San Pedro. With that accomplished the Los Angeles Terminal Railway assumed control of all traffic on the east side of the main channel. This was an intruder that could not be intimidated, and it must have caused deep consternation within the previously omnipotent Southern Pacific.

In retrospect, although few realized it then, Collis Huntington's master plan had begun to unfold two years earlier. The Los Angeles Chamber of Commerce was organized in 1888, and its first priority was the urgent need for a deep-water port to generate foreign commerce. It was generally agreed that San Pedro should be the site for such a harbor. This, of course, would require construction of a breakwater, which would cost between four and five million dollars to build.

Chances for such a large federal appropriation appeared slim at the time because Congress already was being inundated by river and harbor improvement bills from various sections of the country. Even so, the Los Angeles

San Pedro residents pause in their buggy during the 1890s near stacks of cut lumber that will be used for harbor construction. In 1912 San Pedro Bay became the biggest lumber importing port in the world. Courtesy, Historical Society of Long Beach

Chamber reacted eagerly when it had the opportunity to host a visit by Senator William B. Frye of Maine, chairman of the Senate Commerce Committee and the single most powerful man in Congress when it came to a decision on port appropriations.

A San Pedro tour was hastily arranged, and among the Los Angeles officials who accompanied the senator to the port, one of San Pedro's most enthusiastic boosters was Leland Stanford, president of the Southern Pacific Railroad. The hometown delegation was in for a shock. After inspecting the desolate looking bay with its acres of mud flats, Frye stunned everyone within earshot with his snide putdown:

Well, as near as I can make out, you propose to ask the government to create a harbor for you almost out of whole cloth. The Lord has not given you much to start with, that is certain. It will cost four or five millions to build, you say. Well, is your whole country worth that much? It seems you made a big mistake in the location of your city. You should have put it at a point where a harbor already exists instead of calling on the government to give you what Nature refused.

The crowning insult, which really wounded the city's provincial pride, was the senator's suggestion that Los Angeles be moved to San Diego which, as everyone knew, had an excellent natural harbor needing no breakwater. Los Angeles and the local press roared with anger; San Diegans howled with glee at their northern neighbor's expense. Fry attempted to make light of his demeaning remarks, but as Senator Jones' houseguest in Santa Monica during his visit, he looked out over Santa Monica Bay and commented on what a much better site that would be for an important harbor.

Finally Collis Huntington was ready to launch his rocket, and he moved with uncommon alacrity and energy for a man nearly seventy years of age—or any age, for that matter. Dissension split the Southern Pacific braintrust. Pro-San Pedro advocate Leland Stanford was abruptly deposed as president and Huntington took control of the company. Work suddenly stopped on a big new wharf the Southern Pacific had been building in San Pedro.

Huntington now shifted his attention to Santa Monica. He applied for a wharf franchise there with a $5,000 bond and purchased one-half of Senator Jones' extensive waterfront property in Santa Monica, as well as additional land in the vicinity. Although they did not yet know exactly what Huntington was up to, the Los Angeles business community realized he had embarked on some extraordinary venture, and they awaited his next move with interest and some apprehension.

At about the time Huntington was preparing to unleash his monumental power play, Congress sent a three-man War Department Board of Engineers, led by Colonel G.H. Mendell, to select a site for a deep-water port somewhere between Point Dume and Capistrano. Only San Pedro and Santa Monica were seriously considered. The board unanimously recommended San Pedro, which "in its natural condition affords better protection both from prevailing winds and from dangerous storms than Santa Monica Bay . . . [which] protection can be secured at less cost for equal development of a breakwater at the former than the latter." The report did not mention another serious shortcoming in Santa Monica—the fact that the porous, sandy bluffs behind the beach offered no firm ground for shoreside development. Those bluffs still collapse periodically on the highway below.

Huntington chose to ignore this official judg-

ment. He went on purchasing more land, including a 100-foot right-of-way across the Bonifacio and Pasquel Marquez beachfront property, and even 249 acres for his personal estate, from which he would be able to survey his future domain like a feudal lord.

Only a month before the Mendell board rendered its decision in favor of San Pedro, Huntington had electrified the community by revealing that the Southern Pacific would construct a huge wharf extending nearly a mile into the ocean at Santa Monica. Even then, it still had not dawned on most Los Angelenos that Huntington actually intended to override the government's choice of San Pedro and attempt singlehandedly to make Santa Monica the official port for Los Angeles.

Work began on the much publicized Long Wharf in February 1892, and it soon became a major attraction with thousands traveling to Santa Monica to watch the longest wooden pier in the world take shape.

Soon after the start of Long Wharf construction, the Senate Commerce Committee was considering a $250,000 appropriation for harbor improvements in San Pedro. During the hearing Senator Frye, by now an open ally of the Southern Pacific, produced a telegram allegedly from the railroad's chief engineer, stating that the floor of San Pedro Bay was so rocky that piles could not be driven into it, and that had made the company decide to build the new wharf in Santa Monica.

The source of that telegram was never authenticated—indeed, years later the same engineer said he had had no trouble with the bottom of San Pedro Bay—but on that dubious evidence alone, the $250,000 appropriation was rejected. It was a chilling display of Huntington's power to control legislation to suit his purposes.

The San Pedro-Santa Monica dispute continued to heat up, and another government board of five engineers headed by Colonel William P. Craighill was formed in the spring of 1892 to make yet another decision on the location of the deep-water harbor. That December the Craighill board recommended to a man for San Pedro. Huntington simply plunged resolutely ahead, and the following spring officially named his unfinished wharf Port Los Angeles, a firm indication of the rail tycoon's complete confidence that he could force his private harbor on the city as its official port-of-entry.

Within a week after its christening by Huntington, the Secretary of the Treasury made Port Los Angeles a sub-port of entry for the Customs District. This meant foreign vessels

Above
The Southern Pacific's Long Wharf broadened to its full width of 130 feet for the last 1,300 feet. The large structure on the right was a giant coal bunker, with a capacity of 8,000 tons. The building in front of it with the tall smokestack is the powerhouse, which provided steam to operate coal-loading booms. The ship on the left is the Lucipara *from Glasgow. From the Ernest Marquez Collection*

Opposite page
The Southern Pacific's famed Long Wharf in Santa Monica became a major tourist attraction during the year-and-a-half it was being built. Completed in July 1893, it was 4,720 feet long, contained four million board feet of piles, and had dockside depths up to fifty feet. Collis Huntington tried to force Los Angeles to accept Santa Monica as the official deep-water port for the city in the dramatic Free Harbor Fight. From the Ernest Marquez Collection

were allowed to land and discharge cargoes there—unheard of recognition for a private, partly-completed wharf that had no qualifications for official stature or approval—but hardly surprising in view of Huntington's singular ability to manipulate policy on every level of government.

Huntington had always played by his own set of rules, ever ready to invest in anyone who was in a position to help his cause. Lawyers who might speak favorably in cases that might benefit the Southern Pacific received checks for nonexistent "legal services." Congressmen could expect generous "campaign contributions" on the eve of legislation involving the railroad for campaigns that might be years away. It was an early version of the modern "payola" syndrome, and Huntington paid and played it like an old master on a vintage violin.

Port Los Angeles was completed in July 1893. It was 4,720 feet long, contained four million board feet of lumber in the form of 5,084 ninety-foot piles, and had dockside depths up to fifty feet, easily able to accommodate the largest craft afloat in those days. Some 300 vessels stopped there during its first year-and-a-half in business, and the Long Wharf was soon siphoning off a large share of seaborne commerce from San Pedro and Redondo.

Once his wharf was fully operational and flourishing, the "huge, miserly millionaire," as one writer described him, dropped all pretense. He made an unannounced visit to the Los Angeles Chamber of Commerce and startled chamber officials with a table-thumping declaration of his position:

You people are making a big mistake in supporting this San Pedro appropriation. The Rivers and Harbors Committee of the House will never report in favor of this place—not in a thousand years. I know them all and I have talked with them about this matter. The same is true of the Senate Commerce Committee. I do not find it to my advantage to have this harbor built at San Pedro, and I shall be compelled to oppose all efforts that you make to secure appropriations for that site. On the other hand, the Santa Monica location will suit me perfectly, and if you folks will get in and work for that, you will find me at your side. I think I have some influence in Washington—as much as some people, perhaps. I don't know for sure that I can get this money for Santa Monica. I think I can. But I know damned well that you shall never get a cent for that other place.

Every development made front-page news, and by then all of the local newspapers were hip-deep in the controversy and had taken sides. Lined up with the *Santa Monica Outlook* in favor of Port Los Angeles were the *Los*

Opposite page
A large crowd came from Los Angeles by special trains in 1893 to greet the collier San Mateo *as the first ship to stop at the Southern Pacific's new Long Wharf in Santa Monica. The steamer carried both passengers from San Francisco and a load of coal from British Columbia. Collis Huntington named the new wharf Port Los Angeles in an effort to identify it as the official deep-water port for the city. From the Ernest Marquez Collection*

Above
Welcoming crowds and unlookers came down to the Long Wharf when the San Mateo *became the first ship to dock at Port Los Angeles in 1893. The ship is unloading coal into cars by using booms mounted to its masts. The huge coal bunker is still under construction at the left. From the Ernest Marquez Collection*

Angeles Herald and *Los Angeles Express,* although the *Herald* was soon sold and its new owners switched sides. Standing firmly for San Pedro was the *Los Angeles Times,* which stated in an early editorial:

The influence of the Southern Pacific at Washington may be great—perhaps greater than it should be—but it cannot reach the extent of upsetting all the established precedents that govern harbor appropriations and even if it were so all-powerful, it would still be the plain duty of the people of this section and their representatives to oppose a scheme to use government funds against the advice of its technical authorities for the special use and benefit of a single corporation.

The Los Angeles Chamber of Commerce decided in the spring of 1894 that it would help settle the affair once and for all by polling its membership, which included all of the city's leading businessmen. Of 464 ballots cast, 328 favored San Pedro and 128 were for Santa Monica. That should have finished the dispute, but incredibly the crafty Huntington, far from defeated, was merely biding his time.

In June 1894 the Senate Commerce Committee again pondered the wearying harbor issue. Anticipating nothing unusual, Los Angeles spokesmen routinely presented their case for San Pedro, whereupon Huntington suddenly appeared and requested a four-million-dollar appropriation for a breakwater in Santa Monica, neglecting to mention official recommendations to the contrary. One of his engineers followed with a detailed explanation of how such a breakwater could be constructed with the Southern Pacific's help at Huntington's private port. Frye and his cronies again shelved the matter.

The harbor controversy expanded and some of the nation's largest newspapers offered some withering comments regarding Huntington's brazen attempt to ram through Congressional approval of his personal harbor as the deepwater port-of-entry for Los Angeles. Observed the *New York World:*

It will be seen that Mr. Huntington's Santa Monica enterprise throughout its entire extent is as exclusive as if it were surrounded by a Chinese Wall.

The *St. Louis Globe Democrat concluded:*

If the appropriation goes to Huntington, it throttles all chances of competition, besides permanently injuring the growth of California and adjacent states and territories.

This was tame, however, compared with the broadsides leveled almost daily against Huntington and the Southern Pacific by the *San Francisco Examiner.* There were few more vituperative publishers in the business than the *Examiner's* William Randolph Hearst when he attacked his prey, and the Southern Pacific had long been a favorite Hearst target.

The entire pro-San Pedro campaign nearly went down the drain when the Los Angeles Chamber formed a new group called the Free Harbor League to carry on the fight while the chamber attended to new business. Naively assuming that the fiery septuagenarian might be tiring of the battle and informed that no major appropriation could be made at that time, the League requested a mere $392,000 to deepen the San Pedro inner harbor to minus twenty-five feet.

Huntington pounced again in another of his unscheduled appearances before the Senate Commerce Committee with a stunning request for $3,098,000 for a Santa Monica breakwater. Once more, his power at controlling legislation prevailed. What emerged was a recommendation that both the $392,000 for San Pedro improvements and the $3,098,000 allocation for Santa Monica be approved. If granted, this would give Huntington's Port Los Angeles the precious breakwater funds and leave the historic Bay of San Pedro out in the cold.

However, an aroused citizenry refused to accept such a whitewash. The proposed double allocation of almost $3.5 million for two harbors less than twenty miles apart precipitated such a public uproar that both appropriations were hastily stricken from the bill. The watered-down proposal was then passed by the House and forwarded to the Senate Commerce Committee.

Huntington again called the tune and the committee performed like puppets. With Senator Frye in another term as chairman, the committee dismissed all testimony favoring San Pedro and voted, nine to six, to restore the breakwater allocation for Santa Monica to the 1896 Rivers and Harbors Bill.

The way was now clear for a Southern Pacific victory and the San Pedro side was in grave danger of losing everything at that point—until Senator Stephen M. White of Los Angeles arrived like a knight in shining armor to save the day. There is little doubt that had it not been for White's timely intervention and brilliant political strategy, the coveted breakwater funds would have gone to Huntington's personal harbor in Santa Monica.

Senator White initially requested that still another board of engineers be sent to choose the best harbor site and that the entire appropriation be spent there. When the Commerce Committee refused, White took the matter to the Senate floor, where the Huntington team no longer had control.

There he again presented his amendment for the special board to make the final site selection, but with the key proviso that if Santa Monica should be chosen, the Southern Pacific would be required to allow any other railroad to use rail access and Port Los Angeles facilities for a reasonable fee—a condition that would shatter Huntington's dreams of a blanket monopoly over all Los Angeles shipping and transportation.

Following introduction of his amendment, White argued eloquently and forcefully for two full days on behalf of the San Pedro cause, while pointedly stressing what everyone realized, that if Santa Monica should be selected, the Southern Pacific would almost certainly restrict free competition and inflict lasting damage on maritime commerce and area trade as a whole. Frye and Huntington both tried to get White to modify his demands, but the stalwart senator refused to budge, and the amended Rivers and Harbors Bill was enacted in June 1896.

Rear Admiral John C. Walker was chairman of the five-man board of engineers assigned final choice of the breakwater recipient, and Walker's group deliberately took plenty of time in arriving at its crucial decision. On March 1, 1897, almost a decade after Los Angeles business leaders first requested federal funds for a deep-water harbor, the Walker board made public its four-to-one recommendation in favor of San Pedro.

The announcement touched off widespread celebrations in Los Angeles and San Pedro, and also in Long Beach, which had been watching with undivided interest as the breakwater battle between San Pedro and Santa Monica unfolded. There was dancing in the streets, whistles tooted, and bells were rung. The afternoon train arrived in Long Beach with its whistle wide open.

Long Beach still considered itself basically a resort at that point, and its port and sister city on the bay was San Pedro. The location of the official deep-sea harbor only five miles away was bound to benefit Long Beach in the way of prosperity, increased population and other improvements, as well as job opportunities for Long Beach residents. Little thought had been given to the possibility of Long Beach having industries of its own, much less its own seaport. Thus the city was rooting enthusiastically for San Pedro from the beginning, and had appropriated municipal funds for use by the San Pedro and Washington Harbor Committee had they been needed.

In an uncharacteristic display of sportsmanship for such a fierce competitor, Collis Huntington was reported to have personally congratulated Senator White on his remarkable tactical victory, but Huntington's supporters were not so magnanimous in defeat. As luck would have it, Secretary of War Russell A. Alger, an old Huntington friend, was the government official responsible for putting the breakwater project in motion, and he used every device he could think of to delay the start of construction and somehow get Congress to reconsider its breakwater vote.

Joy turned to anger as the public realized that Alger was dragging his feet, and there ensued another battle almost as bitter as the original struggle for the appropriation itself. Most of the invective was directed at Alger, but many suspected that Huntington was engineering the delay until he could acquire all available land the Southern Pacific did not already own along the San Pedro waterfront and attempt another takeover there.

Alger hemmed and hawed and dipped and dallied, and by the fall of 1897 each of his lame excuses triggered a storm of derision and outrage. His claim that there were no funds to advertise for bids and he had to wait for Congress to grant them brought a deluge of offers from the Los Angeles Chamber and private citizens to pay for them, and offers from all Los Angeles and San Francisco papers to print them free of charge.

Hounded on all sides, Alger finally ran out of room to maneuver. When he sought "opinions" from various government officials who had no authority in the matter, protests reached such a crescendo that President William McKinley himself issued a sharp order to Alger that he act at once. He had no alternative but to obey this time, and bids were finally opened in February 1898, just one month short of a year after the Walker board had rendered its decision. Alger eventually got around to ap-

Above
Twenty-thousand people, many wearing pins like this one, swarmed into San Pedro for the festive weekend jubilee and barbecue that marked the official start of breakwater construction in 1899. It was one of the biggest and most memorable celebrations in harbor history, shared by San Pedro and Long Beach alike. From the Ernest Marquez Collection

Top
Pins and buttons such as this were worn by San Pedro and "Free Harbor" supporters in the long-running battle to prevent the Southern Pacific from achieving a complete monopoly over Los Angeles area shipping by making Santa Monica the official deep-water harbor for Los Angeles. From the Ernest Marquez Collection

proving a bid of $1,303,198 from Heldmaier & Neu of Chicago and drawing up a contract in July 1898.

On April 26, 1899, more than 20,000 people swarmed into the harbor area for a festive jubilee marking the official start of breakwater construction. President McKinley pressed a button in the White House at 11 a.m., dumping the first bargeload of stone for the San Pedro breakwater. An enormous barbecue followed in one of the biggest and most memorable celebrations in harbor history. With one thing and another, including a change in contractors because the work was too slow, another eleven years were to pass before the breakwater was completed.

Grateful citizens of Los Angeles raised $25,000 after the death of Senator Stephen M. White to cast this statue in bronze to honor the man who defeated the Southern Pacific's attempt to make Santa Monica the deep-water port for Los Angeles instead of San Pedro. The statue has stood for years in downtown Los Angeles. Recent efforts to have it moved to the harbor have so far been unsuccessful. From the Ernest Marquez Collection

Stephen M. White, the hero of the deep-harbor fight, was accorded a princely reception on his triumphal return from Washington. A train decorated with banners and flowers met him as he crossed the state border. Crowds lined the tracks and applauded as he passed through. A huge parade in his honor was held through the streets of Los Angeles. The pro-Republican *Los Angeles Times* made a rare concession in calling the Democratic legislator "the greatest man this state has produced in its half-century of existence."

Sadly, Senator White did not have long to enjoy the acclaim of his grateful constituency. He returned to private law practice shortly afterward, but his health had been irreparably damaged by the rigors of preparing his one-man defense against the big Southern Pacific machine with almost none of the staff assistance a congressman has at his disposal today. His condition deteriorated steadily, and he died in 1901 at the age of forty-eight. A bronze statue of Senator White has stood in downtown Los Angeles for many years, and recent efforts have been made, so far unsuccessfully, to have it moved to what some consider a much more appropriate location overlooking the harbor he saved in San Pedro.

Loss of the deep-water port was an unprecedented setback for Collis Huntington, who himself died in 1901 at seventy-eight. His Southern Pacific juggernaut had rarely been challenged, much less defeated with so much at stake. It marked the end of the railroad's stifling control over area transportation and the dawn of a new era of competition and growth that never could have been achieved under the previous commercial monopoly. The Southern Pacific never accumulated such power again.

Stephen White not only tamed "The Octopus," he also preserved the future of San Pedro and Long Beach.

The Pine Avenue Pier was rebuilt as a much stronger structure using concrete piling, with a lower level for shops and restaurants. Courtesy, Historical Society of Long Beach

C H A P T E R V

COMING OF AGE

There was good reason for optimism as the Bay of San Pedro sailed into the new century. The titanic breakwater struggle had been won and the bay's preeminent maritime role in the booming commerce of the area was assured. Even as its fate was being decided thousands of miles away, San Pedro continued to improve its facilities. New wharves were built, and almost the entire length of the present-day main channel was dredged to a depth of eighteen feet.

In Long Beach there had been talk of a separate ship canal from San Pedro to Long Beach via a deepened harbor at Wilmington, and even wistful speculation that San Pedro, Wilmington, and Long Beach might one day be combined as a single mammoth commercial city on the bay—so much for wishful thinking, particularly when so many diverse interests are involved, but first things first.

In 1900 the *Long Beach Press* spearheaded a successful campaign to secure a federal appropriation for the inner harbor deepening in Wilmington on the theory that a canal accessible to Long Beach would help the city in its first attempts to attract industry. A delegation from the Rivers and Harbors Committee visited the bay and in 1903 granted a $300,000 appropriation for the necessary dredging of the inner harbor.

Some Long Beach citizens were not so diplomatic about furthering the city's interests. In 1903 an impulsive expansionist, William Galer, urged the city to annex Terminal Island, which would give Long Beach a ready-made port of its own and immediate access to harbor commerce. A number of Terminal Islanders liked the idea, but San Pedro would have none of it. Land-grab fever became infectious. San Pedro not only clung tenaciously to Terminal Island, but retaliated by trying to annex the western end of Long Beach.

Next, the two rivals attempted to annex the pivotal territory of Wilmington, which neatly sidestepped the issue by incorporating itself in 1905. That same year Long Beach began a series of annexations through which it absorbed Alamitos Beach, a new town that John Bixby had established in 1886, adjoining Long Beach at its eastern boundary, Alamitos Avenue. Finally, Los Angeles tried several different approaches in an all-out effort to annex Long Beach itself, but the bay city enjoyed its municipal independence and refused to succumb to the siren's song from the big city. After nearly twenty years of trying to seduce Long Beach into the fold, Los Angeles finally got the message and gave up.

Los Angeles was much more successful in its bid to acquire the commercial side of the

Above
Steam vessels were already vying with sailing ships for space in this turn-of-the-century photograph of the main channel in San Pedro. From the Charles F. Queenan Collection

Opposite page
This view of the main channel in San Pedro was taken shortly before the official founding of the Port of Los Angeles in 1907. Courtesy, Security Pacific National Bank Photograph Collection/Los Angeles Public Library

bay. In 1906 the city annexed a long, narrow strip of land that came to be known as the "shoestring," one mile wide and roughly parallel to the present Harbor Freeway, from the southern edge of the city limits to the boundaries of San Pedro and Long Beach.

The official founding of the Port of Los Angeles and creation of the first Board of Harbor Commissioners took place on December 9, 1907, with approval by the Los Angeles City Council of City Ordinance No. 19128. George H. Stewart, J.E. Carr, and F.W. Braun were appointed to the first Harbor Commission the following March.

Los Angeles city fathers were correct in assuming the next step would be the most difficult. The proposed consolidation of San Pedro and Wilmington met strong reactions in both towns. The waterfront was largely populated by free spirits, and none wanted to surrender con-

trol over local government and become part of a large metropolis nearly twenty miles away. The issue precipitated everything from genteel parlor debate to saloon-wrecking brawls down on the docks.

Realistically, the position of the two harbor towns was untenable. Both were badly in need of help. The harbor provided jobs and was the backbone of the local economy, but maritime commerce was operated by big outside companies—railroads, shipping lines, and the like—which owned the wharves and nearly all the ocean frontage and carried the bulk of their handsome profits elsewhere. Neither town had any other industries to speak of, and both were hard pressed to finance their own basic services. They could never hope to improve anything on their own.

Los Angeles, on the other hand, would solve all those major problems with a pledge of one million dollars a year for harbor improvement over the next decade, an adequate water supply for a steadily increasing harbor population, new schools, new police and fire stations and equipment, and a municipally owned and operated San Pedro-Terminal Island ferry. Along with this impressive list of valuable benefits came the gentle reminder that Los Angeles had already annexed the small waterfront town of Harbor City and could build its own port if forced to go it alone.

Cooler heads prevailed and the vote for consolidation was carried in both towns. President Howard Taft was the guest of honor at consolidation ceremonies on August 28, 1909, and the entire San Pedro population of several hundred turned out to greet the President's four-car motorcade as it wound its way through the dusty streets of the town.

Meanwhile, a series of events were beginning to unfold that would ultimately result in the development of Long Beach's own harbor. In 1903 C.J. Walker and Stephen Townsend formed a syndicate to purchase 800 acres of lowland west of Long Beach for $250,000 from the Seaside Water Company for use as industrial sites. Their company was called the Long Beach Land and Navigation Company, and the word

Left
Charles H. Windham was one of the earliest champions of Long Beach harbor development, who pressed the cause as city manager of Long Beach and was later honored as "The Father of the Port of Long Beach." He later moved to Florida and founded its city of Hollywood. Courtesy, Long Beach Harbor Department

Opposite page
The new steamship Camino *rights itself after a sideways launching at Craig Shipyard in Long Beach about 1915. Craig relocated from the Midwest in 1906 as the first major industry in Long Beach Harbor. Courtesy, Long Beach Harbor Department*

Below
Workers at Craig Shipyard in Long Beach paused for this group photograph during construction of the General Hubbard. *Craig was the first major industry in the new harbor. Courtesy, Long Beach Harbor Department*

"navigation" in the name strongly suggests the eventual goal of its founders was harbor development.

Long Beach Land and Navigation's immediate plan was to convert Cerritos Slough into a ship canal and persuade the Santa Fe Railroad to run through the flats to attract new industries to that side of Long Beach. Offers to industry to locate there were most attractive. First to move there was a smelter, which received free land, and the Pacific Electric Railway, which was gifted with a private right-of-way through what came to be called the Riverside tract.

In mid-1905 Henry P. Barbour and Dana Burk, two other local developers, took an option on part of the Riverside tract with the intention of building a pleasure resort of lagoons and canals like those in Venice to the north and Ocean Park. Yet developments on the same theme in Alamitos Bay caused them to drop the resort idea and raise their sights instead to a much more far-reaching and ambitious goal—the development of a deep-water harbor which would enable Long Beach to become the big seaport city envisioned several decades earlier by a luckless entrepreneur named Willmore.

Barbour and Burk formulated a detailed plan for the dredging of three channels and a 1,400-foot turning basin that would create 27,000 feet of water frontage on the tidal flats west of the city. Channels were to be deepened to minus twenty feet at low tide and dredge material used to raise the level of the flatland. The harbor would have room for at least five slips for warehouse and dockage installation. The channel of the Los Angeles River would be dredged to a depth of thirty feet and 300 feet wide for five miles. It would turn the shallow, muddy stream into a canal able to accommodate the largest steamers afloat. Once completed, this would give Long Beach more dockage area than San Pedro, second only to that of San Francisco on the West Coast.

Enthusiasm ran high, and that fall the Los Angeles Dock and Terminal Company—no kin to the city of the same name—was organized to make the plan a reality, with Burk as president and Barbour one of the directors. Another director was Charles H. Windham, one of the earliest advocates of a Long Beach harbor who also helped push that development to a successful conclusion as city manager of Long Beach.

The new company purchased 800 acres of westside flats from the Long Beach Land and Navigation Company, and promptly awarded the contract for the first dredging phase that would deepen the Los Angeles River entrance. The first dredger arrived but was forced to wait until the Salt Lake bridge over Cerritos Slough could be removed to let it pass. The problem of railroads interfering with maritime movement in the harbor was a recurrent one, beginning when the Southern Pacific ran its track across the marshes and down the west side of the channel, closing off the West Basin and preventing any development of that area until the railroad was forced to install a drawbridge almost thirty years later.

Shortly after dredging had begun in 1906, the first major industry was installed in the new harbor. John F. Craig, a second-generation owner of the prominent Craig Shipbuilding Company of Toledo, Ohio, visited Long Beach for his health and was eager to relocate his

Above
Fishermen of various nationalities came to San Pedro in large numbers shortly after the turn of the century to make the harbor one of the nation's leading fishing and canning centers. Courtesy, Southwest Instruments

Top
A colorful, multiracial community made up of Japanese, Italians, Yugoslavs, Portuguese, and Scandinavians grew up on Terminal Island to work in the fishing and canning industries. These Japanese women are making fish cakes from barracuda at an early cannery. Courtesy, Southwest Instruments

Opposite page
Southern Pacific tracks and cargoes of lumber occupied most of the west side of the main channel in this early 1900s photograph of San Pedro. Courtesy, Los Angeles Habor Department

plant on the coast. San Diego offered him eighty free acres, but Craig turned it down and accepted a bid from the Long Beach group of $300,000 and forty acres of land in a location where direct ocean access was blocked by a Salt Lake Railway trestle connecting Long Beach to Terminal Island. The only route to the sea was via Cerritos Slough and the Port of Los Angeles, and it was clear that Craig was not about to let himself be boxed in for long.

Boat building was already a growing industry in San Pedro, where Phineas Banning had founded the first boatyard well before the turn of the century. The steady growth of commercial fishing in the harbor had given further impetus to boat building, as a number of small yards were opened to service and repair the increasing volume of fishing and pleasure craft based in the harbor.

At first commercial fishing produced only a limited catch that supplied the local market. In 1893 the Golden Gate Packing Company tired of the slim harvest in San Francisco Bay, packed up its equipment, and moved south to open the first cannery in San Pedro Bay on Terminal Island. Fishing and canning took off virtually overnight in 1903 when Albert P. Halfhill, co-owner of the California Fish Company, discovered a method of steaming albacore to make it look and taste like chicken.

Marketed as a new delicacy called tuna, the unusual fish product soon became a national favorite. Much of the credit for the popularization of tuna should be given to Frank L. Van Camp, the dynamic owner of Van Camp Sea Food Company, who led the campaign to build fishing and canning into major harbor industries and make the Bay of San Pedro the leading commercial fishing center in the United States. Another key figure in the cannery industry was Martin J. Bogdanovitch, founder of the French Sardine Company, which became the largest fish cannery in the world under its new name, Star-Kist. Sadly, that huge cannery recently went out of business, the victim of ru-

inous foreign competition.

In San Pedro lumber had long since replaced everything else combined as the harbor's biggest import. It arrived in such astronomical quantities—eleven million board feet as early as 1874—that it literally swamped the western end of the bay. It was needed everywhere—in Los Angeles and other fast-growing cities in the area, by the railroads, the mines, and the harbors themselves. A dozen lumber firms worked frantically to keep the avalanche of cut wood moving. Even so, the huge piles of timber never seemed to diminish, and the port appears in many early photographs as one vast lumber yard. Some had only to be shipped the few miles around the bay to Long Beach, which was building at a feverish pace to keep up with a population that had mushroomed from 564 in 1890 to nearly 20,000 in less than two decades.

In Long Beach the presence of Craig Shipbuilding generated other applications for commercial space in the new harbor, all of which put increasing emphasis on the need for a drawbridge that would clear the passage to the outer harbor. The War Department finally issued the order, and in 1908 the Salt Lake Railroad installed a 187-foot bascule bridge, one of the largest single-span drawbridges constructed up to that time.

The Los Angeles Dock and Terminal Company continued its development work, barely weathering one financial crisis after another to meet the enormous expense of keeping the three inner channels, the turning basin, and the entrance channel in navigable condition. Only the constant sale of property enabled the firm to defray the immense costs of maintenance and regular dredging required to offset the flooding and tons of silt swept into the bay from the Los Angeles River.

While the company waged its no-win battle, it had become increasingly apparent to local leaders that the city should have a stronger voice and a more influential role in a project of surpassing importance to Long Beach's future. On September 9, 1909, the first Long Beach municipal bond issue for harbor improvement and commercial development passed by a six-to-one margin. Of the $245,000 issue, $200,000 was for purchase of 2,200 feet of frontage on Channel 3 and the rest for construction of a wharf there.

Within a few months a movement was underway for the outright purchase of the entire harbor, with civic leaders predicting it would bring "tremendous" profits to the city. Furthermore, it would give the city the freedom to offer special inducements to lure new industries that otherwise might purchase property from the railroads, which held some of the waterfront land.

Yet despite the financial pressures, the harried Dock and Terminal Company was not yet ready to surrender, and city officials decided to wait until the harbor entrance was completed before giving it another try while they continued to press for federal assistance from the Rivers and Harbors Committee.

Craig gave the new harbor badly needed credibility by producing a powerful electric dredger for harbor development within a year after it set up operations in Long Beach, and then in 1911 building and launching the 256-foot *General Hubbard,* the first steel steamship built in Southern California. The *General Hubbard* became the first ship to sail through the newly-dredged ocean entrance to the harbor.

A pair of historic "firsts" preceded the official founding of the Port of Long Beach. On May 3, 1911, the steam schooner SS *Casco* arrived with the first shipment by steamer in Long Beach harbor. It was a familiar cargo—275,000 feet of lumber for Craig Shipyard, to build the first floating drydock south of San Francisco. A month later, the first lumber delivered at the new 500-foot municipal dock—280,000 feet of redwood—was brought in by the SS *Iaqua.*

The formal opening of the new municipal dock marked the official founding of the Port of Long Beach on June 24, 1911. The event was attended by thousands of Long Beach citizens and featured music by the municipal band and a succession of long-winded speakers who rhapsodized in glowing terms about the "practical utilization of the great Long Beach harbor."

Use of the word "great" was premature, to put it mildly, but Long Beach could well be proud of its accomplishments. With drive and leadership it had achieved in little more than a decade a stage of municipal and port development that had taken generations in San Pedro. That quaint little community preferred to preserve its picturesque, small-town atmosphere, while Long Beach funneled its abundant ener-

Above
Craig Shipyard, the first major maritime industry in Long Beach harbor, built the first floating drydock south of San Francisco in 1912 from lumber that had made up the first cargo delivered by a steamer in Long Beach. The 3,500-foot drydock remained in use until 1970. Courtesy, Long Beach Harbor Department

Top
In the background is the sandbar that was swept out to sea by a storm in 1909, clearing the opening of the inner harbor to the open ocean. The dredge in the foreground had been working in that direction when nature took over and completed the job. Courtesy, Long Beach Harbor Department

Opposite page
Long Beach leaders were out in force, including pioneer landowner Jotham Bixby (with beard in the front row at the left) and shipyard owner John F. Craig (hands in pockets beside him) when the Craig yard launched the 256-foot General Hubbard, *the first steel steamship built in Southern California, in 1911. Courtesy, Long Beach Harbor Department*

gies in single-minded pursuit of growth, progress, prosperity, and the promise of a shining future.

While Long Beach was still regarded as the prime seaside attraction in the area, another resort of the same type but on a much smaller scale put in an appearance on the south side of Terminal Island. It was called Brighton Beach, and it came into being when the Los Angeles Terminal Railway ran its tracks across to Terminal Island. The beach there was sheltered, the water extremely shallow and ideal for wading by those who disliked the breakers that rumbled ashore from the open sea in Long Beach.

More than 200 summer homes were eventually built there but alas, the colorful little resort became yet another victim of progress. Harbor development continued the enlargement of Terminal Island, and as more and more dredge material was added to it, the waterline retreated farther and farther back from the natural shore, completely obliterating the original beach. Brighton Beach lost its biggest asset, and the summer homes were later sold or rented to the ethnic immigrants who would soon develop the second largest fish canning industry in the world. Brighton Beach disappeared without a trace—except perhaps for the founding of the area's first recreational boating group in 1901, then called the South Coast Yacht Club and now known as the Los Angeles Yacht Club.

Yet while Brighton Beach was sinking slowly into the sunset, Long Beach was entering into the period of its greatest growth as an entertainment and resort center. Previously the city had bristled with activity during the summer months with the two permanent Chatauquas and the Methodist summer assembly, but it "died," as they say in resort parlance, during the off-season. It badly needed some sort of permanent attraction to keep the action going for those lean months as well.

Enter, as if on divine cue, one Colonel Charles R. Drake, a remarkable gentleman from Arizona who came to Long Beach to retire in 1901 and instead spent the next thirty years tirelessly building its beach into one of the most popular and long-running year-round recreational meccas on the West Coast.

A former president of the Arizona Territorial Senate and a man of wealth and influence, Colonel Drake was a born showman, entrepreneur, promoter, and businessman, and he lost no time in becoming the Barnum of Long Beach. A superb tactician and skilled negotia-

Above
A popular weekend pastime shortly after the turn of the century was a stroll in one's Sunday best on the Long Beach wharf. At left is the original auditorium, with a sign advertising an upcoming Chatauqua meeting. The temporary archway was erected for a Shriners convention. To the right of the auditorium is the "Unique Penny Arcade," and the Sun Parlor is at the end of the wharf. Courtesy, Long Beach Historical Society

Opposite page, top
The Virginia Hotel was one of Long Beach's most elegant beachfront hotels for years. Built in 1908, the palatial hostelry ran into financial problems in 1932 and was demolished in 1933. From the George Metivier Collection

Opposite page, bottom
A typical Sunday scene in Long Beach is seen circa 1900: beach, breakers, buggies, and bathers – with the Pine Street Pier at the left. Courtesy, Historical Society of Long Beach

tor, Drake first appeared as spokesman for a syndicate headed by Henry Huntington, nephew of the late Southern Pacific leader, and I.W. Hellman to propose a new streetcar line connecting Long Beach with Los Angeles. Again, opposition to further despoiling Ocean Avenue with a trolley line was as swift and shrill as it was when the Los Angeles Terminal Railroad came in, but the Long Beach City Council wisely recognized the value of a convenient, inexpensive means of transportation for area residents to reach the city. The Pacific Electric Railway won the contract and construction on the tracks began at once.

With mass transportation assured, Drake next organized the Seaside Water Company, which promptly purchased the Long Beach Development Company and its extensive properties. This priceless coup gave him exclusive ownership of 1,600 acres, including all of the beachfront in the original township site and two water companies. He was now prepared to turn the Long Beach waterfront into a West Coast version of the famed boardwalk in Atlantic City.

Drake's basic blueprint called for a mile-long pleasure and entertainment strip connecting a new bathhouse and a new luxury hotel, the one thing Long Beach sorely needed to qualify as a first-class resort. First to be built was the bathhouse, a huge structure that contained the largest indoor swimming pool west of the Mississippi. The bathhouse was nearly completed when the Pacific Electric Railway sent its first red car rolling into Long Beach on the Fourth of July in 1902, as some 50,000 holiday celebrants piled into the city on that day alone. It was a time for rejoicing and Drake, ever the master diplomat, gave the crowd a thrill by opening the bathhouse prematurely that day.

Long Beach leaders realized what Drake was doing for the city and gladly joined in upgrading existing city-owned facilities on the beach. The popular Pavilion was improved and doubled in size. The nearby Pine Avenue Pier had taken ten years of pounding from the sea and infestation by termites and was badly in need of renovation as well. A $100,000 bond issue was passed to reconstruct the pier as a two-level wharf with shops and restaurants below, and even though a violent storm severely damaged it when it was nearly completed, it was again rebuilt and ready for a gala opening in 1904.

Nature perversely kept trying to rain on Long Beach's buoyant parade. This time it was fire that destroyed the renovated Pavilion two months after its opening, but dauntless Long Beach residents quickly approved another bond

Left
Drake's "Walk of a Thousand Lights" – better known as the Pike – was the area's most popular weekend attraction by the time this panoramic photograph was taken in 1909. The white-columned building on the left is the Bath House (The Plunge), the Pavilion is in the center, the Sun Pavilion is at the end of the pier, and the band shell is at lower right, where the nation's first city-supported year-round municipal band played to audiences on the beach. Courtesy, Historical Society of Long Beach

Opposite page, bottom
For decades, and for years before the automobile, Pier Day was a festive annual event in Long Beach, as in this 1904 photograph, with crowds flocking to the new pavilion adjacent to the Pine Avenue Pier. From the George Metivier Collection

Below
Long Beach was still very much a beach resort when this aerial photograph was taken in the mid-1930s. Since then the beachfront hotels and most of this area have been taken over by modern development. From the George Metivier Collection

issue to rebuild it. The original tabernacle and sometime community center was showing its age by then, so the new Pavilion was built as a vast auditorium to serve as a temple as well as a popular spot for group gatherings in its 39,400-square-foot assembly hall.

Next came the icing on the cake—that elegant first-class hotel that would complete the beachfront. Again, it was the dynamic Drake who organized the Long Beach Hotel Company, with the city's foremost citizens, including several Bixbys as directors. The new hotel, to be named the Bixby in honor of that distinguished pioneer family, was designed as the most luxurious hostelry of its day. The city's great expectations were shattered when thirteen workers were killed in the collapse of part of the building during construction.

Long Beach was stunned by the tragedy, and the Bixbys asked that their name not be used. The hotel was renamed the Virginia. It was completed and opened in 1908, and it was everything Drake and his admirers hoped it would be and more. It was the scene of a succession of glittering social events as one of the most palatial hotels on the West Coast and a proud Long Beach showpiece for many years. It was closed in 1932 and razed in 1933.

Meanwhile Drake's so-called "Walk of a Thousand Lights" quickly lost that pretentious identification and came to be known affectionately by generations of fun-seekers as simply the Pike. Its popularity grew as privately-owned and operated concessions of various types rapidly filled in the brightly-lit promenade. The star attraction was the roller coaster, the first of which was installed in 1907 and proved to be an immediate sensation. The Pike had something for everyone—except the thirsty—and even the ban on liquor did not seem to dampen its appeal. It was like a carnival that came to town and never left.

The Pike's appeal was greatly enhanced in 1911 when Charles Looff, creator and operator of the first carousel in this country at Coney Island in New York, moved west and opened the Hippodrome merry-go-round, which featured his own collection of exquisite, hand-carved horses. It provided an artistic balance to the earthier aspects of the Pike, and for more than three decades Looff's masterworks brought pleasure and excitement to millions of children and adults alike.

Things were much quieter and more businesslike across the bay, where Los Angeles had approved the first general obligation bond issue of three million dollars for full-scale harbor improvement on the San Pedro side. Harbor boundary lines, however, had to be established first and the delicate matter of land ownership resolved. Most of the waterfront land was owned either legitimately or by squatters who much earlier had moved in unchallenged and in time had come to regard it as their own.

Furthermore the old State Admissions Act, passed when California first joined the Union but largely ignored since then, was revived and interpreted to mean that all claims to the tidelands and other valuable property along the main channel were invalid and that the land legally belonged to the state. It was a devastating blow to some waterfront operators, especially those who could not afford to contest the decision in court, but these matters had to be settled because no sensible businessman would invest in land of uncertain title. The court battles that ensued were long and bitter, and some have still not been settled to this day.

Of the many exciting events for bay residents during that first decade of the new century, one of the most memorable was the visit of the Great White Fleet, the flotilla of American battleships, during their round-the-world goodwill trip sponsored by President Theodore Roosevelt in 1908. Excitement turned to dismay and sadness when ten crewmen were killed in an explosion aboard the USS *Tennessee.* A solemn procession of navy whaleboats carried the victims ashore for burial in San Pedro.

Construction of the breakwater had been in

progress for ten years and seemed to go on forever, but the initial 8,500-foot segment was finally completed in 1911 at a cost of $2.9 million.

That sum was lower than had been anticipated, and enough money remained to extend it another 750 feet. The breakwater began at a point 1,800 feet off Point Fermin, the gap left open to prevent silt from accumulating in the harbor, but when that proved not to be a problem, the gap was filled in all the way to the shore. The breakwater was sixty-two to sixty-six feet high from the bottom, 200 feet thick at the base, and twenty feet wide at the top. From low water to fourteen feet above that level, it consisted of huge granite blocks, those on the ocean side weighing at least eight tons each. The breakwater was never seriously damaged until 1983, when towering, storm-driven waves smashed several holes in it.

A major evolution had taken place in the Bay of San Pedro during those first dozen years of the twentieth century. The dynamics of growth, progress, and expansion were evident everywhere around the bay. Waterways were improved. Important industries arrived. Others were born on the waterfront. A bustling new city hit its stride and charted its future. What were destined to become two of America's most productive ports-of-call became official entities side by side within a few years of each other. For those who lived and savored them, those were exciting, action-filled, unforgettable years, but the best was yet to come.

Above
For the first full decade of the new century, trains rumbling through the port with huge rocks for breakwater construction were a common sight in San Pedro. The first 8,500-foot segment of the breakwater was completed in 1911 after construction had begun in 1899. Courtesy, Southwest Instruments

Top
Pictured is a view toward the entrance of San Pedro harbor about 1915. In the foreground is the Southern Pacific wharf, the first major docking facility in San Pedro, built in 1912. Across the channel is Terminal Island and the Los Angeles Terminal Railroad depot. In the distance is Deadman's Island and the first completed segment of the breakwater. Courtesy, Historical Society of Long Beach

Another in a seemingly endless series of oil strikes in the mid-1920s continued when this Union Oil well blew its stack on Signal Hill. Courtesy, Long Beach Historical Society

CHAPTER VI

FOIBLES AND FORTUNES

San Pedro Bay's two ports—one an ancient entity in the maritime world, the other still largely in the planning stage—now stood on the threshold of significant growth, each in its own fashion and on completely divergent paths.

Centuries old and a hallowed landmark in the area, San Pedro had become a subsidized ward of Los Angeles and the beneficiary of the big city's bounteous financial resources. In addition, the quaint little town still basked in the national attention and congressional endorsement it had received as the official deep-water port for Southern California in the protracted and widely-publicized free-harbor affair.

Long Beach enjoyed none of the advantages of identity or history. A relatively new community that had worked hard to establish its image as a resort, Long Beach still faced a frustrating struggle to create a harbor of its own, and only the persistence and determination of its leaders—and a timely stroke of geological good fortune—brought it all to reality.

For Long Beach the obstacles were formidable and disheartening, to put it mildly. The land where the city wanted to build its harbor was privately owned by a company that stubbornly refused to give it up. Indeed, that company's operations had demonstrated the futility of keeping any new harbor in that location functioning with the heavy flooding and silting that kept clogging its channels and made the exorbitant cost of constant dredging a total waste of money and effort.

Even more discouraging, the irreversible mind-set of government engineers could find no grounds to justify federal participation in the improvement of another port so close to the accepted deep-water site in San Pedro. Long Beach was not yet capable of financing the staggering expense of harbor development and maintenance on its own—even if it had been able to acquire the land it needed.

With the Tidelands Act of 1911 transferring most tidelands and other valuable waterfront property to Los Angeles to be held in trust, the city's first three-million-dollar general obligation bond for harbor improvement was put to work on the San Pedro waterfront. The width of the main channel had become an increasing problem as traffic grew, and in 1912 the original 500-foot-wide entrance was broadened to 800 feet in some places.

The channel was dredged to a depth of thirty feet for its full length to accommodate world-class vessels. The Southern Pacific Railroad completed the first major wharf in San Pedro, with facilities that enabled ships and freight cars to load and unload on either side of the wharf simultaneously. That same year the Port of Los Angeles became the world's biggest lumber importer, with 720,882,630 board feet pouring across its San Pedro docks.

In Long Beach, Craig Shipbuilding, which since 1906 had stood in lonely isolation on the otherwise barren mud flats, finally began to get some company. The Southern California Edison Company, the first large, non-maritime industry to locate in the new harbor, began construction on a new plant in 1910 across the channel from the Craig yard. Edison's steam generating Plant No. 1, which included a vertical steam turbine and two 250-foot steel towers, built high enough to clear the masts of sailing ships, went into operation in 1912.

Long Beach officials eagerly sought to solicit additional business for the city's new municipal wharf. That same year the city council voted to give free dockage to the North Pacific Steamship Company if its steamer *Santa Clara* would make Long Beach a regular port-of-call on its San Diego-to-Santa Barbara run. The ship was welcomed in its inaugural visit with full municipal pomp and ceremony, but service was discontinued after a few weeks for lack of business.

The city had had its full share of setbacks, and Long Beach residents were used to taking waterfront mishaps like storm-damaged piers and buildings destroyed by fire in stride, but no one was prepared for anything like the Municipal Auditorium tragedy on May 24, 1913. Thirty-six were killed and 174 injured in the city's worst catastrophe up to that time. Sadly, it was Empire Day, one of the most festive events of the year, when large crowds were on hand for the downtown parade and program at the auditorium. The parade over, a happy throng had gathered in front of the main entrance to the auditorium waiting to get in, when a forty-square-foot section of the entrance approach suddenly collapsed, hurling 350 people through the lower deck platform onto the sand below. The death toll eventually reached fifty, and the shock of that disaster haunted the city for months.

One of the most extraordinary and tortuous achievements in the history of civil and maritime engineering—the Panama Canal—was then nearing completion across a pestilential stretch of jungle in Central America, and both harbor cities were awaiting its opening with great anticipation. With its fortuitous location as the first big American harbor north of the West Coast side of the canal, and the curvature of the earth placing it only seventy miles off the Great Circle Route between the canal and the Orient, San Pedro Bay would be the first important Pacific stopover for most of the traffic using the new fifty-mile waterway. The benefits to both ports would be considerable.

Alas, that incipient windfall was suddenly put on hold, superseded by international political violence elsewhere. Only eleven days before the Panama Canal was officially opened on August 15, 1914, England had declared war on Germany. Other European nations quickly took sides, and World War I soon engulfed the continent. With most ocean commerce concentrated in the Atlantic Ocean during the conflict and sections of the new waterway blocked by rock and dirt slides, the canal was closed and remained so during the war and for several years afterward.

Both harbor communities turned their full energies to war work, and when the demand rose for workers in East Coast munitions plants, the only war-related jobs available in large numbers in the Los Angeles area were in the shipyards. On the San Pedro side, Southwestern Shipbuilding Company produced nineteen cargo vessels and six tankers, Los Angeles Shipbuilding & Drydock Corporation built thirty-five vessels of various types, and Ralph J. Chandler Shipbuilding produced six cargo vessels. By 1918 four shipbuilding yards in San Pedro had contracts in excess of $115 million to build steel and wooden ships and employed more than 20,000 workers.

In Long Beach a new corporation, Long Beach Shipbuilding Company, temporarily took over the Craig yard for nearly two years in 1916 to 1917 and built five submarines—among the first to be built on the West Coast—as well as eleven large freighters, three smaller freighters, and a lighthouse tender. Meanwhile, Craig built another plant just east of its original yard in 1917 and built three submarines that were launched in 1918. By the end of that year, John F. Craig and his associates had regained control of both shipyards, with thousands of men employed in the two yards. Elsewhere, Golden State Woolen Mills was producing two million dollars' worth of military clothing, five canneries were supplying canned tuna and other fish to the military, and four plants were producing war materials from kelp.

Silting continued to plague Long Beach Harbor. An increasing volume of lumber came in at Long Beach's municipal dock in 1914, and the need to keep the channels navigable became more acute than ever. A lively campaign was mounted for a new bond issue of $650,000 for harbor improvement, maintenance and expansion, and one dollar bills were given away to attract and hold crowds to hear arguments for the bond issue. The vote was well over the margin required, but the issue was never used because it was based on the condition that the government assist Long Beach with its harbor program, or at least supervise expenditure of the bond money. Again, the ranking district engineer had ruled there was "no need" for a second deep-water harbor so close to San Pedro and rejected the request for federal aid.

Despite the rejection, some of the more forceful local organizations demanded that the money be spent on the harbor anyway, but the bonds were never sold. What this latest disappointment did clarify was that far more could be achieved by having harbor matters handled by an organized body rather than various civic-minded volunteers. This well-founded proposal worked its way slowly through the bureaucratic maze, and on June 29, 1917, the city government created a new board of harbor commissioners. Its first members were Mayor W.T. Lisenby, James R. Williams, and C.J. Hargis, commissioners respectively of public property, public safety, and public works.

Earlier, Nature had taken a firm hand—albeit a violent one—in breaking down the beleagured Dock and Terminal Company's resistance when the City of Long Beach could not. A series of savage storms in 1914 and 1916 hammered the waterfront, battering the beach and swamping the Dock and Terminal Company's struggling harbor property with silt and debris. The company could no longer continue, and its only alternative was to withdraw. The dredging project was turned over to the city in 1916, along with the deed to the channels and a 4.7-acre tract of land lying near Slip 5.

Finally, gratefully, Long Beach had the harbor property it had sought so desperately for so long. The happy citizens easily passed a proposed bond issue of $300,000 for harbor improvement, but a loud dispute arose over whether the city had a right to spend taxpayer money on improvements that would benefit adjacent, privately-held property. The case went to the State Supreme Court, which ruled in the city's favor. In addition, harbor channels had become so clogged with silt that the California Shipbuilding Company complained that it had been unable to finish wartime work on two new submarines, including the L-6 which was so firmly imbedded in the mud that it could not be moved. Once unstuck, the L-6 recovered its dignity and went on to fight with distinction, winning credit for sinking a German U-boat in the English Channel. Other harbor firms also protested, and Craig Shipbuilding was given an emergency dredging contract to clear the channels so that vessels could move safely about the harbor without running aground.

Yet there was plenty of action other than maritime around Long Beach and its waterfront. Despite its religious origins and strait-laced ordinances, the city flirted coyly but mischieviously with the prevailing fads and fancies of the day. It took some of the edge off that righteous image and added a refreshing dash of spice and excitement to the local scene.

To most of the world the movies have always been the private preserve of Hollywood, at least until the present era of out-of-town and foreign production. Yet Hollywood had no corner on early film-making, even after its pioneer principals moved west from New Jersey and New York in search of better weather, more light, more space, and an infinite variety of locations to match stories set everywhere in the world.

While some of the founding fathers set up shop and studio in a little suburb of Los Angeles that would become known as Hollywood, other moviemakers found their way to Long Beach. The city's brief but titillating fling with the movies lasted well under a decade, but it was great fun while it lasted.

First to set up an operating film studio in Long Beach was J. Searle Dawley, who opened Balboa Films at the corner of Alamitos and Sixth Street in 1911. He sold the studio two years later to H.M. Horkheimer, a much more stable and ambitious businessman. It was the era of silent movies, and under Horkheimer's astute management Balboa ground out dozens of quickie one-reelers and expanded at a phenomenal pace.

By 1917 Balboa was the largest movie studio in the business, occupying a large section of downtown Long Beach and with a half-dozen films being shot simultaneously on the city's streets, fields, and beaches. It became the city's biggest enterprise and a marvelous tourist attraction. Charlie Chaplin, Buster Keaton, and other great comics worked regularly at Balboa. Stars like Theda Bara and Roscoe "Fatty" Arbuckle lived in Long Beach and could be seen driving through the streets and eating at local restaurants. Where else could the visitor spend the day watching a film being shot or lounging on the beach, then wrap it up with an evening sampling the varied attractions on the Pike? The city's bluenoses had a fit, but the average citizen and the tourists loved it.

Unfortunately, like all good dreams and the industry itself, Long Beach's affair with the movies was fragile, fleeting, and illusory, and it all ended as abruptly as the films it produced. Less than a year after Balboa hit its peak as the world's biggest studio it suddenly went bankrupt, and no one ever really knew why. Perhaps it was that powerful religious faction that still wielded plenty of clout in Long Beach and always deplored the shenanigans of the movie people as a public offense against morality—their particular version of morality, anyway.

The other diversion of the time that immediately captured public imagination and enthusiasm was the hair-raising and death-defying new pastime of powered flight. Only a few years after the Wright brothers made history at Kittyhawk, what was advertised as the country's first international air meet drew an average daily crowd of 25,000 to Dominguez Field in 1910. Dashing young daredevils in their rickety, open-air aerial contraptions thrilled their earthbound audiences and rivaled the popularity of today's rock stars among the youthful and adventure-minded population. Frenchman Louis Paulhan soared to an incredible 1,100 feet, "the greatest height for an aeroplane yet recorded in America," the front pages shouted. Roy Knabenshue reached 800 feet in his bid for a dirigible record in another highlight of the first international meet.

Aviation fever gripped Long Beach like an epidemic. The Bay of San Pedro was a perfect stage for these aerial heroes, who performed out over the harbor as thousands watched breathlessly from the beach. There was a rash of do-it-yourself airplane construction. Bernard Birnie put together the first "big airship" built in Long Beach in a barn in 1910. Charlie Day built his in the old tabernacle building. Other planes were built in the basement of the Virginia Hotel, and from 1913 to 1915 the beach in front of the Earl Apartments was used as a landing field.

It was aviation at its most primitive stage, and a suicidal road to fame and glory. Most of those fearless stuntmen died young and violently. Calbraith "Cal" Rodgers made Long Beach the aviation center of the world for a time when he completed the first transcontinental flight ever made with a perfect landing on the sand in 1911. He was killed a few months later in a crash into the surf near the Pine Avenue Pier. Earl Daugherty and Frank Champion were among the first local men to qualify for aviation licenses. Champion later died in an accident in Japan. Famous altitude pilot Archie Hoxsey put on a dazzling display, then went into a flat spin and crashed to his death at the second annual international air meet at Dominguez Field in 1911.

These freewheeling activities in Long Beach made San Pedro seem tame by comparison, but the steady infusion of Los Angeles subsidies enabled port development to continue. In 1914 construction began on the first of two of San Pedro's most famous and most visible landmarks. Ground was broken for Fort MacArthur on a large piece of land adjacent to Cabrillo Beach that had originally been set aside for military use by the Spanish and later designated as an unnamed military reservation by President Grover Cleveland at the request of the War Department. Named for Lieutenant General Arthur MacArthur, father of General Douglas MacArthur, it became a permanent harbor defense installation until it was closed in 1981 and the land deeded to the City of Los Angeles as the site of the new Cabrillo Beach Recreational Complex.

After never previously being able to offer much more than limited facilities for shallow-draft lumber schooners, the Port of Los Angeles in 1915 began building its first warehouse, the massive, six-story Warehouse No. 1, which still stands like a fortress alongside the entrance to the main channel. It marked the transition in class from a small, poorly-equipped landing point to a legitimate seaport with onshore capabilities for deep-sea vessels with varied cargoes.

Flooding and silting remained a seasonal blight that affected both Long Beach and Los Angeles harbors, but was especially severe in Long Beach. The condition became so critical in 1913 to 1914 that Long Beach leaders seriously wondered whether they would ever be able to develop a harbor there. It was recognized that the only way of alleviating this perennial problem was proper flood control of the Los Angeles River. In 1917 a newly-created Los Angeles County Flood Control District proposed that a channel to divert floodwaters be built through Long Beach to the ocean. After some discussion on where the diversion channel should go, a route through the west side of the city was chosen, and county voters approved a $4.5-million bond issue to finance it.

Said Walter H. Case in his definitive *History of Long Beach and Vicinity:*

Construction of the flood control channel through the industrial district made continued and permanent harbor development possible for Long Beach. Pending completion of the project, city officials continued to experience great difficulty in maintaining adequate channels for boats plying to plants on the harbor.

With completion of the flood control channel in 1923, however, the problem of extensive silting was permanently controlled in both ports.

While Long Beach had at last taken full charge of its own harbor and was formulating plans for its full-scale development, harbor traffic in San Pedro had skyrocketed after the war. The port had handled about two million tons of cargo in 1913, and that total had diminished during the war years. From a meager 150,000 tons per month at the end of hostilities, the total leaped to more than 2.5 million tons per month within a few years, as goods stockpiled all over the world were abruptly freed for delivery, and business and building activities were suddenly reactivated.

Maritime activity was soaring in San Pedro, but a much more significant eruption took place on the other side of the harbor on a quiet June night in 1921. With the property in hand, Long Beach was facing the impossible task of raising the millions of dollars it would take to create a harbor of international stature—an utterly unrealistic goal for a city the size of Long Beach, especially since the government had shown no inclination whatsoever to help fund that costly work.

The solution to that dilemma, and many of Long Beach's other financial problems, arrived with a thunderous roar on the evening of June 23, when Shell Oil Company's Alamitos No. 1 well at the corner of Temple Avenue and Hill Street in Signal Hill came in at 2,745 feet. The strike hurled an eighty-foot geyser into the night air, drenching the neighborhood with a layer of sticky black crude for four days before it was controlled. The discovery of oil on Signal Hill, which one harbor historian referred to as "the intervention which might be termed a miracle," turned the town upside down and completely disrupted its normal way of life. Suddenly, it resembled a frontier town all over again. Speculators arrived in droves. Land values went out of sight, and many citizens of limited means suddenly found their humble holdings in great demand and worth a small fortune. People who would not know oil from axle grease were clamoring to get into the hectic new business.

Signal Hill had developed a reputation as one of the more desirable residential districts of the city before the oil strike, and many families who had recently completed expensive homes there moved out and leased them to the oil developers who surrounded them on all sides. The scramble for land leases and purchases after the first well came in was intensified as one after another roared into production. For a time, there seemed to be no dry wells. Excitement grew as the field of production became wider, and land values leaped higher and higher.

Even after they were controlled and capped, the wells were notorious for their dangerous and unpredictable behavior. During that frantic first six months, three wells had gas blowouts and were ignited, creating an awesome sight at night with towering pillars of flame that could be seen for miles. Daring workers used dyna-

Shell-Martin No. 1, one of the earliest of the Long Beach oil strikes, came in with a whistle and a roar and blew its derrick to smithereens as it erupted skyward in 1921. Courtesy, Long Beach Historical Society

mite and pumped in mud to put out the fires, and there was considerable damage from explosions as the perilous technique of extinguishing oil well fires had to be learned through trial and error. By the end of 1921 Signal Hill had dozens of derricks, with six in production pumping 75,000 barrels of oil.

Production rose as explosively as the geysers themselves in 1922, when the forest of derricks multiplied and expanded by the day, and the great black bonanza pumped out a total of more than 18,500,000 barrels that year. Highlighting that yield was the most spectacular geyser to date, General Petroleum's Black & Drake well, which blew in January 1922 and rained 9,000 barrels of dingy film on fields, streets, and many homes for a mile or more before it sanded up.

Scores of new wells kept coming in, and production reached an incredible total of nearly sixty-nine million barrels in 1923. While there seemed no end in sight, the output slowed a smidgen in 1924 to slightly over sixty million barrels. Even so, it gave the city of Long Beach royalties and revenue from lease rights of $1,204,119, the first in a number of years when the city received over one million dollars in oil royalties.

It was undeniably dirty and messy, but this gold from the earth was pure manna from heaven as far as Long Beach was concerned. Suddenly, the city was bathed in the warm glow of prosperity, its coffers overflowing after years of struggling with its municipal budget. All kinds of things were possible—including that big, expensive harbor that the city never could have financed from its ordinary revenues. In 1924, by an overwhelming majority, the people of Long Beach approved a five-million-dollar bond issue for harbor improvement. Proceeds were used to build a 7,284-foot breakwater and for construction of east and west moles and bulkheads for protection of the entrance channel into the inner harbor, all of which were completed by 1928. It was the size of financial outlay that usually only the government could afford, and it marked a major milestone in the port's development.

While not as direct a recipient of petroleum riches as Long Beach, San Pedro had long had a piece of the oil action and had begun serving the industry years earlier. Oil had previously been discovered at a number of other locations in Southern California. In 1909 Union Oil Company has built a subsidiary called Outer Harbor Dock & Wharf Company in the Port of Los Angeles, and by 1911 Union Oil, Standard Oil Company, and Associated Petroleum were shipping a million barrels a year through port facilities. Union began building a refinery on 260 acres of port property, and by 1921 Standard had storage for 460,000 barrels in the port and could load two tankers simultaneously at the rate of 12,000 barrels per hour.

Then came a number of major strikes in 1921, including the nearby Signal Hills blast, and production completely swamped the limited onsite storage and refining facilities available at that time. The huge volume had to be shipped out as fast as ships could carry it away. Fortunately, the Panama Canal also reopened in 1921, and the sea lanes between the harbor and the canal became an endless parade of tankers carrying oil eastward to Gulf and East Coast refineries. Their tolls alone were responsible for putting the canal on a paying basis.

Still, the big beneficiary of the oil largesse was and remains the city of Long Beach. It has brought the harborside community wealth and opportunity beyond belief. That same subterranean treasure would misbehave years later, twisting the topography, frightening the populace, and seeming to punish the city for its excesses, which some religious zealots doubtlessly must have found most appropriate and well-deserved. No matter, in terms of the city's future it had the greatest single impact on Long Beach of any development in the community's history. In the view of one historian, it made Long Beach the "richest city in the world."

The Long Beach Curtain Cleaning Company and French Laundry did most of the fancy cleaning and laundry work around the city in the decades between 1910 and 1930. It was then owned by E. Morita, pictured in front of his delivery truck, with his family-type team of employees at right. The company was later sold and the name changed. Courtesy, Long Beach Historical Society

C H A P T E R V I I

FEAST OR FAMINE

As the bay's new millionaire municipality launched its massive harbor improvement program, Los Angeles city fathers were taking a long, hard look at their own port operations and came to the inescapable conclusion that it had not yet come close to achieving its enormous potential.

Certainly, the statistics were impressive. A 1922 joint study by the University of Southern California and three local banks stated that the port had poured about $100 million into the local economy from all sources during the previous year. Boxcar tonnage statistics placed it near the top among American seaports, but lumber made up nearly all of that huge import figure; outgoing petroleum almost alone accounted for a staggering export volume in the tens of millions of tons. Otherwise, the port had done almost nothing to promote itself or generate other business.

There were reasons for this, and it was not entirely the fault of port administrators. Before 1920 the Los Angeles area was still largely agricultural and had not yet developed a diversified economy. It had little two-way trade to offer, and ship captains were reluctant to stop in a port unless they could also pick up outgoing cargo.

Another factor found most new arrivals among the fast-growing population in Los Angeles from inland areas where people were completely unfamiliar with the functions and commercial possibilities of a seaside city. Furthermore the location of most of the city's residents twenty or more miles from the harbor did not encourage the familiarity with waterfront operations to be found in cities like San Diego and San Francisco, where their ports are a physical part of the community.

For these reasons the Los Angeles port's trade was almost entirely a one-way process. Ships carrying cargoes to South American ports, which could have brought back a variety of goods, not only sailed back empty but bypassed Los Angeles and carried Latin American merchants up the coast to San Francisco. Lumber ships would unload in Los Angeles, leave empty and stop in San Francisco to pick up supplies and goods for the well-heeled Northwest lumber cities.

An important element in San Francisco's domination over West-Coast trade was its virtual monopoly over direct trade with the Orient. Before 1920 virtually all shipments to what would later become the great markets of the Far East had to go through established trans-Pacific lines in San Francisco and occasionally Seattle. This enabled San Francisco to take millions of dollars in maritime commerce away from Los Angeles, by default more than anything else. There was simply no competition.

The Los Angeles Chamber of Commerce

tried hard to remedy these glaring inadequacies shortly after the war. In an effort to establish the port's first direct line with the Orient, they persuaded fifty citizens to invest $1,000 each in a new Los Angeles Pacific Navigation Company. The shipping firm chartered three large steamers and scheduled sailings to major Far East ports every sixty days, but an economic downturn and competition from other Pacific lines effectively put the new operator out of business in 1921.

Another local group, founded in 1920 as the Los Angeles Steamship Company, fared much better. It acquired the *Yale* and *Harvard* when the two passenger steamers were released from wartime naval duty and used them to introduce a popular coastal cruise from Los Angeles to San Francisco. Buoyed by that success the company bought a pair of confiscated German liners, rechristened them the *City of Los Angeles* and *City of Honolulu,* and became the first to become involved in the cruise business between Los Angeles and Hawaii on a large scale.

Once aware of its commercial and maritime shortcomings, the Los Angeles business community scrambled to make up for lost opportunity. It came at the right time, too, because Los Angeles was then turning from agricultural to industrial interests, and with the change came a growing awareness of the harbor as a direct terminal for the import of raw materials and the export of finished goods to the distant markets of the world. The city needed industry and the chamber dangled an enticing package of inexpensive fuel and electrical power, exceptional year-round climate and a steadily growing labor force before big inland corporations thinking of relocating. Goodyear Tire & Rubber Company was one of the first major industries to make the move to Southern California.

Of all the excesses brought on by the liberation of the Roaring Twenties, one most sorely beseiged and ferociously guarded was the tottering bastion of female modesty, and nowhere was it more rigorously tested than on the beaches. In this modern era when women's bathing suits are more rumor than fact and the material in them diminishes every year, it is amusing to consider the furor that the battle over ladies' beach attire caused at that time. An ambivalent city like Long Beach was a natural battleground for such a confrontation.

Long Beach women had frequently complained about being swaddled from chin to ankle in such a shapeless tonnage of heavy cloth at the beach that it is a wonder more did not drown, much less learn to swim. The Women's Christian Temperance Union took a proprietary interest in the issue and had plenty to say, and the controversy raged on until the city decided in 1920 to set some official guidelines for beach dress and get rid of the problem once and for all.

What followed was one of the most hilarious episodes in Long Beach history, a comedy classic that couldn't have been funnier if it had been hatched in the antic imagination of a Woody Allen or a Mel Brooks. It had to be someone with a wry sense of humor who chose the author of the beachwear ordinance—one William Peek, a local mortician who also served as the city's commissioner of public safety.

When the laughter had died down, Mr. Peek came up with an ordinance that demonstrated an innate talent for linguistic gobbledygook and an almost total disregard for periods, commas, and other basic aids to clarity and readability. His work required a long attention span to get all the way through it:

No person over the age of six shall appear on any highway or public place or on sand or beach or in the Pacific Ocean in Long Beach clothed in a bathing suit which does not completely conceal from view all that portion of the trunk of the body of such person below a line around the body even with the upper part of the armpits except a circular arm hole for each arm with the maximum diameter no longer than twice the distance from the upper part of the armpit to the top of the shoulder and which does not completely conceal from view each leg from the hip joint to a line around the leg one-third of the way to the knee, and without such bathing suit having a skirt made of opaque material surrounding the person and hanging loosely from the waistline to the bottom of such suit. Every person violating any of the provisions of this ordinance shall be deemed guilty of a misdemeanor and upon conviction thereof shall be punished by a fine not exceeding five hundred dollars or by imprisonment in the city for not more than six months, or by both such fine and imprisonment.

Having delivered himself of this masterpiece, Mr. Peek presumably returned to his somber duties at the funeral home while the townsfolk came up with various interpretations of the new law. Some of them were still trying to figure it out three years later when the ordinance was repealed, bathing suits were carved down to fit the figure, and women were given a fighting chance to swim rather than sink.

The preservation of female modesty took another drubbing in 1925 when the city council resolutely overrode the horrified objections of local church authorities and approved an application by the Long Beach Amusement League to hold the city's first bathing beauty contest. Several hundred girls participated before a gaping crowd in a mass display of female flesh unprecedented in Long Beach.

That was only part of the city's "deplorable moral disintegration." Bootlegging had long been an illicit way of life in bone-dry Long Beach when Prohibition became the law of the land in 1920. Thus, when the rest of the nation's amateur distillers were just learning the tricks of the trade, Long Beach's long established cadre of illegal booze-makers had been making and surreptitiously distributing the stuff for years.

Before Prohibition it had been only a minor inconvenience for Long Beach residents to slip down to Seal Beach or over to Wilmington or San Pedro for a legal drink. The friendly neighborhood bootlegger had been a popular fellow then, but with the ban on booze everywhere he soon achieved that special level of prestige and respect reserved only for people like butchers and service station owners during wartime rationing.

The illegal liquor business began to flourish as never before, blind pigs proliferated in the most unlikely places, and there was enough nighttime boat traffic and furtive landings all around the bay to have staged a full-scale amphibious assault. "Rum ships" operated brazenly off the coast, one of which was reported to have made Long Beach its home port for several years. Overworked harbor police intercepted countless vessels trying to unload illicit liquor. Smaller boats with the same cargo were capsized. Stiff sentences were doled out for drunken driving, as well as bootlegging and possession.

City records for fiscal 1925 to 1926 list 415 liquor raids by police, twenty-five stills destroyed, 7,783 gallons confiscated, and 415 arrests for bootlegging; in 1926 to 1927, 350 raids and 500 arrests. One of the most sensational raids took place in December 1926, when police stormed a four-story molasses feed factory and found equipment producing 10,000 gallons daily behind an elaborate facade of false walls and secret panels. After thirty-three legally dry years Long Beach eventually voted, 37,170 to 26,890, to repeal the Wright Act, also known as the Little Volstead Act, in November 1932. That same year the city also legalized dancing on Sunday by a slim majority of thirteen votes.

While Long Beach was making plenty of racket kicking over the traces during the twenties, the only truly loud noise in San Pedro during those years came from Fort MacArthur, of all places. After the flurry of World War I activity, the fort had assumed that air of patient inertia that prevails in all armies when there is no war to fight. In 1926 two giant,

Above
Formal military services were held at Fort MacArthur in San Pedro in 1924 for the fifty-six navy men killed in an explosion aboard the battleship USS Mississippi *during gunnery practice off Catalina Island. Courtesy, Los Angeles Harbor Department*

Opposite page
The Port of Los Angeles had not achieved its potential, but it was a busy harbor all the same when this photograph was taken from above the breakwater in 1925. Courtesy, Title Insurance and Trust Company

fourteen-inch coastal defense guns were installed, and it was decided to test-fire them. Although the army later insisted it had issued plenty of advance notice of the tests, the concussion from the first blast sent the community into a near panic, and the army dutifully paid for thousands of broken windows. Another few firings brought such vehement objections that all further tests were canceled and the big guns cut up and sold for junk.

That eminently sensible but utterly unworkable suggestion that the entire Bay of San Pedro should be administered as a single port by one combined administration made another appearance during the mid-1920s. This time the proposal gained more credence and momentum than in the past, carrying all the way to Sacramento. The State Legislature in 1925 passed a Port District Enabling Act, under which Long Beach and Los Angeles harbors could be controlled by a joint powers agreement if both cities approved. Straw votes on endorsing the plan found a decided majority in Los Angeles, but a cautious fifty-fifty vote in Long Beach. That opposition was based on the long-held feeling that Long Beach could not be assured of an equal voice in running harbor affairs. Long Beach was also then flush with new oil money and feeling more independent than ever—so much for the port district plan.

Besides, Long Beach was much too preoccupied with its own harbor development to think about sharing it with anyone else. Work from the city's initial five-million-dollar bond issue for harbor improvement had been completed, and the Long Beach electorate approved another bond issue of $2.7 million for construction of additional piers, wharves, and other terminal facilities in 1928. Work began immediately on reconstruction of Pier 1, then known as the municipal wharf, in the inner harbor, and on new Piers A and B in the outer harbor. The seven berths at these new outer harbor facilities would provide total dockage space of 3,500 feet, enough to accommodate five large vessels at one time.

While growth was necessarily slow at the beginning, Long Beach Harbor commerce steadily began to pick up momentum. From 1.1 million tons valued at slightly under eleven million dollars in 1926, volume rose rapidly to four million tons worth almost seventy million dollars in 1930. Lack of storage space became critical. Two million tons of cargo moved through Long Beach in fiscal 1928 to 1929, even though the port's only municipal transit shed was a fifty-by-sixty-foot wood-frame structure on the wharf. That cargo consisted mainly of pipe, case oil, steel, lumber, and other products that did not need covered storage.

The Port of Los Angeles was undergoing its own massive expansion at that time. The Chamber of Commerce pushed its Foreign Commerce and Shipping Department to renewed efforts, and in 1923 organized the Marine Exchange, which has given valuable support to the local shipping industry over the years. Each member of a "Greater Harbor Committee of

200" contributed $1,000 for development of an in-depth plan that would insure the future growth of the port.

With lumber and oil monopolizing its facilities, the Los Angeles Harbor Department used a fifteen-million-dollar obligation bond to initiate the biggest construction program in the port's history in order to offer other local industries room to operate in the harbor. In four years municipal wharf space more than doubled, from 13,900 lineal feet in 1921 to 30,884 lineal feet in 1925. Still, those two big commodities continued to dominate harbor traffic. In 1923 the 1.1 billion board feet of lumber imports and 21.5 million tons of outgoing petroleum made Los Angeles the tonnage leader on the West Coast, replacing perennial front-runner San Francisco.

With the reopening of the Panama Canal in 1921, the Bay of San Pedro reclaimed both its geographic importance and its former access to East Coast and European trade. While Long Beach was building its harbor with all possible haste, maritime traffic in San Pedro was mushrooming sevenfold in less than a decade. Ships that once came to San Pedro only for its inexpensive fuel began serving the port as scheduled carriers. Forty-three steamship lines used the port in 1922, and by the end of the following year ninety-three lines—including nineteen carrying both passengers and freight—were regular customers.

The sudden surge in maritime commerce was no aberration of the times. With a brief postwar economic slump over and world ports reactivated and improving rapidly, the international business community now recognized and appreciated the enormous advantages of shipping by sea—namely, that it was by far the least expensive method of transportation available anywhere. Comparative prices were astonishing. It cost six dollars to ship a ton of cement by train from the harbor to Needles, California, a distance of 311 miles; by sea, you could ship that same ton for the same price 7,721 miles from the harbor to Belgium. It also cost four times as much to transport steel rails overland from Pittsburgh to Los Angeles as it did by ship from Belgium to Los Angeles, about one-third the distance. Charges for ocean-going freight averaged from five to ten dollars less than shipment by land. Even at a minimum five dollars, shippers saved an estimated $130 million on the twenty-six million tons that moved through the port in fiscal 1923 to 1924.

The flurry of harbor activity was causing increasing congestion in the main channel. It was still only 500 to 800 feet wide, and with ships tied up two and three abreast at wharves on both sides, passage through that key access was much too narrow. Many of the shacks inhabited by fishermen and artistic itinerants on Terminal Island were demolished to make way for widening of the channel to 1,000 feet in 1925.

With the channel broadened and improved, that venerable old landmark Deadman's Island was a worse navigational hazard than ever and, sentiment to the contrary, it simply had to go. Before demolition started in 1927, the dead buried there were disinterred, including the remains of a couple of long-dead sea captains, the last survivor of the Indians on offshore San Nicolas Island, the six marines who died in the Battle of Rancho San Pedro in 1846, a female skeleton with flowing blond hair, two cavaliers wearing conquistador-style clothing and boots, and a skeleton with an arrow piercing its skull. All were reinterred ashore, and debris from two years of steady blasting was used to add sixty-two acres to Reservation Point on Terminal Island.

A few miles to the east Long Beach was applying the fruits of its oil royalties wisely. Generous bond issues were approved for new high schools, a community hospital, a large new park, and other fine municipal facilities. But for all the riches it provided, oil did have its darker side—literally. If, as has been written, the petroleum find made Long Beach the rich-

Opposite page
The office of the chief harbor engineer at the Port of Los Angeles was housed in this building at Berth 90 in 1923. Note the vintage Model-T Fords parked nearby. Courtesy, Los Angeles Harbor Department

Below
Boatloads of sailors cruise through the harbor during the early stages of the demolition of the famed landmark Deadman's Island. It took two years of steady blasting from 1927 to 1929 before the old navigational hazard was finally removed and the debris used to add sixty-two acres of landfill to Terminal Island. At left is one of the cranes at Bethlehem Shipyard, now Southwest Marine Inc. Courtesy, Southwest Instruments

Below
Terminal Island was home to the nation's leading fishing and canning industries in 1925. Seaside Avenue runs out to the shore, with Fish Harbor at upper left. Bethlehem Shipyard and Deadman's Island are at upper right. In the foreground are the homes of fishermen and cannery workers, the neighborhood grocery is at the right, and also a small shop (with white trim) where a Japanese woman barber gave haircuts for twenty-five cents. Courtesy, Los Angeles Harbor Department

est city in the world, it soon made it one of the grubbiest looking as well. Oil developers, not the tidiest of humans, were notoriously careless about picking up after themselves. Oily water lay in pools in vacant lots and streets, or found its way into flood control channels. Broken and discarded equipment littered some sections of the city. Fire prevention measures in the oil field were lax. The city responded by issuing stern warnings and passing and enforcing stiff ordinances to make the petroleum people clean up their act.

Despite identical goals, Los Angeles and Long Beach had had little to do with each other in developing their individual ports. Civic pride strongly influenced this mutual decision to go it alone, especially in Long Beach. The only time they had worked together previously was in the 1918 dredging that turned Cerritos Slough from a shallow ditch into the 200-foot-wide Cerritos Channel and made regular navigation between the two harbors possible. The next cooperative project that benefitted both principals was the creation of the Harbor Belt Line Railroad in 1929, which merged the operation of the Southern Pacific, Union Pacific, Santa Fe, and Pacific Electric Railway throughout the harbor.

Backdoor booze and uninhibited bathing beauties were only part of the local Long Beach scene during the twenties. Distance swimming became a major spectator sport, thanks largely to the successful crossing of the English Channel by America's Gertrude Ederle. With its long love affair with water sports and that twenty-six-mile stretch between the harbor and Catalina Island an ideal course, Long Beach was soon in the swim. Chewing gum magnate William Wrigley, Jr., whose family also owned Catalina Island, brought national attention to the city in the summer of 1926 when he posted a $25,000 first prize for the winner of a race to Catalina. The event was held the following January amid tremendous ballyhoo and many months of priceless promotion and publicity for Long Beach. From a field of almost a hundred experienced swimmers, an unknown Canadian teenager named George Young staggered ashore first on the rocky Catalina coast after battling the treacherous cross-channel currents for nearly sixteen hours.

Something always seemed to be happening in Long Beach as the decade wore on. The ultra-exclusive Pacific Coast Club opened on Ocean Avenue with an elaborate dedication ceremony in 1926. The Lone Eagle himself—Charles A. Lindbergh—led the list of distinguished visitors when he stopped by in 1928. A surge of elation swept through the city when it was announced that none other than the Ford Motor Company, the reigning giant of American industry, had purchased forty acres of choice harbor property and would erect an auto-assembly plant there. One sad note during those exhilarating times was the death of the city's foremost aviation pioneer, Earl Daugherty, in a crash near the municipal airport, which was later named in his memory.

Long Beach was riding a new high of prosperity and optimism and the future shone with promise when the honeymoon ended abruptly with the financial crash of 1929. The awakening was rude and painful, but not as catastrophic as in other places where the collapse of a single large employer wiped out countless company towns all over the country. The tourist business fell off sharply. The proud Virginia Hotel was forced to close its doors in 1932. Traffic on the Pike continued; you could still stroll the strip, even if you could not afford to sample its pleasures, but longtime concessionaires were dropping out one after another. Oil production also took a nosedive, but at least there still were jobs there.

Two developments that would have had a much greater impact in happier days occurred in 1930. There was the official opening of the new Ford plant with 2,000 badly needed jobs in April, and two months later ground was broken by Proctor & Gamble for a new five-

Above
The Long Beach inner harbor was studded with oil derricks and largely undeveloped in 1930. The largest industries shown in this photograph were Craig Shipyard, at lower left, and the Proctor & Gamble plant, at right. From the George Metivier Collection

Right
Environmentalists fought bitterly against allowing the railroad to be built along Ocean Boulevard, and it was still an unusual sight when this photograph was taken in 1929. From the George Metivier Collection

Above
Many of America's capital warships, including a number that were sunk or damaged at Pearl Harbor, were a common sight at anchor inside the breakwater in Long Beach during the late 1930s. The breakwater then extended halfway across the harbor to Angel's Gate lighthouse. The final section was begun in 1946 and completed in 1949. Courtesy, Long Beach Harbor Department

Opposite page
The Breakers Hotel, at right, was one of the tallest buildings on the Long Beach oceanfront around 1930, and is one of the few still surviving today. From the George Metivier Collection

Below
The 1933 earthquake wrecked many buildings throughout Long Beach. Fifty-two people were killed and 700 were injured. Damage was estimated at forty-five million dollars. From the George Metivier Collection

million-dollar, fifteen-acre factory that promised to employ another 1,200. Long Beach was deeply grateful for these important new sources of employment and income, but hard times cast a pall over both ceremonies.

One mainstay during the Depression years was the presence and the spending power of the United States Navy. A city with a weakness for inspirational names, Long Beach had been calling itself the "Home Port of the Battle Fleet" since 1919. That was changed to "Navy Capital of the United States" in 1932, when the harbor became the home anchorage for nearly fifty ships of the Pacific fleet. There was some basis for that grandiose title. About 900 naval officers and their families lived in Long Beach, more than in any other American city, in addition to the families of thousands of enlisted men. Long Beach made them welcome by building an $80,000 navy landing at the foot of Pico Avenue and spending another $15,000 for a nearby navy athletic field. Their service dollars were a valuable addition to the local economy.

Two harbor events during the early days of the Depression helped raise the morale to some degree, or at least distracted bay residents from their anxieties. One was the 1932 Olympics in Los Angeles, with the rowing competition held in the new Marine Stadium in Long Beach. The athletes performed to a lot of empty seats during the five-day event, but a mighty crowd estimated at 1.5 million overran San Pedro in 1933 to watch the USS *Constitution* sail into the harbor during its only visit ever to the

West Coast. This one was free, and nearly a half-million people clambered aboard to inspect historic "Old Ironsides" during its three-week layover.

What Long Beach needed least during those troubled times was a disaster on the scale of the Empire Day tragedy twenty years earlier, but it got one all the same. A violent earthquake, which originated miles under the ocean at a point about four miles off Newport Beach, shook the city at 5:55 p.m. on March 10, 1933. The initial shock lasted eleven seconds and registered 6.3 on the Richter Scale, with thirty-four aftershocks during the night. In Long Beach fifty-two people were killed and 700 injured. The quake caused extensive damage throughout the city. Many buildings collapsed or were wrecked beyond repair, and damage was estimated at forty-five million dollars.

One seventy-five-year-old Long Beach resident, a seaman aboard the aircraft carrier *Saratoga* anchored in the harbor at the time, recalls the huge vessel shuddering as though hit by a torpedo at the instant the quake hit and seeing the entire Long Beach skyline sway as in a strong breeze. No one knew what it was, but general quarters was sounded and every battle station manned within a minute or two.

Although the stricken city was without telephone or telegraph service that first night and runners had to be used for communications, help came promptly and from many sources. The Pacific fleet, which had just returned from a six-month cruise, sent medical supplies, food, blankets, tents, and 2,000 navy personnel and marines to guard against looting and assist in any way possible. The Army at Fort MacArthur also sent men and supplies, and the Red Cross, Salvation Army, American Legion, and other civic organizations set up emergency aid, shelter, and food stations and rendered valuable assistance.

Long Beach's limited number of harbor facilities suffered little, but the quake caused approximately $250,000's worth of damage to Los Angeles port property and knocked down copings on buildings and chimneys in San Pedro. All told, the quake killed 119 people in Los Angeles and Orange counties, and a nerve-wracking series of small aftershocks rattled the area for the next three months.

The collapse of the American economy had a far-reaching domino effect, paralyzing the world monetary system and causing a precipitous decline in international trade. Ocean traffic was curtailed and fewer ships sailed, throwing thousands of merchant seamen out of work. Many drifted into San Pedro or were stranded there, and the state set up emergency relief camps at Timm's Point to provide temporary shelter for them. Their situation did not improve until the late 1930s when business began to revive and nations preparing for an impending war developed a growing need for American commodities.

Relations between waterfront labor and management had always been tenuous and cold, with management in total control. Disputes over wages and working conditions invariably ended with the worker being forced to accept whatever crumbs a contemptuous employer condescended to throw his way. It was no contest in 1910, when Craig Shipyard workers wanted a little more pay and the work day cut from ten to eight hours. Craig bluntly refused to meet with the workers or even discuss it. The complaisant city council quickly passed a local law prohibiting picketing, and several doz-

Oil pumps, like these pictured on Pier A in 1953, bobbed away constantly, bringing in the millions in oil revenues which enabled Long Beach to build its harbor into one of America's leading international ports. Courtesy, Long Beach Harbor Department

en workers were thrown into jail.

Working conditions had not improved much over the years. Hiring procedures were still flagrantly corrupt and unfair, wages still so low that the average worker had trouble supporting a family. Tough company bosses treated workers ruthlessly; practices such as forcing men to move a load and run back for the next one were common. Labor remained at the mercy of management until 1933, when federal law enabled them to unionize for the first time.

In 1934 the International Longshoremen's Association flexed its newly acquired muscle with a demand for an end to inhumane labor conditions in San Pedro. When a strike was called shipowners ignored their demands and hired dozens of strikebreakers. Private guards supported the police, and the strikebreakers were lodged in a company compound in Wilmington. On May 15 union members attacked the compound. Two longshoremen were killed, five seriously wounded, and dozens of others beaten and arrested, as guards and police met them with a barrage of gunfire and tear gas. Management was held accountable and was forced to grant major concessions in subsequent contracts with the longshoremen. That tragic incident came to be known as "Bloody Thursday," and the date is observed each year with memorial marches and services in San Pedro, San Francisco, and other port cities.

Slowly but unmistakably, the grim, discouraging ordeal of the Depression years began to subside and the harbor mists were growing brighter. Construction of a 12,500-foot extension of the San Pedro breakwater was completed to a point south of the Long Beach outer harbor construction in 1937. Lack of funds seriously hampered further harbor expansion during the middle Depression years, but several projects were completed in Long Beach Harbor with the aid of the government's Works Projects Administration (WPA). The port joined with the WPA to finance construction of a concrete and steel passenger and freight terminal at Pier A, in addition to a new 560-foot wharf and other improvements at Pier B.

In San Pedro total port traffic went up over the twenty-million-ton level in fiscal 1937 to 1938 for the first time in seven years. The overall value of cargo for the year nearly matched the one-billion-dollar level it had first attained during that calamitous year, 1929. Gross revenues and ship arrivals were up, money was back in circulation, and big, beautiful passenger ships like the *President Hoover* and *President Coolidge* of the Dollar Line and Matson's *Lurline* and *Matsonia* made romantic cruises to the Pacific isles available again. The huge, forty-two-ton Pan American World Airways clippers became an awesome attraction, as was the sight of row upon row of massive grey ships of war anchored inside the breakwater.

Long Beach and its harbor development program reached another milestone in 1936, when oil was discovered in the harbor area just west of the city limits and north of Cerritos Channel by General Petroleum Corporation. On March 8, 1938, the Westgate-Greenland Oil Company brought in the first Long Beach Harbor Department well, producing an uninterrupted flow of riches that would generate a plethora of wealth and problems in equal abundance.

The container crane, seen here through a porthole in the Port of Long Beach, symbolizes one of the greatest advances in maritime commerce. Containerization increased manpower productivity many times over, cut ship turnaround time from days to hours, and virtually eliminated pilferage and handling damage. Courtesy, Long Beach Harbor Department

Opposite page, top
Juan Rodriguez Cabrillo is shown aboard his flagship El Salvador, *accompanied by* La Vitoria, *both small, hand-hewn caravels, sailing along the Alta California coast. Cabrillo died as a result of a fall at San Miguel Island in 1543, only six months after he sailed from Mexico. The log of his voyage lay unrecognized for centuries in the archives in Madrid. Courtesy, Los Angeles Harbor Department*

Opposite page, bottom
The waters of San Pedro Bay were so shallow that early traders had no choice but to anchor well offshore and transfer goods via small boats, an onerous chore which Richard Henry Dana described so graphically in his classic Two Years Before the Mast. *The fortress-like outcropping in the bay was Deadman's Island, sometime graveyard and navigational hazard until it was dynamited out of existence in 1928. Courtesy, Los Angeles Harbor Department*

Above
The historic landing of Juan Rodriguez Cabrillo in 1542 is reenacted each year at Cabrillo Beach in San Pedro by a group from the Los Angeles Department of Parks and Recreation. For years, the role of Cabrillo has been played by Juan Rodriguez Olguin, who was named after the explorer. Courtesy, Los Angeles Harbor Department

Above
The Buccaneer *is one of several replicas of colorful old sailing ships available for charter in the harbor. An exact reproduction of the* Bounty, *used in the filming of* Mutiny on the Bounty, *is berthed in the Port of Long Beach. Courtesy, Los Angeles Harbor Department*

Above
Star-Kist, originally founded in 1971 by Martin Bogdanovich as the French Sardine Company, became the largest cannery in the world, but was forced to close several years ago because of ruinous foreign competition. Courtesy, Los Angeles Harbor Department

Right
The collapse of the tuna industry had a domino effect on the local fishing industry, which relied on the canneries to take most of its catch. Soaring fuel costs and territorial disputes with Mexico have caused more woes for the fishing fleet. Courtesy, Los Angeles Harbor Department

Opposite page, left
The container ship and sailboat sharing space on the main channel represent two of the harbor's principal activities – maritime commerce and recreation. Large areas of the waterfront are devoted to recreational purposes, including marinas with thousands of berths for small boats. Courtesy, Los Angeles Harbor Department

Opposite page, right
Sea birds have a wide choice of convenient landing points on the many thousands of vessels of every size and description that visit the harbor each year. Courtesy, Los Angeles Harbor Department

PORT OF LONG BEACH
CALIFORNIA
ADMINISTRATION BUILDING

Opposite page, top
The handsome fresco adorning the front of the Port of Long Beach administration building depicts the long and colorful history of the Bay of San Pedro, from Cabrillo's landing at right to the modern era of containerization at left. Courtesy, Long Beach Harbor Department

Opposite page, bottom
The Port of Long Beach administration building was officially opened at dedication ceremonies on March 40, 1960. The department may move its headquarters to the new World Trade Center and use that valuable space on Pier J for additional container facilities. Courtesy, Long Beach Harbor Department

Above
President Ronald Reagan gave a brief address after signing the Export Trading Company Act of 1982 at the Sea-Land container terminal at Berth 228, Pier G at the Port of Long Beach on October 8, 1982. Reagan made a second visit to the Port of Long Beach as guest speaker at a dinner in the Spruce Goose Dome. Courtesy, Long Beach Harbor Department

Opposite page, top
The Oyster Wharf is one of the latest and most popular additions to the mile-long stretch of public recreational facilities along the north side of the main channel, extending from the Los Angeles World Cruise Center to the new Cabrillo Beach Recreational Complex, both now under construction. Courtesy, Los Angeles Harbor Department

Opposite page, bottom left
Ports O' Call Village alongside the main channel began with the opening of Ports O' Call restaurant in 1961 and grew so rapidly that within a few years it had become one of Southern California's leading tourist attractions, visited by more than two million people annually. Courtesy, Los Angeles Harbor Department

Above
After years of bitter controversy and staggering financial losses, the stately Queen Mary is back on an even keel and operating profitably under Wrather Port Properties. Adding to its tourist appeal is the nearby geodesic dome, which houses Howard Hughes' legendary Spruce Goose. Courtesy, Wrather Port Properties

Opposite page, bottom right
Ports O' Call developed into a twenty-four-acre complex of cobblestoned streets and quaint shops and restaurants, with a Whalers Wharf section in an early Cape Cod motif added in 1964. Its picturesque environment has been a favorite location site for movies and television. Courtesy, Los Angeles Harbor Department

L. A. PILOTS

Opposite page, top left
Fighting dock fires is all in a day's work for harbor firefighters, who are trained to handle nearly any type of mishap that might occur along the waterfront. Modern concrete wharf construction has minimized the threat of fire in the docks. Courtesy, Los Angeles Fire Department

Opposite page, top right
Although they perform completely behind the scenes, port pilots are among the most important specialists in harbor operations, as they are shuttled out to guide giant vessels safely to and from their berths. Courtesy, Los Angeles Harbor Department

Above
Cargo ships, their decks piled high with containers, are a familiar sight in the Port of Long Beach, which has been the busiest container port on the West Coast for several years. Long Beach's revenue tonnage exceeded fifty million tons for the first time and its container volume rose an astonishing 44 percent in fiscal 1984. Courtesy, Long Beach Harbor Department

Opposite page, bottom
An electric dredge with a cutter head resembling a sea monster deepened the San Pedro main channel from minus 35 to minus 45 feet in the early 1980s, in the first major dredging of that harbor in fifty-three years. The extra ten feet opened the harbor to the 35 percent of the world's container ships which could not use the port at its previous depth. Courtesy, Los Angeles Harbor Department

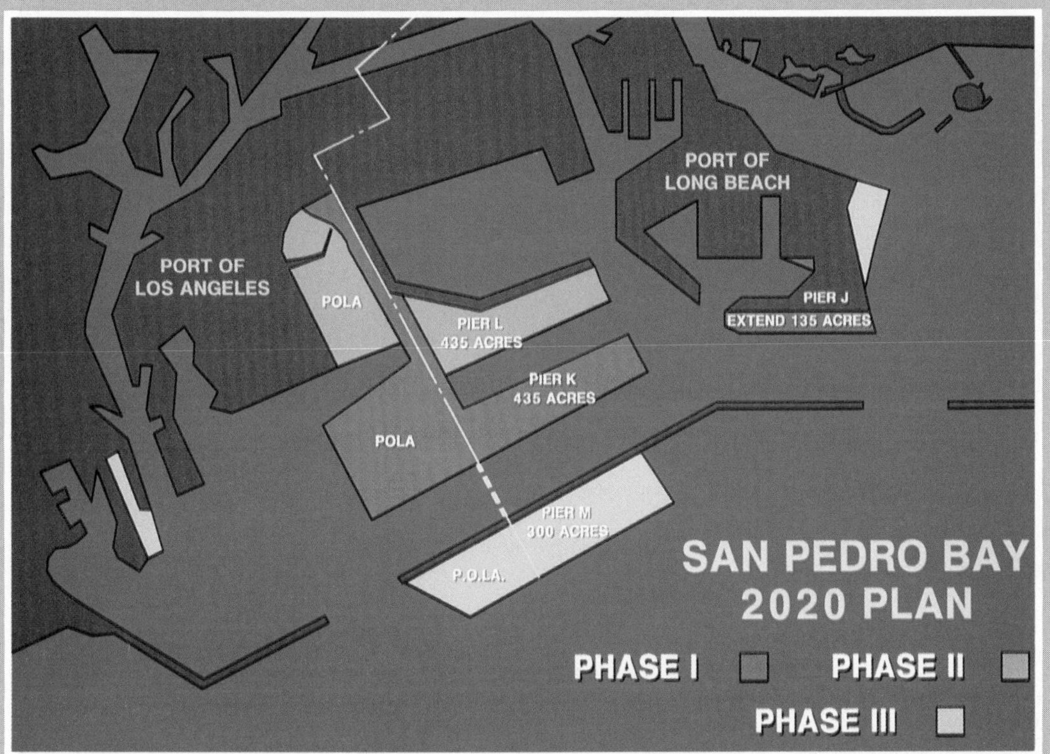

Left
The controversial 2020 Plan as seen in this artist's rendering would add 2,600 acres of landfill to the harbor in order to provide additional land to handle the projected growth of commerce in the bay by the year 2020. The plan is still subject to revision. Courtesy, Long Beach Harbor Department

Bottom
The Spruce Goose, *the largest airplane ever built, casts oblique shadows inside the biggest geodesic dome in existence at the Port of Long Beach. The* Spruce Goose, *with Howard Hughes at the controls, made one brief, memorable flight in 1947 and never flew again. Courtesy, Long Beach Harbor Department*

Opposite page, top
Brilliant sunshine after a summer shower brings out a beautiful rainbow over the tall buildings of downtown Long Beach in this view of the waterfront from across the harbor. Courtesy, Long Beach Harbor Department

Opposite page, bottom
Small boats still have plenty of room to maneuver in the marina and lagoon at Long Beach Harbor. In the background is the plush Hyatt Regency Hotel, the harbor's newest hostelry. Courtesy, Long Beach Harbor Department

Above
Terminal Island, shown at night in this view from the Vincent Thomas Bridge, was originally a narrow sandspit called Rattlesnake Island. Today it is one of the most valuable pieces of property in the Port of Los Angeles and the center of much of port's container activity. Courtesy, Los Angeles Harbor Department

Opposite page, top
The combined ports of Los Angeles (left) and Long Beach (right) form one of the largest man-made harbor complexes in the world. In fiscal 1984 they combined to make the Los Angeles Custom District the leading customs collection center in the United States, after years of placing second to the New York/New Jersey district. Photo by Pacific Aerographics

Opposite page, bottom
Gorgeous sunsets like this late afternoon view across Long Beach Harbor are a regular treat for residents of the waterfront communities of Long Beach and San Pedro. The growth of the two ports in the Bay of San Pedro is one of the most colorful chapters in the history of the region. Courtesy, Long Beach Harbor Department

The superliner America, *one of the giants of its day, is pictured during a visit to Long Beach Harbor in 1939. American flags were painted on the sides of United States ships at that time because Europe was already at war and German U-boats were ranging all over the Atlantic right up to the East Coast. Courtesy, Long Beach Harbor Department*

CHAPTER VIII

WAR AND PEACE

It was heartening that the worst financial crisis in the nation's history was ending, but there were disturbing signs that the world was heading for another outbreak of international violence as the 1930s drew to a close. The United States Navy was quietly strengthening its Pacific fleet, and Long Beach was taking on more and more the appearance of a navy town.

The number of ships based in the harbor was increasing by the month, and growing numbers of navy blues were seen on the Pike and on the streets of the city. Residents can still remember driving along Ocean Avenue during the latter part of the 1930s and seeing the two giant aircraft carriers, *Saratoga* and *Lexington,* looking absolutely enormous as they rode at anchor in the harbor.

Until it built its own naval base, the Navy had to cope with a severe housing shortage, and many of the top navy brass were quartered in the towering, sixteen-story Villa Riviera, the huge pink landmark built in 1929 that still stands on Ocean Avenue. Some of the most famous naval leaders of the Pacific War lived there, and many a young officer checked in at the Villa Riviera. Its needle-like tower was an ideal wartime lookout post as well as a marvelous target that even the most myopic bombardier could never miss, although it was assumed that the enemy would never be foolish enough to destroy such an excellent directional guidance point.

In 1940 the United States government had acquired 104 acres of the east end of Terminal Island in addition to a large segment of adjacent water area for a token one dollar, while the city retained the mineral rights. The Navy eventually added about 288 acres to that property, with top priority given to new shore facilities and a shipyard. The new Terminal Island Naval Base was commissioned on September 1, 1942. The Navy also leased Allen Field on the Los Angeles section of Terminal Island and renamed it Reeves Field, for Admiral Joseph Reeves, a former Chief of Naval Operations.

War had broken out in Europe in 1938, as Hitler sent his German armies rolling across neighboring countries against little or no opposition, to occupy them in days or even hours. The Battle of Britain was soon underway. England fought with its back against the wall, expecting an invasion at any moment. The German Air Force began the savage bombing of London and other British cities.

This was before the days of television, and newspapers and radio brought gripping reports of heroic Spitfire pilots fighting hordes of enemy bombers. German submarines ranged with impunity all the way across the Atlantic, their

By 1939 Pier A, in the foreground, the first section of the Long Beach middle harbor, and the beginning of Pier B had been completed. Between them is the navy landing, with dozens of oil wells in the background. Courtesy, Long Beach Harbor Department

torpedoes turning defenseless freighters into deadly bonfires within sight of the American East Coast. Yet it was still a war of headlines and newsreels on the West Coast until the incredible Japanese attack on Pearl Harbor on December 7, 1941. Perhaps no other community in the nation suffered such a crushing sense of loss from the Pearl Harbor disaster.

Hundreds of the men who died at Pearl Harbor and thousands of others who eventually would be killed in the bloody Pacific fighting were career servicemen who had become permanent residents of the Long Beach area. The community had adopted them as its own. Their children went to local schools. Thousands of service wives worked there, while their men were at sea and then went off to war. It was almost impossible to believe those mighty battleships that seemed so indestructible when they anchored regularly in the harbor were now part of the twisted and battered wreckage on the bottom of Pearl Harbor.

Even before the Pearl Harbor attack the harbor was fast approaching a wartime footing. A few months prior to the legendary Day of Infamy, the old cross-channel ferry that had been operating since the city annexed San Pedro in 1909 was replaced by a modern vehicular and passenger ferry service. With the sharp increase in shipbuilding and military activity on Terminal Island, the Ford Avenue Bridge and the Heim Bridge were hastily built to improve access to the island.

As soon as war was declared, the Navy took full control of the harbor. A port director was installed with total command over all shipping operations, including movement of commercial vessels. Emergency security measures went into effect. Lighthouses were extinguished for the duration. Strict blackout orders were enforced. Across the harbor from Rainbow Pier to the federal breakwater, the Navy stretched an antisubmarine net, which had to be lowered to permit passage of each large ship to the Navy base.

All commercial improvement work in the harbor was put on hold, except for the naval base and naval shipyard that the Navy was then rushing to completion. Otherwise, the only other major installation during the war years was construction of the Victory Pier at the end of the 7,284-foot Long Beach breakwater by the Army for the loading of munitions for the China-Burma-India theatre of war. It was the farthest point from populated areas where that dangerous operation could be located.

Shipbuilding in the harbor already had started on a massive scale. No shipyard before or since has matched the performance of California Shipbuilding Corporation, the largest and most productive yard in the harbor and the second biggest emergency shipyard in the nation during World War II.

In cooperation with the United States Maritime Commission, Calship, as it came to be called, was organized in 1940 by a team of experts who specialized in building bridges, oil refineries, and huge dams, but never ships. What they lacked in technical savvy they more than made up for in energy and organizational genius. Calship occupied 175 acres of semi-marshland on Terminal Island. It began building Liberty ships in May 1941, and launched its first vessel the following September.

Once Calship production got rolling, it picked up speed at an amazing rate. Before long it was launching up to a dozen new ships every month. It broke the existing record by delivering fifteen Liberty ships in June 1942, and finally reached the point where it was building a complete ship a day. At its peak, Calship had 55,000 full-time employees.

Another large-scale harbor producer was Consolidated Steel Corporation, which operated another emergency facility on ninety-five acres of Wilmington mud flats, in addition to leasing Craig Shipyard in Long Beach during the war. Consolidated hit its production climax on May 29, 1944, when it launched three large ships during one hectic two-and-a-half-hour period, and later finished its 500th vessel under the company's wartime construction program.

At the main Craig yard, Consolidated made dozens of small freighters, using a technique of building two ships at a time that kept new vessels sliding down the ways at a steady pace. The Craig company itself was fully occupied with wartime work, converting large yachts and other craft for use as patrol boats and gunboats, and later converting them back to their original state after the war.

Another highly productive yard was Bethlehem Shipbuilding Corporation, which had acquired Southwestern Shipbuilding Company in 1922. Bethlehem enlarged the yard to forty acres and 3,000 feet of berthing space, and was ideally suited for the war effort with its location at the head of the main channel. Bethlehem produced twenty-six destroyers and converted a large number of cargo vessels into transports and supply craft. Besides destroyer construction, Bethlehem specialized in repairs, working with such phenomenal speed that it was repairing and returning to duty two ships for each wartime work day.

The long-established Los Angeles Shipbuilding & Drydock Corporation ran into financial grief when ship production dried up during the Depression and lost control of the company in 1939. Todd Shipyards took over management under government orders in 1943, and built, launched, and outfitted a dozen large naval vessels and repaired or converted 2,376 other ships to combat use during the war.

While the big shipyards drew most of the plaudits and recognition with their dazzling production records, every smaller maritime company responded with equal patriotic fervor and total dedication. Each working hour went into the production of hundreds of auxiliary vessels—sub-chasers, patrol boats, PT boats, landing craft, rescue boats, barges, and tugs—all necessary to the effective execution of the war and a valuable contribution to the overall effort. At its busiest, harbor shipbuilding employed about 90,000 workers, not counting those at the naval shipyard.

A few miles from the harbor, Daugherty Field in Long Beach bristled with Army Air Force activity and adjacent aircraft production. Rechristened Long Beach Army Airfield for the duration, it was turned into an army ferry command center and headquarters of the Ferrying Division of the Air Transport Command. ATC pilots, including a number of women, flew thousands of aircraft all over the world to keep the Allies' overwhelming superiority in air power at full strength.

Delivery was just a step away from the airport at the adjacent wartime Douglas Aircraft Company plant, which the government had built and leased to Douglas for the emergency production of urgently needed aircraft for friendly nations already at war. With operations beginning in August 1941, the Douglas plant achieved feats of production comparable to the prodigious shipbuilding output down at the harbor.

The first finished aircraft rolled off the Douglas assembly line in December 1941—only a couple of weeks after Pearl Harbor—and production from then and throughout the war soared along with its high-flying product. When it was all over the Douglas plant had produced nearly 9,500 military aircraft and thousands of light bombers and transport planes in one of the great home front performances of the war.

As one of the closest major American ports to the Pacific battleground, few places in the nation were busier or more fully caught up in the war than the Bay of San Pedro and its waterfront cities. Enormous ship and aircraft production went on day and night. The harbor teemed with movement, criss-crossed by vessels constantly arriving, leaving, newly launched, or limping home from battle for repairs.

Over fifteen million tons of war equipment and supplies poured across the waterfront, and hundreds of thousands of service personnel passed through going to or returning from the war. For all the furious activity there were remarkably few serious accidents in the harbor during the war years. The worst occurred in 1944 in Wilmington when a welder's torch touched off an explosion and fire in which sixteen died and thirty-five others were seriously injured.

As if things were not hectic enough, harbor folk got a real-life taste of battle about two weeks after the Pearl Harbor bombing when the coastal steamer *Absaroka* was torpedoed in broad daylight less than two miles off Point Fermin. It was the worst possible choice for a Japanese sub-commander seeking the distinction of sinking a United States vessel so close to the American shore because it was carrying a load of lumber and simply would not go down. Hundreds of fascinated residents watched the floundering vessel from vantage points on the Palos Verdes Peninsula, and newspaper reporters assigned to nothing more violent than the city hall or county beat suddenly found themselves covering honest-to-goodness combat action from rowboats. The *Absaroka* was finally towed in to Bethlehem Shipyard for repairs.

War hysteria took strange forms around the harbor. The *Absaroka* attack and other signs that the enemy was lurking off the coast made everyone nervous, and anti-aircraft batteries and every other gun of any size in the area let off a lot of steam one February night in 1942 by banging away for six hours at what was thought to be an armada of unidentified aircraft on the first air raid ever on the United States mainland. No one really saw anything, nothing was hit, and the only damage was to some homes from falling shrapnel, but it was indicative of the tension and fear that permeated the bayside cities during the early days of the war.

A month later United States military leaders implemented one of the most shameful decisions ever made in this country in peace or war. In a flagrant violation of their constitutional rights, thousands of American citizens of Japanese descent, including 3,000 residents of Terminal Island, were shipped off like common criminals to relocation camps, and in the process lost most of their homes, businesses, and possessions.

The end of the war brought its own adjustments, as the high drama of the war years began to wind down. Production schedules at the shipyards and aircraft plants were curtailed sharply and thousands of jobs were dissolved. The pressure on woefully inadequate housing facilities that had been bursting at the seams for several years suddenly relaxed. The first Japanese prisoners-of-war returned, and older San Pedro residents recall the outpouring of warmth, sympathy, and gratitude that greeted the emaciated and dispirited survivors of years of mistreatment in the infamous prison camps in the Philippines and Japan.

The war's end did not see the volume of traffic in Long Beach Harbor diminishing—at least not right away. For a year or more the harbor was crowded with naval vessels of every description, all back from the war and waiting to be reassigned, dispersed, or dismantled. Calship's facilities were acquired in 1947 by National Metal & Steel Corporation, and fifty-five of the 306 Liberty and Victory ships built at Calship, which survived some of the most harrowing duty of the war, later returned to the National Metal & Steel breakers yard and were dismantled and scrapped on the site where they were built.

San Pedro was left with one legacy of the war that was an embarrassment, an eyesore, and a blight on the city's reputation for years afterward. Beacon Street had been one of the community's oldest thoroughfares and the main business district of San Pedro. Unfortunately, Beacon Street was also no more than a few hundred yards from the docks, and when swarms of sailors and merchant seamen starved for excitement after months of dangerous combat duty in the Pacific stepped ashore, Beacon Street was the closest oasis. The vultures were ready, and a string of seedy saloons like Shanghai Red's and the Bank Cafe—in a former bank building after business retreated north to Pacific Avenue and Gaffey Street—became known in ports around the globe. The brothels and pawnshops were not far behind and, to the utter dismay and anger of the townspeople, Beacon Street became known as one of the toughest waterfront streets in the world. That disreputable identification clung to San Pedro for years, until a badly-needed new redevelopment program obliterated that sordid stretch of dives and flophouses for all time.

Although not as directly involved in war production as shipbuilding and airplane production, the Edison plant in Long Beach was providing the all-important electric power that kept those industries operating at full capacity. Edison did make its own unique contribution when two original units from Plant 2 were appropriated by the Treasury Department, dismantled, and shipped to Russia to help the Soviets in their war effort. Long Beach Harbor got something back when the world's largest marine crane was transported from Germany to the Long Beach Naval Shipyard in 1946. The 385-ton self-propelled floating crane, nicknamed "Herman the German," continues to serve the Navy today, down to its original cable and operating instructions in German.

Even after wartime activity had abated, something always seemed to be happening in Long Beach Harbor to make headlines and enliven the local scene. Howard Hughes made the city an international dateline when he personally piloted a brief, historic flight in his famous *Spruce Goose,* the largest airplane ever built. Technically called the H-K 1, the giant aircraft was the result of a 1942 contract between the War Production Board and the Kaiser-Hughes Corporation for construction of three massive troop transport flying boats at a time when German submarines were taking a deadly toll of United States troopships and cargo vessels.

By 1944, when the first of the flying boats was nearing completion, the Allies were winning the war and the U-boat threat was minimal. Henry Kaiser withdrew from the project, but Howard Hughes completed the aircraft at his own expense. The plane was built in sections at the Hughes plant in Culver City, and a site on Terminal Island was chosen for its assembly. Schools along the route brought children out to watch the huge sections being trucked to the harbor. Power and telephone lines had to be cut and respliced to permit them to pass, and a special pontoon bridge was built to move the parts onto Terminal Island.

Fully assembled, the *Spruce Goose* was a sight to boggle the imagination. It had a wing span of 320 feet—wider than the length of a football field—with wings 11.5 feet thick, made entirely of wood except for the motor mounts and fittings. It was 218.5 feet long, 79.5 feet high, weighed 300,000 pounds, and was powered by eight 3,000-horsepower engines. Fitted as a hospital plane, it would carry 350 stretcher patients and a full medical crew. Only taxi and flight tests were left to be done.

On November 2, 1947, Howard Hughes maneuvered his gigantic brainchild away from its moorings, ostensibly for taxi tests and to check out equipment. Suddenly, he gave it full throttle, and the enormous craft picked up speed. It thundered halfway across the harbor and lifted slowly into the air. It was airborne for about a mile and reached an altitude of eighty-five feet before Hughes eased it gently back down into the water.

The *Spruce Goose* never flew again. It was lodged in a corrugated steel structure at Pier E in Long Beach, as ownership changed hands several times. In 1961 the Hughes Tool Company (now SUMMA Corporation) leased the plane and paid rent on its quarters. However, the Long Beach Harbor Department notified SUMMA in 1972 that it needed that space for a new tanker terminal. Three years later SUMMA and the Smithsonian Institution drew up

The Spruce Goose *was trucked in sections from the Hughes plant in Culver City to Terminal Island, where it was assembled. Howard Hughes made his historic flight on November 2, 1947. Courtesy, Long Beach Harbor Department*

an agreement to dismantle the historic plane and distribute parts of it to eight aviation museums around the country, but a flood of petitions from national organizations and letters from private citizens saved the huge aircraft from dismemberment. The *Spruce Goose* is now a major tourist attraction in Long Beach Harbor—housed, appropriately, in the world's largest aluminum geodesic dome, next to the world's largest passenger ship, the *Queen Mary.*

No chronicle of Long Beach would be complete without the fascinating episode of "The Sinking City," as *Time* magazine called it—its cause, the grave concern and extensive damage that resulted, the eventual solution, and the happy ending to what had steadily assumed the proportions of a full-blown catastrophe.

Long Beach officials, of course, had been ecstatic when oil was first discovered in the harbor area and the first well began to pump black gold in 1938. Long Beach Oil Development Company became the city's major oil operator in 1939, and by early 1943 the company had 126 harbor wells producing 17,000 barrels per day and city revenue from oil production was exceeding ten million dollars annually. However, this torrent of riches had its price.

Subsidence—the gradual lowering or sinking of the earth's surface—had been detected in the harbor area at various times before 1940, but it was only a few hundredths of a foot and not worth bothering about. By August 1941 a survey showed the east end of Terminal Island near where the naval installations were located had settled up to 1.3 feet, with sinkage diminishing toward downtown Long Beach. Measurements made several months earlier for the paving of Seaside Avenue showed movement of as much as .2 feet over a distance of 1,000 feet.

The cause was generally attributed to some temporary geological shift in the area and of no great import, especially with America's imminent entry into the war uppermost in everyone's mind.

The subsidence situation was largely ignored during the war years, although Craig executives noticed early in 1945 that water on the launching ways was creeping slowly upward and high tides seemed progressively higher. Meetings of the engineers in both ports were held, and the same condition of unusually high tides did not exist on the San Pedro side of the harbor. That July a United States Coast and Geodetic Survey confirmed that the east end of Terminal Island had dropped a total of 4.2 feet between 1931 and 1945.

By war's end, the problem had become serious and there was genuine alarm. Some remedial steps had been taken as early as 1940 when a few new Harbor Department buildings were built at slightly higher levels to keep them above the rising tides. The survey and other evidence made it clear by the end of 1945 that the subsidence would be much greater than had been anticipated, and intensive remedial work was begun on the approximately forty miles of Long Beach waterfront in the subsidence area.

Extensive flooding was making more and more valuable harbor land useless, and every conceivable engineering device was used to counteract the subsidence. Wharves were raised, sections of others were built up, and some were completely replaced. Seawalls were heightened. New rail lines and streets had to be built to reach facilities after tidewater had risen to cover normal access. Earthen dikes and concrete walls were hastily constructed to protect low areas from flooding, including a large section of the naval shipyard. Craig raised its buildings three or four times, as did other harborside industries.

In addition to the vertical change, there was also a horizontal movement of the earth of a half-dozen feet or more in some places that caused widespread damage to harbor buildings, wharves, streets, railroad tracks, and various underground systems. Pipes buckled. Buildings cracked. Clay and concrete sewer and drain lines broke. Wharf underpinnings crumbled. Loading platforms heaved. The 250-foot towers on the lift bridge to Terminal Island were pushed together, tilted, and racked out of position, making the bridge inoperable. The naval shipyard suffered heavy destruction. The same irresistible forces caused extensive subsurface damage estimated at over twenty million dollars to oil wells, with at least 136 wells severely or irreparably damaged.

More bad news arrived when the Navy filed what came to be known as the Anchor Oil Suit, suing the city of Long Beach and a long list of oil companies for damages caused by the subsidence to the navy base and shipyard. The city had retained the oil rights when the Navy took over that property in 1940, and now Long Beach was being held responsible for the havoc caused by the extraction of petroleum from under the site. Worse, Navy authorities in Washing-

Above
Capped oil wells appeared like newly-planted sprouts when subsidence caused the land to sink, leading to millions of dollars in damage to Long Beach Harbor Department property. Courtesy, Long Beach Harbor Department

Left and following page
Subsidence dropped Long Beach wharves so far that high tide reached dock level. Lateral movement of the subsidence cracked buildings and roads, and twisted rail lines. Oil well caps, normally standing just above ground level, exposed a dozen or more feet of underground pipe as the earth sank beneath them. Courtesy, Long Beach Harbor Department

ton, D.C., were thinking of closing the shipyard because of the damage. The yard had 6,500 employees and an annual payroll of over thirty million dollars, the loss of which would be a severe blow to the local economy. The Navy did shut down the Naval Shipyard in 1950, much to the city's dismay, but along came the Korean conflict and it was reactivated in 1951.

By 1966 an area of over twenty square miles had subsided from two up to twenty-nine feet at the epicenter, roughly in the shape of an oval bowl, with a major northwest-southeast axis six miles long and a minor axis about four miles long. It included the fringes of Los Angeles Harbor, all of the developed portions of Long Beach Harbor, the lower reaches and outlet of the flood control channel, and the southwest section of the city, with a lasso-like loop encircling Signal Hill on the edge of the subsidence area. The Edison plant, Craig Shipyard, and the Navy facilities were all located near the deepest point of subsidence.

Obviously, drastic measures were called for to put an end to what had become a geological nightmare. The subsidence had to be halted or controlled at all costs. Damage almost beyond comprehension would result if the land continued to settle. The miraculous source of wealth, which had appeared decades ago to solve some of the city's insurmountable financial problems, had turned into a monster that now threatened to destroy most of the valuable assets it had made possible.

Engineers, geologists, soil experts, mathematicians, and scientists combined their cumulative expertise in the preparation of some thirty major technical reports, and the consensus held that the massive injection of water into the subsurface area would have the best chance of restoring underground pressure and stabilizing the earth. A limited water injection program was started in 1953, and when that proved successful large-scale water injection was begun in 1958. Within a few years the largest water injection plant in the world was pumping a million barrels of water a day into the area under the harbor.

The results were, and continue to be, reassuring. From a maximum subsidence rate of 2.4 feet annually in 1951, the yearly sinkage rate has declined to millimeters and has stopped entirely in most of the subsidence area. There have even been dramatic examples of the land being elevated in some places.

Today the Long Beach Harbor Department monitors the affected area every three months to make certain the repressurization program has controlled the problem, and their reports seem to indicate that it has. Yet the battle to save the harbor from sinking into oblivion—literally—has been waged at tremendous cost, with a conservative estimate of nearly $100 million already spent to remedy the effects of subsidence. Thus, what the oil hath given, the damage its removal has caused hath taken a goodly portion away. On the other hand, engineers estimated that by the end of 1960 the water flooding program had already forced six million barrels of oil into a position where it could be recovered that could not be produced under ordinary drilling methods.

Even with the landmark crisis over subsidence apparently solved or at least forestalled, Long Beach's petroleum problems were far from over. With major harbor expansion curtailed during the war, the Harbor Department had accumulated tens of millions of dollars in oil royalties, and it immediately embarked on a vast building program. For years the federal government had tried to claim title to the tidal oil lands. The Tidelands Law of 1953 prevented acquisition by the federal government, but Long Beach's hold on oil revenues had been loosened by an earlier action.

In 1951 the State Legislature had passed an amendment to the original 1911 tideland grant to the city, which authorized use of half of the tidelands oil income for non-harbor purposes. Four years later the State Supreme Court decreed that when the Legislature had released half of the oil revenue and all gas income from terms of the 1911 tideland grant, these revenues should go to the state and not to Long Beach.

Early in 1956 the state filed suit to recover its share of the oil income. City and state representatives worked out a compromise, later passed by the State Legislature as Assembly Bill 77, whereby the city agreed to use tideland oil and gas revenues only for harbor improvements, and the state agreed that the remaining half of the oil income could be spent by Long Beach for state trust purposes.

For the city of Long Beach and its harbor, the stakes were astronomical. The harbor's share from Long Beach Oil Development Company production reached a high of nearly $23.5 million in fiscal 1951 to 1952. The highest annual royalty payment to the city from Richfield Oil Corporation, which also became a city operator under contract in 1948, was $8.7 million in 1956 to 1957.

By the end of June 1960 total income to the city from both operators had amounted to $345.4 million from the production of 264 million barrels of oil, in addition to the natural gas that had been produced. By fiscal 1959 to 1960, this annual income from both contractors had declined to just over thirteen million dollars before the tidelands compromise bill went into effect.

The enactment of AB 77 resulted in more than $120 million being turned over by the city to the state, along with a commitment to pay half of all oil revenues and all revenues from the sale of natural gas to the state. For its part the state would pay part of the cost of subsidence repair.

The day was not far off when the legislature would slash the city's income from its tidelands oil even further and eventually turn off the spigot for good, but the big postwar expansion program would soon return rich dividends and enable Long Beach Harbor to flourish and prosper on its own.

Construction on the $21.4 million Vincent Thomas Bridge was started in 1960 and completed in 1963. Courtesy, Los Angeles Harbor Department

C H A P T E R I X

ACHIEVING WORLD STATURE

The disruption and disorientation of the war years seemed almost like a dream, as both ports resumed peacetime operations and began putting their priorities back in order when the military returned the harbor to its civilian owners late in 1945. Their ultimate postwar goals were identical—membership in that elite society of world-class ports-of-call. There were shared advantages to be exploited and individual challenges to be overcome before either would achieve that distinction.

Many factors were involved. The Bay of San Pedro had a favorable location second to none on the West Coast. Because of this geographic endowment, it first was the natural conduit for the movement of hides and tallow from the ranchos, then for the mountains of incoming lumber to build the city of Los Angeles and outgoing petroleum when oil was discovered throughout the area. It was the closest and most convenient major West Coast port to the Panama Canal. After nearly losing everything, it had been designated as the official deep-water harbor for the Southern California megalopolis.

No less important was the continuing demand to excel in fierce side-by-side competition for the fabulously profitable maritime traffic to and from the second largest concentration of population, finance, and industry in the United States and the administrative talent to run those complex operations. Although generally circumspect but correct, the relationship between the two ports has been sharp and acrimonious at times, and neither hesitates to invade the other's territory in pursuit of an important harbor tenant who expresses any sign of dissatisfaction with its existing accommodations.

Both ports were fortunate during that crucial period after World War II to have men of experience and skill in those arcane executive positions that require the broad technical expertise to operate an international harbor and a large measure of patience and diplomacy to deal with local politicians and harbor commissioners. The latter are political appointees, usually successful in their own fields, who tend to become instant experts in maritime affairs and the bane of port professionals while they allegedly guard the public interest against private ambition.

Eloi J. "Frenchy" Amar, San Pedro-born and president of the Los Angeles Board of Harbor Commissioners for five years, jumped ship to become general manager of the Long Beach Harbor Department in 1940. He retired in 1958 and was followed by Charles Vickers, who held the position for nearly a dozen years before bowing out in 1969.

At the Port of Los Angeles Arthur Eldridge

was appointed general manager in 1934 and headed operations until he died in his office in 1954. He was succeeded by his assistant, Bernard J. Caughlin, who presided over two decades of the port's greatest expansion and retired in 1974.

While the Port of Long Beach was waging its desperate battle against the ravages of subsidence, the Los Angeles Harbor Department launched a broad restoration program. Much of its property was in urgent need of general maintenance that had been delayed during the war to conserve scarce materials and manpower. Wear and tear on various facilities had to be repaired. Pavement, foundations at emergency shipyards, and temporary buildings that had no peacetime use had to be removed.

Construction also began on new reinforced concrete wharves for general cargo use, improvements on Fish Harbor, and dredging and reclamation of low-lying areas to provide more space for pleasure boats. A critical shortage of berthing accommodations had been created by the return of many pleasure craft that had vacated the harbor when the Navy took over during the war, and the many new boats that needed mooring. Reclaimed land in the East Basin provided more than 600 badly needed berths.

The Port of Los Angeles also turned its attention to matters of safety and developed its first official set of traffic rules for a harbor where vessel movement had usually been a matter of courtesy, size, and whoever got there first. Speed limits were set for every type of vessel from giant tankers and passenger liners to tugs and tiny speedboats, as well as right-of-way rules for specific situations.

The port also cracked down hard for the first time on careless oil spills and the casual dumping of trash and debris, which was rapidly polluting the harbor, and they apparently picked the right man to see that the rules were obeyed. Coast Guard Real Admiral Frank Higbee, who had been the first captain of the port during the war, was named Port Warden for the Port of Los Angeles in the summer of 1946. He enforced the new regulations with such efficiency and dispatch that several shipping lines, labor unions, and others that had felt the sting of his authority tried quietly but unsuccessfully to have him removed.

That same year the Los Angeles Harbor Department began pressuring the Southern Pacific Railroad to remove the drawbridge that had long hindered development and full use of the West Basin. Years earlier the railroad had been obliged to remove part of the trestle and install the drawbridge, but now ships were being built bigger by the year, many could scarcely fit through, and some ship captains were reluctant to try. Dealing with the Southern Pacific had always been tedious and time-consuming, and it took another ten years before the drawbridge was finally removed.

It took far less time for completion of the final 13,360-foot leg of the breakwater, which began in 1946 and was completed in March 1949. Prices for breakwater construction had gone up considerably over the years. The first leg had cost approximately $335 per linear foot when it was built between 1899 and 1910. This last section went for more than double that at

$726 a foot.

Eastward, the Long Beach Harbor Department was fully engaged in its titanic struggle on two fronts—trying to cut its losses from the dread subsidence, and at the time attempting to build a modern harbor that would enable it to compete with its older neighbor for the mushrooming postwar maritime trade. The greatest concentration of new construction and subsidence remedial work in Long Beach Harbor took place during the 1950s, all financed by that tidal wave of oil money that continued to roll in.

Damaged wharves were replaced and thousands of feet of modern new docks installed, with the cumulative result that quite literally,

Above
More than 100 wartime craft, ranging from landing craft to a heavy cruiser, jammed the National Metal & Steel Corporation docks on Terminal Island in 1947, all headed for the scrap pile on the same site where California Shipbuilding Corporation built nearly a ship a day at the height of World War II. Courtesy, Los Angeles Harbor Department

Opposite page
Eloi J. "Frenchy" Amar was president of the Los Angeles Harbor Commission before he crossed the bay to become general manager of the Port of Long Beach in 1940. He served for eighteen years, retiring in 1958. Courtesy, Long Beach Harbor Department

Long Beach built a new harbor on the old. All new harbor construction was carefully sited at a higher level and existing facilities were raised about twenty feet to compensate for past subsidence and allow for any further settling. In the process reinforced concrete replaced the old timber wharves that had always been so vulnerable to both fire and astonishing damage by a variety of underwater insects, especially the voracious marine borer.

Thus Long Beach, with its old penchant for high-sounding titles, began calling itself "America's Most Modern Port," and with some justification. In the contest for new tenants, the possibility that a harbor-based shipping line might move from the fire-prone timber wharves of the Port of Los Angeles to the new fireproof Port of Long Beach was a persuasive selling point.

The emphasis on its modern construction was a key factor in the rapid growth of Long Beach Harbor in the 1960s, when the facilities were in place to handle soaring traffic and total cargo tonnage quadrupled in a single decade. Two of its big early projects were on Pier A, where the first of nine huge clear span transit sheds was completed and Pierpoint Landing began what eventually became one of the world's largest sportfishing operations.

The new awareness of traffic safety and orderly vessel movement had been working effectively, but it could do nothing to prevent the worst fire in Los Angeles Harbor history on June 22, 1947. On a quiet Sunday morning reminiscent of that fateful day at Pearl Harbor, the oil tanker *Markay* erupted in a ball of flame at the Shell wharf in Wilmington. Oil spewed across the water and the surface was soon in flames, which crept across the channel and completely destroyed the American President Lines warehouses at Berths 153-155.

Heroic harbor firemen drove fireboats through sheets of flame to battle the fire from the other side and keep it from moving deeper into the slip. Eleven were killed and twenty-two were hurt in the $2.5 million fire, and it could have been worse. A firm lesson had been learned from the disastrous Texas City fire, where a number of ships were lost because they were headed in and could not be moved without tugs. The new Los Angeles Harbor safety rules stated that all vessels had to be docked heading out, and several were saved in the 1947 fire because they could be moved quickly out of harm's way.

The cruise business recovered soon after the war, and in 1950 the first phase of the luxurious new APL passenger-cargo terminal was completed, and that same year construction was begun on the forty-five-acre Matson passenger-cargo terminal in Wilmington. Once their vessels were returned from wartime troopship service, both Matson and APL restored passenger schedules. Romantic Matson sailings to Hawaii were back in style, and APL resumed its round-the-world passenger-cargo service that had first been inaugurated from Los Angeles in 1924 by the old Dollar Line, predecessor to American President Lines.

One of the most significant developments of the early postwar years, which has directly affected commerce in the harbor since then, was the resumption of full-scale maritime trade with Japan. The defeated nation desperately needed machinery and other commodities to rebuild its war-ravaged cities, and less than a year after the signing of the Japanese Peace Pact in 1951, the number of Japanese cargo ships stopping in the harbor had increased by 140 percent and ocean commerce with Japan had nearly doubled. Among the first of the Japanese imports arriving on a large scale were Toyota automobiles, which had recently been introduced in this country and had quickly become popular.

Long Beach had lost none of its love of a spectacle during the war years. The same community that had defied its powerful religious sector by allowing a group of brazen young women to flaunt their charms in the city's first bathing beauty contest in 1925 got back into the beauty business a quarter century later when Long Beach became host to the new Miss Universe Beauty Pageant in 1952.

Designed to compete with the Miss America Pageant on an international level, the first Miss Universe contest was a resounding success. With thirty-four entrants from around the world, including a Miss USA as a patriotic favorite, the show included parades, floats, public appearances, and all the trappings of a big-time spectacular, much to the delight of crowds that included thousands of appreciative sailors from the naval station. Joining Long Beach as sponsors were Catalina swimwear, United International Studios, and Pan American World Airways.

Yet, as often happens with the fine-tuning of such events, the pageant never again ran as smoothly as it did in the debut of its eight-year stint in Long Beach. Pan-Am and U-I dropped out as sponsors after a couple of years, leaving Catalina and the city as sole backers. Catalina began to grumble that the raft of favorable publicity Long Beach was getting out of the pageant was worth far more than the city's miserly $30,000 annual investment. Local citizens who worked on the pageant retorted with some heat that the time they spent on the event was worth far more than any financial expenditure involved.

Catalina hit the roof when some of the more conventional of the participating nations agitated to replace the swimsuit competition with clothing more ladylike and less revealing. No need to mention the swimwear company's response to that one. The pageant also had other woes. The young women behaved properly enough, but inevitably their qualifications came under fire. There were snide allegations involving padding and silicone and other unkind speculation about the authenticity of what the tape measure showed. One contestant was found to be only seventeen, a year younger than the minimum age. In the most startling exposé of all, instead of being a paragon of pristine American girlhood, one heavily-favored Miss USA was revealed by an unforgiving former mother-in-law as a twice-married mother of three children.

The original Miss Universe contract expired in 1959, and Catalina and Long Beach had had enough of each other by then. The city refused to accept Catalina's terms when the contract came up for renewal, and the Miss Universe Pageant found a new home in Miami. Something called the International Beauty Congress was brought in as a substitute for the departed Miss Universe affair, but it never really caught on and was discontinued in 1967.

In 1952 the French Sardine Company, for thirty-five years one of the largest canneries in the harbor, officially changed its name to Star-Kist Foods Inc., and opened its huge new plant on Terminal Island. Tens of thousands of local residents worked there over the next three decades. However, ruinous foreign competition, based on a much lower wage scale in some of the Pacific islands, eventually forced the cannery to cut back on its work force in the early 1980s. Production was sharply curtailed and temporary layoffs were invoked in a final effort to survive. Star-Kist finally closed for good in 1984, virtually marking the end of the great canning industry that had flourished in the harbor during the first three-quarters of the century.

A happier occasion marked the dedication in July 1953 of the massive new Matson passenger terminal in Wilmington, one of the most modern facilities of its kind, with the latest design in separate accommodations for both passengers and cargo under one roof. Thousands of older local citizens still cherish fond memories of leis and alohas and the strains of "Blue Hawaii" wafting through that terminal. Alas, along came the low cost and speed of jet-air travel and the Hawaii cruise business went down the drain as one after another of the big passenger liners slipped off into the sunset to be scrapped or converted to commercial use as

Contestants are pictured lined up in front of the Port of Long Beach administration building for the 1964 International Beauty Congress, the successor to the departed Miss Universe Pageant. The IBC never quite achieved the popularity of the Miss Universe event and was discontinued in 1967. Courtesy, Long Beach Harbor Department

freighters.

Size had become a factor of surpassing importance in the postwar maritime industry's efforts to refine its operations, and the obvious actuality was that larger ships could carry much more cargo at less cost per ton. The latest trend was to build ships much bigger or, if possible, enlarge existing vessels. Todd Shipyards completed one of the first "jumboizing" conversions when it added forty-one feet to the center section of the oil tanker *Ticonderoga* in 1954.

Labor troubles hit most of the major Pacific ports in the late 1950s, and the Bay of San Pedro was affected along with the others. A tugboat strike threatened to close down harbor traffic and the Navy was asked to use its five

tugs to prevent complete paralysis of commerce in the bay. While other walkouts hindered activity at key West Coast ports and in Hawaii, the Port of Los Angeles was having worsening problems with stevedoring unions. There were angry charges of goldbricking and featherbedding, that Los Angeles Harbor had the highest pilferage rate in the world. Cargo thefts became so serious in 1959 that Japanese shippers with berthing facilities in the harbor were unloading cargo in San Francisco and San Diego instead and shipping it overland to Los Angeles destinations.

A five-year American President Lines study found that pilferage and handling damage accounted for fully 10 percent of the company's operations, and the harbor became so notorious for its high pilferage rate that a Port of Los Angeles trade mission to Europe was repeatedly questioned about it. Los Angeles Mayor Norris Poulson called for an investigation, and meetings were held between Los Angeles and Long Beach harbor officials, union leaders, and shipping representatives in an effort to eliminate this rampant thievery.

As maritime leaders were pondering a solution to the insidious problem of waterfront larceny, part of the answer arrived with one of the most remarkable advances in the ancient history of the shipping industry. Containerization—called "as dynamic a change in shipping as the development of the rocket in space travel" by one leading industry expert—was a revolutionary new technique which would drastically alter

Above
The battleship Missouri, *"Mighty Mo" of World War II fame, drew long lines of visitors when it stopped in the Port of Long Beach on a goodwill visit in 1954. Courtesy, Long Beach Harbor Department*

Opposite page, top
Congressman Craig Hosmer presented the first honorary Long Beach Port Pilot Award to President Eisenhower in 1954. Courtesy, Long Beach Harbor Department

Opposite page, bottom
Expansion through the 1960s continued to increase as the Port of Los Angeles adapted its facilities to the container age. This 1964 photograph shows construction on a concrete wharf on Terminal Island at Berths 218-225, just beyond the Vincent Thomas Bridge, which had been opened a year earlier. Courtesy, Los Angeles Harbor Department

maritime transportation, change traditional terminal design, and affect the appearance of ports throughout the world.

The instrument of all this was a huge sealable metal box, twenty or forty feet long, carried to and from ships by trucks and transferred directly to the ship by huge, specially-designed cranes. Except for unusually large commodities like automobiles and earth-moving equipment, thousands of smaller items were ideally suited for containerization. Once the box was filled, it was sealed and remained safe and secure until it reached its destination.

This streamlined new processing technique caused dramatic changes in manpower requirements, speed of handling, and to a drastic degree, shipping charges. Labor costs were reduced precipitously and productivity improved immeasurably. While the average longshore gang of sixteen to eighteen men could handle eight to ten tons of cargo in regular packaging, a five-man team could move 450 tons of containerized goods and expend only a fraction of the effort and energy doing it. This enormous increase in productivity cut the normal five- to seven-day turnaround time for a ship in port to today's average stay of eight hours. With the daily cost of operating a large vessel running into many thousands of dollars, the saving to the operator was enormous.

The new shipping system brought a special ray of sunshine to those harbor officials harrassed by thievery on the docks. The goods were packaged in sealed, tamper-proof metal containers, which virtually eliminated re-handling, handling damage, and, that old nemesis, pilferage, once and for all. With shipping and insurance costs reduced, and the unprecedented speed of handling with containerization, rate structures were completely overhauled.

The mechanical catalyst in this marvelous new technique was a spidery, four-legged metal structure that resembled a giant erector set. Called a gantry crane, it cost $1.5 million and up, and its gaunt, towering figure soon became a familiar fixture on the skyline of all ports handling containers.

The most profound impact of containerization in terms of replacement costs was felt among oceangoing properties around the world. Many thousands of vessels became obsolete surplus, and entire commercial fleets were consigned to the scrap heap, since the holds of

Above
The $2.5 million Koppel Bulk Terminal on Pier A at Long Beach was the largest grain-loading facility on the West Coast when it was built in the early 1960s. Koppel is no longer in business at the port. Courtesy, Long Beach Harbor Department

Top
By 1961 the Long Beach outer harbor had grown considerably with constant landfill additions over the previous decade, as shown in this aerial photograph of Long Beach Harbor. The curve of Santa Monica Bay is seen at upper left, with the Santa Monica Mountains beyond. Clusters of oil tanks form the checkered pattern in the center. The oval-shaped Rainbow Pier and drive on the beach at right is now the site of the Long Beach Civic Center. Courtesy, Long Beach Habor Department

regular cargo ships were not designed for container stowage. Special holds were designed for containers and many more could be carried on flat, open decks. Comparatively few ships could be adapted for container use; the rest were rendered inoperable.

Commercial wharves underwent their own metamorphosis in design and construction. Containers had to have docks that could bear far more weight than ever before, not only for the fully-packed steel boxes but also for the huge cranes, for which rails had to be installed in the wharves.

Just behind the docks another complete face-lift took place. Unlike the old boxes and crates that required the shelter of transit sheds, the waterproof containers did not need any cover at all. All they had to have was open space and plenty of it. From the look of an army camp with its conglomeration of barracks-like cargo sheds, terminals turned into acres of plain open space with rows of stacked containers or boxes stored on truck chassis.

Actually, containerization did not appear as a sudden inspiration to an unsuspecting shipping industry. Some American companies had been experimenting with containers to a limited degree and the military had routinely been using them to ship servicemen's household goods from one assignment to another, but the innovative Matson company is generally credited with introducing containerization on the West Coast.

Matson made its first shipment of twenty containers aboard the *Hawaiian Merchant* in August 1958 from a temporary container dock at Berth 135 in the Port of Los Angeles, and the following year construction began on the first Los Angeles container terminal for Matson. The terminal was partially destroyed by fire as it neared completion, but the undamaged section went into use in August 1960. A few months earlier Matson's *Hawaiian Citizen* began service as the first all-container vessel in the Pacific. A total of 7,000 of the new metal boxes moved through Los Angeles Harbor in 1960, the first full year of container traffic.

Long Beach Harbor might have had its vast oil riches, but the Port of Los Angeles had access to the financial resources of a great city. In 1959 a City Charter amendment was approved by the voters that authorized the Harbor Department to finance port improvements with revenue bonds, a source which was expected to enable port planners to spend fifty million dollars on new facilities over the next five years and add one-third to the port's estimated value of about $106.4 million. A year later the Los Angeles Harbor Commission approved a five-year, thirty-seven-million-dollar expansion plan for the construction of fifteen new berths and five general cargo terminals, the modernization of thirteen existing berths, and the upgrading of various other facilities.

San Pedro was also the site of the fastest-growing special event on the waterfront during that period. The annual Fishermen's Fiesta and blessing of the fishing boats by the Archbishop of Los Angeles began as a small local event shortly after the war. It quickly grew to such phenomenal proportions and attracted such huge crowds that by the 1950s it was rivaling the Tournament of Roses parade as a yearly celebration. It finally became so commercial and unmanageable that it was discontinued twice, once for nine years. The Harbor Department revived it in 1981, but on a limited scale and with its original hometown flavor restored.

There was constant activity in both ports during the early years of the 1960s. The Long Beach Harbor Department occupied its new headquarters building, construction was begun on the $2.5 million Koppel Bulk Terminal, the largest grain-loading facility on the West Coast, on Pier A, and one of the largest shipments of foreign cars—1,152 Volkswagens—arrived at the new twenty-three-acre Pier E terminal. Construction also began on Pier J and the $2.8 million Pier F transit shed, and almost as soon as the Koppel terminal was dedicated, work was underway to double its capacity.

Across the bay, huge waves triggered by an earthquake off Chile in 1960 caused millions of dollars in damage in Los Angeles Harbor, tearing many pleasure boats from their moorings, sinking several dozen, and smashing wharves and anchorages. That same year the state began sinking piles for the Vincent Thomas Bridge, the first direct road connection between San Pedro and Long Beach. The $21.4 million bridge was opened to traffic on November 15, 1963, and on that day the cross-channel ferry service was discontinued and the ferryboat *Islander* retired after twenty-two years of service.

Petroleum companies and their shipping operations were given a stern warning when it was determined that an average of two oil spills per week in harbor waters was causing more than $500,000 damage annually to docks and boats and in cleanup operations, in addition to the lethal effect it had on fish and waterfowl. The problem was part of the harbor scene because Los Angeles had long been the largest refueling port in the nation, and nearby refineries had been habitually dumping residue into channels

Above
In addition to millions of tons of regular commodities, some unusual cargoes have crossed the Los Angeles waterfront. They have included the last surviving Japanese Zero fighter plane from World War II, Sir Winston Churchill's funeral car, armaments such as tanks, and many live animals. Courtesy, Los Angeles Harbor Department

Top
Dozens of regular passengers crowded the ferryboat Islander *for a nostalgic last trip when the ferryboat ended twenty-two years of service on November 15, 1963, the day the new Vincent Thomas Bridge over the Los Angeles main channel was opened to traffic. Courtesy, Los Angeles Habor Department*

Opposite page
The pike, with its roller coaster and the Rainbow Pier, were still major Long Beach attractions in the late 1950s. From the George Metivier Collection

leading into the harbor without giving it a second thought.

San Pedro's biggest permanent waterfront attraction began on a modest scale with the opening of the Ports O' Call restaurant opened alongside the main channel in 1961. From that humble start the Ports O' Call Village grew rapidly, and by 1965 it was a twenty-four-acre complex of cobblestoned streets and quaint shops with an annual attendance of more than two million visitors. Shortly afterward the *Princess Louise,* a former Canadian cruise ship, opened as a floating restaurant, first on the east side of the channel and, after its shortest voyage ever, almost directly across on the opposite shore.

All the while both ports were busy with their large-scale expansion programs, and as Long Beach steadily acquired major league status, competition for the big shipping companies grew more intense. An occasional public skirmish was unavoidable. One such beef flared into the open in 1964 when articles in the Long Beach *Independent Press-Telegram* quoted charges against the Los Angeles Harbor Department of mismanagement, "hidden losses," and favoritism in awarding contracts.

The Los Angeles side retaliated with a claim that Long Beach Harbor, awash in tidelands oil gravy, was using cutthroat tactics in the battle for new tenants. Long Beach said Los Angeles was raising the issue to cover up for its own operational shortcomings. A few months after this exchange, the Los Angeles City Council resurrected an old refrain and again proposed the consolidation of the two ports under a single authority. The state had been making threatening gestures in that direction, and Los Angeles Mayor Sam Yorty supported the proposal, stating that separate operations were "wasteful" and "it would be much better from the standpoint of competition to have one great harbor run by a local agency and not the state." Unimpressed, the Long Beach City Council unanimously opposed the consolida-

tion as "just another effort in Los Angeles to get our oil money to develop that port."

The Long Beach Harbor Department put the last word to its rival's accusation that it was floating on petroleum royalties rather than earning its way. By 1965 oil money no longer funded port projects; henceforth, the entire harbor operation was financed from its own income.

Los Angeles had good reason to take its opposite number seriously. With the subsidence threat very much under control, Long Beach Harbor's growth over the next half-dozen years was truly phenomenal. In fiscal 1965 Long Beach handled a total of 13.6 million revenue tons while Los Angeles processed almost double that amount—25.1 million tons. Barely six years later Long Beach's traffic had skyrocketed to 26.1 million tons as Los Angeles inched forward to 27.2 million tons. Almost overnight, the brash newcomer was running neck-and-neck with the old-timer on the other side of the bay.

Long Beach may have been making giant strides in the maritime world, but perhaps its most cherished and durable harborside institution for over a half-century—the grand old Pike—was in a sad state of decline. The aging amusement center was still running strong and attracting large crowds right into the 1950s, until Mickey Mouse's famous father decided to open his own theme park in suburban Anaheim. The old pros along the Pike chortled over the foolishness of Walt Disney's choice of a site where it was beastly hot in summer and also hard to reach over a narrow two-lane road, and the fact that untrained kids probably would be running the rides. However, the freeway came in and Disneyland was a smash hit from the beginning. Knott's Berry Farm alertly picked up on the trend and added kiddie rides, and the new Magic Mountain added to the competition. Clusters of motels sprang up around these attractions, and the tourists headed there instead of to Long Beach.

The days were clearly numbered for the granddaddy of all Southern California fun centers, which had begun with the saltwater plunge

Above and opposite page
Pierpoint Landing, a major recreational project in Long Beach Harbor during the early 1960s, eventually grew into one of the world's largest sportfishing centers. From the George Metivier Collection

in 1902 and reigned through the 1940s as the largest amusement park west of the Mississippi. The departure of the Navy was a stunning setback to the city and a fatal blow to the Pike, which had always drawn a large share of its customers from that youthful, free-spending source. The Pike's biggest single attraction, the hair-raising Cyclone Racer, was dismantled in 1972. A few years later it was announced that the eleven-acre east end of the strip where the rides were located would be closed and condominiums and highrise buildings erected there. A decade has passed and the site is still awaiting a developer.

In its heyday, when it regularly drew 50,000 on a weekend, the Pike had everything the seeker of entertainment could want. It had twenty major rides, including fifteen for the kiddies, four dance halls, three bowling alleys, at least a half-dozen restaurants, six theaters, three barbershops, three pool halls, and dozens of novelty and specialty shops. It had thirteen

bingo games, which local church officials roundly condemned at first but have since piously approved as a prime source of their own income. Spiritual help was only a few steps away in the early days, when crowds of up to 10,000 attended George Taubman's Sunday Bible classes on the beach. All that now remains of the Pike are two buildings, both earmarked for removal in the near future. In one of them, the last concessionaire from the Pike's glory days—a true survivor named Al Brown, who started working on the strip sixty-one years ago—still operates a game similar to bingo.

While the Pike was disintegrating, Long Beach Harbor was acquiring an atmospheric new attraction in the 1960s that often causes first-time visitors to do a double-take. What at first glance appears to be a series of tropical islands are actually offshore oil-drilling operations in disguise. A consortium of major oil companies, including Texaco, Humble, Union, Mobil, and Shell and known under the acronym THUMS, submitted the bid that would bring the highest return to the city to produce all the petroleum under the harbor east of the harbor district. The search had to be handled with extreme care. The ecologists were out in full cry, and THUMS was given strict orders: no drilling on the beach or despoiling that precious asset in any way, and immediate repressurization after drilling to avoid any repetition of the fearsome subsidence.

To soften the visual impact on local sensibilities, some of which detested the idea under any circumstances, THUMS camouflaged its offshore drilling installations in South Seas raiment, complete with palm trees and waterfalls lighted at night. Each of the four islands has 200 wells in concentric circles, with another 200 wells on Pier J for a total of 1,000 potential sites.

Scandal rocked the Los Angeles Harbor Department in 1968 when a Los Angeles County Grand Jury indicted three former harbor commissioners for alleged criminal misconduct regarding a proposed two-hundred-million-dollar World Trade Center complex on Terminal Island and the contractual arrangements involved. The three ex-commissioners were convicted in Superior Court trials. One died while his appeal was pending, a second had his conviction reversed by an appellate court, and the conviction of the third was sustained on appeal. The harbor community was shocked when, a year earlier, commissioner Pietro Di Carlo, founder of the Di Carlo bakery chain and one of San Pedro's leading citizens, accidentally drowned in the main channel.

At about that time Long Beach took off on one of the most bizarre and controversial adventures in its colorful history. In 1967, its coffers overflowing with oil revenue and badly in need of a shot in the arm to regain its old appeal after the subsidence trauma, the city made an investment that still generates strong emotions almost twenty years later.

One of Long Beach's enduring charms is that it seems always game to try something new as long as it is big and/or different. Growth had stalled during the 1960s. New business was leery of relocating to a place where the earth had been sinking. Somewhere out there, there had to be an extraordinary showstopper with the magical power to put the city's commerce and tourism back on the track.

Some Long Beach leaders felt they had indeed located that one-of-a-kind attraction when they learned the legendary *Queen Mary,* the most luxurious passenger liner of the 1930s and then the fastest passenger liner afloat, had been put up for sale by the Cunard Steamship Company. Transatlantic jet service had cut deeply into surface travel, and Cunard had been losing up to two million dollars per year on the stately old vessel when the company decided to sell.

An enthusiastic Long Beach delegation made up of business manager of the *Independent Press-Telegram* Sam Cameron, Harbor Commissioner H.E. "Bud" Ridings, and City Councilman and Vice Mayor Robert Crow joined the bidding and won out over several East Coast cities and various European interests with a high bid of $3.45 million, 10 percent above the Philadelphia bid.

The acquisition made headlines everywhere, and it was sensational news for the City of Long Beach. The trio who had pulled off this spectacular coup returned in triumph. This was no penny-ante game of chance, to be sure. Yet, it was only oil revenue, which the city had plenty of, and after a few more million dollars to get the *Queen* into shape to welcome the public—about five ought to do it—it was anticipated that the renowned ocean liner would be the star attraction in Long Beach's renaissance.

There were congratulations all around, and civic pride soared. Robert Crow had his picture in *Life* magazine as "the man who purchased the *Queen Mary,"* decked out in bowler, cane, and all the finery of a debonair international financier. The local sales and marketing club honored the bidding trio as "Salesmen of the Year." The next big thing was for those who had the time and could afford it to fly to England and take the *Queen*'s "Last Great Cruise" from Southhampton to Long Beach.

It was a memorable voyage, but it had its forgettable moments. Instead of traveling across the cool North Atlantic as it had in its previous 1,001 crossings, the ship had to go down around Cape Horn since it could not fit through the Panama Canal. The *Queen* was not air conditioned for the tropics, and its passengers spent some hot and sticky days and nights along the coast of South America. The *Queen*'s impeccable shipboard service faltered at times, while some of the crew decided to enjoy themselves on their final cruise since no one could fire them afterward.

The *Queen Mary* sailed majestically into Long Beach Harbor on the morning of December 9, 1967, to an unforgettable reception. Hundreds of boats of every size and description accompanied the mighty vessel the last few miles as it cleared the breakwater and arrived to a gala welcoming celebration for passengers and crew. The tumult and the shouting eventually died down, and the entire city waited in eager expectation for the next steps that would transform this gigantic luxury liner into Long Beach's prize exhibit.

A closer and more objective analysis revealed that there were unexpected complications involved in making the *Queen* a viable and profitable tourist attraction, as well as the seeds of disagreement from the very beginning. Some

Long Beach's purchase of the Queen Mary, *shown sailing grandly into Long Beach Harbor accompanied by hundreds of small boats, turned into the most controversial project in the city's history. Courtesy, Long Beach Harbor Department*

harbor officials had advised against the purchase, but had been overruled. Others resented what they considered grandstanding by those who took credit for the purchase. A harbor commissioner who also headed one of the biggest shipbuilding firms in the bay was miffed because he had not been consulted on the conversion of the *Queen* into a public drawing card.

A basic issue concerned the sheer size of the ship—almost the length of three-and-a-half football fields—and where one put such a leviathan. No one quite realized how big it was until it arrived, and the question was where the monster should be parked without using up too much precious waterfront space that the Harbor Department dearly needed for commercial development.

Rear Admiral Jack Fee, commander of the Long Beach Naval Shipyard, retired from the Navy to head the newly-created Queen Mary Department of the city. It was finally decided that the ship should have its permanent berth at Pier J. Construction began on the costly Queens Way Bridge to give direct access from downtown Long Beach. The Harbor Commission advised the city that it could not allocate any of its own space on Pier J to the project, and acres of landfill were added there, as well as special wharf facilities—all at enormous expense.

The *Queen Mary* soon became a bitter bone of contention. Its detractors referred to it as the "city's folly." The initial estimate of about five million dollars to convert the ship disappeared as quickly as a ripple on the beach, as huge sums of tidelands oil money went into the renovation. Three years would pass and about fifty million dollars would be expended on the retired "Queen of the High Seas" before the first paying customer would step aboard.

Pictured is a ship which participated in TOPSail '84. Some spectators watched the parade of tall ships from the stern of the Queen Mary. *Courtesy, Long Beach Harbor Department*

PROMISE OF THE FUTURE

Impetus for the continued growth of San Pedro Bay received a mighty thrust forward in 1970 with huge revenue bond issues totaling over fifty million dollars for harbor expansion and improvement in both ports. The thirty-million-dollar Long Beach issue financed a large-scale, three-year program that included three new container terminals, a container freight station, and enlargement of its existing container operations. Los Angeles voted a twenty-five-million-dollar issue for various expansion projects, including further enlargement of the massive Los Angeles Container Terminal and the purchase of scarce land within the port complex.

Both harbor departments were proceeding with all possible speed in the construction of additional container facilities. The Port of Los Angeles had a number of older wharves that could not bear the weight of container operations which were easier to replace than remodel and reinforce. Yet Los Angeles had a more serious problem—the restrictive thirty-five-foot depth of its main channel. Container ships were being built larger all the time, and before long fully 35 percent of the world's container vessels drew too much water to enter the main Los Angeles waterway. What was the good of building new container facilities if ships could not reach them? The only solution was the deepening of the channel with the aid of federal financing, and a proposal to achieve that end had for years been working its tortuous way through a congressional morass of permits and approvals.

As a relative newcomer Long Beach Harbor did not have to cope with the debilities of aging, obsolete facilities. Everything Long Beach was now building was new, and with the unlimited promise of the container age abundantly clear, its port planners could tailor new construction to suit those requirements. Even that notorious hobgoblin, subsidence, finally made a positive contribution. While it was wreaking havoc and inflicting appalling damage to man-made facilities, it was also lowering the floor of Long Beach Harbor—which quite handily accommodated the larger, deeper draft ships when they arrived. A major dredging project further deepened the partially sunken harbor floor to sixty feet, making it the deepest harbor fairway in the United States and providing Long Beach with the landfill required for its extensive pier expansion project.

The momentum of growth was temporarily slowed when both ports were hit by a prolonged longshoremen's strike on the first day of fiscal 1971 to 1972. The strike lasted 135 days in the Port of Los Angeles with a three-month interval of work, and although general cargo fell off by nearly two million tons, the two perennial, big-ticket commodities—petroleum and lumber—were not affected. Long Beach was shut down for 142 days and saw its steady rise in total tonnage interrupted for the first time in nearly a decade. However, Long Beach recovered quickly, and a year later it overtook the Port of Los Angeles in total tonnage for the first time in its history, a lead that it retains to this day.

The sorry saga of the *Queen Mary* continued into 1971, when the ship was finally opened to the public nearly three years after its scheduled debut, with astronomical cost overruns in converting it into a tourist attraction and monumental confusion over how it should be run. The city first contracted Diners-Queen Mary to operate the ship, but that firm suddenly withdrew shortly before the opening.

In its haste to secure some form of management and at long last put its oversized white elephant on a paying basis, the city made the mistake of leasing out the ship to three different operators—the hotel facilities to Pacific Southwest Airlines (PSA), all food and other concessions to Specialty Restaurants Inc., and the Museum of the Sea to the Los Angeles Museum of Science and Industry. This tripartite form of operation proved a disaster from the start, as was the grand old lady of the sea herself and what they did to make her a tourist attraction.

It soon became evident that the *Queen Mary* did not have the broad, all-round family appeal of Disneyland or Marineland. Instead of an attraction for all ages, it was basically a nostalgia piece from the past, mostly of interest to older people who remembered the *Queen* from her glory days. Unlike Disneyland, which kept adding new rides to generate return business, one tour of the *Queen* was enough—sometimes too much. Clambering about the ship was exhausting, with its many steep stairways, and impossible for handicapped visitors. The biggest single disappointment was the widely-heralded Museum of the Sea, allegedly masterminded by Jacques Cousteau, the world-famous oceanographer whose underwater explorations had thrilled millions of television viewers. Instead of a fascinating collection of wall-to-wall sea life, the museum was made up mostly of pictures and plastic exhibits, far too technical to interest the average adult, much less children. "Dull—deadly dull," one city official called it.

Conflicts arose from the splintered system of responsibility. PSA operated the 400-room Hotel Queen Mary of converted cabins, but had no jurisdiction over the food or service in its restaurants, which were run by Specialty Restaurants. Complaints began to pile up. Parking charges were too steep, as were prices in the ship's restaurants. Worried concessionaires barely scratched out a profit with rentals so high. Some concession items on board were duplicated in the Mary's Gate Village of shops and restaurants adjacent to the *Queen Mary.*

There were charges of "bungling" against the museum management, which angrily replied that the failure of the museum was due to lack of advertising and poor city policies. A new exhibit, Phantom of the Museum, opened at a cost of $100,000 and closed within a month for lack of business. One city councilman called the *Queen Mary* "the greatest boondoggle in California history." All the while the whole project was being pummeled unmercifully by some of the worst publicity in the annals of the media.

By July 1975, although more than 6.4 million visitors had boarded the ship since its opening four years earlier, the *Queen* had a net operating loss of $6.6 million as of that date. Later that year, with over sixty million dollars in tidelands funds already invested in the giant white albatross, the city seriously considered scrapping the *Queen Mary* and putting an end to the nightmare. "Long Beach Struggles to Keep Queen," headlined the *Los Angeles Times.* The Long Beach *Press-Telegram* told of a "do-or-die effort to save the ship from financial ruin." The Long Beach paper pointed out that the project was a success in the sense that it provided more than 1,600 new jobs and thirty million dollars in economic benefits to the city while belaboring the obvious that "It was an uncharted course and learning the hard way can be expensive and full of mistakes."

A confidential report on the scrapping proposal, which was promptly made available to the press, indicated that while the ship could be sold as salvage for $500,000, more than ten million dollars would be needed to pay off its outstanding debts and the dozens of lawsuits that had been filed against it. Moreover, the report concluded, such an admission of total failure would have a devastating political and psychological impact on the city's image and its residents, as well as its future economic development. On that basis the city decided to keep the *Queen* and try to weather the storm.

In order to end the management dilemma, Long Beach city fathers decided to buy back the leases from Pacific Southwest Airlines and Specialty Restaurants at the lessees' prices, including an agreement that permitted Specialty to pay no rent to the city until its total investment had been amortized. This transaction gobbled up another nine to ten million dollars in tidelands funds, beyond the king's ransom that already had been squandered on the project.

The *Queen* wallowed along with an annual loss of two million dollars in tidelands funds until July 1978, when the Long Beach Harbor Department agreed to assume financial responsibility for the ship on condition that it could take control of the fifteen acres of land and 230 acres of water surrounding the *Queen,* which was to be used exclusively for recreational purposes. Port officials immediately tried to sell or lease the ship but were determined to keep it in Long Beach as a tourist attraction. They contacted a number of hotel chains and others who might be receptive to such an investment. The offers were interesting; the trouble was that each wanted to move the ship elsewhere. A group from the Philippines wanted to purchase the vessel and haul it to Manila while a French cartel submitted an offer to buy the *Queen* and take it to Rio de Janiero. Another wanted to lease the ship and tow it down around the Horn and up the East Coast for berthing in Atlantic City as a gambling ship, with Long Beach receiving a share of the proceeds.

Long Beach port officials decided to bite the bullet and buy out the lease held by the master lessee in order to start from scratch in its search for new management. This strategy paid off. In 1980 the Wrather Corporation took over full operation of the ship, including hotel, restaurants, meeting facilities, tours, and the adjacent British village of Londontowne with its shops and restaurants. After another two years in the red the much-maligned ship finally began to show a profit.

Another spectacular attraction was added to the *Queen Mary* complex in April 1983 when the world-famous *Spruce Goose* of yesteryear returned as a public exhibit inside the largest clear-span aluminum dome ever constructed, just off the stern of the *Queen Mary.* The giant aircraft had rested in complete secrecy in a huge hanger built to its shape since shortly after Howard Hughes' brief but historic flight in November 1947. More than thirty-two years later the plane was moved from the hanger for the first time and lifted onto a nearby site by the largest crane afloat, after which the hanger was demolished. In February 1982 the *Spruce Goose* was moved onto an enormous barge and towed around the entire Long Beach Harbor to its permanent home, where it was carefully backed into its new geodesic home. Wrather now has plans for a new 350-room hotel addition near the *Queen Mary*'s bow, as well as additional shopping and exhibit facilities. The Queensway Bay Hilton Hotel provides another 200 rooms nearby. It appears that the renowned old liner has finally reached calm waters after one of the stormiest voyages on

Above
Oil tank fires sometimes set off some spectacular pyrotechnics, like this waterfront GATX blaze in 1972, which blew an exploding thirty-six-foot tank 250 feet into the air. Over fifty firemen suffered chemical burns, and most of the water to fight the fire was supplied through seventeen hose lines from Port of Los Angeles Fireboat No. 2. Courtesy, Los Angeles Fire Department

Opposite page
San Pedro Bay's worst accident in recent years was the explosion of the tanker Sansinena *in Los Angeles Harbor on the evening of December 17, 1976. The blast drove the fore and aft sections of the ship apart by 150 feet. Nine people were killed and twenty-three were rescued from the water. Courtesy, Los Angeles Harbor Department*

record. Thanks to a thirty-million-dollar investment by Wrather Port Properties in refurbishment of the ship, the village, and the dome for the *Spruce Goose*.

Throughout the long-running *Queen Mary* debacle the Long Beach Harbor Department kept moving steadily ahead with its expansion plans, as did the Port of Los Angeles, despite a new environmental awareness that added more bureaucratic red tape to the approval process for almost every building project. The National Environmental Policy Act of 1969 required environmental impact reports on all projects involving federal participation. Then the California Environmental Act of 1970 required environmental studies on most port developments, and the California Coastal Zone Conservation Act of 1972 involved more time-consuming legal procedures and still another approval before work could proceed. Patient port planners could only hope their pet projects would actually take shape before they were forced into retirement. The Port of Long Beach demonstrated its conservationist concern well enough to win an Environmental Enhancement Award from the American Association of Port Authorities in 1973 for its work in the improvement and protection of the environment, the first harbor in the Western Hemisphere to be so honored.

The turbulent 1970s was a decade of drastic social change in many areas, and one of the burning issues of that era was the mounting pressure for genuine female equality. Women were demonstrating well-trained ability to handle a variety of responsible positions in private industry and governmental functions, and both harbor departments were adding more and more qualified women to their administrative staffs. One of the more significant breakthroughs into a traditional all-male bastion came in 1974, when Gene Kaplan, wife of a prominent Los Angeles attorney, became the first woman ever appointed to the Los Angeles Board of Harbor Commissioners. Five years lat-

er Louise M. Duvall, an expert in corporate and real estate law, former president of the Long Beach Bar Association, and the first woman ever elected to the Long Beach Chamber of Commerce Board of Directors, became the first distaff member of the Long Beach Harbor Department in its fifty-four-year history.

The worldwide economic recession of the mid-1970s, due primarily to the continuing oil crisis, had serious repercussions in international maritime circles. Shipping schedules were cut back, as vessels reduced speed to conserve precious fuel. Petroleum prices went up with the shortage, and new refueling tariffs raised fuel and shipping costs. Cargo volume declined perceptibly, but both ports were offering a recession-proof service and remained the same powerful contributors to the regional economy. An economic impact report financed by the two ports showed that nearly 220,000 area jobs were directly dependent on maritime trade moving through the harbor, that its cargo/passenger movement contributed $2.6 billion to regional payrolls annually, $9.8 billion to local business revenues, and $3.9 billion to local business purchases.

The harbor's many years of accident-free operations came to an abrupt end on the early evening of December 17, 1976. The 70,000-ton tanker *Sansinena* was in the process of discharging petroleum at the supertanker terminal in the outer harbor in San Pedro and fumes were being vented from its tanks. Somehow they ignited and exploded with a force that could be felt for miles around. The blast drove the fore and aft sections of the ship 150 feet apart and hurled the entire central superstructure up onto the wharf, obliterating a guardhouse and raking the area with a hail of shrapnel-like metal. Incredibly, a number of crewmen in the after section of the ship survived without injury. Nine were killed, including a watchman in the guardhouse whose body was never found, and twenty-three men were rescued from the

The catch was still plentiful and profitable when this photograph was taken in 1974, but territorial restrictions and high costs have caused a steady decline in what for decades was the leading fishing and canning center in the United States. Courtesy, Los Angeles Harbor Department

water, after being blown overboard by the explosion, by fast-acting Coast Guard and harbor patrol boats. Damage was actually remarkably light because the accident occurred on the open, outer fringe of the harbor. Port and fire officials agreed the destruction would have been far worse had it happened in a deeper, more enclosed section of the bay.

Both ports continued to win new accolades as the decade moved along. The Port of Los Angeles became the most profitable port in the United States in terms of net income in fiscal 1977 to 1978 with a profit of $25.7 million, an astonishing 82 percent higher than the net for the previous year. The port's bunkering trade had tripled, with 3,000 ships refueling there. Los Angeles general cargo volume was up nearly two million tons to 9.5 million. In 1978 to 1979 POLA again led all United States ports in net income with $28.6 million, and its total operating revenue of $53.6 million was second only to the vast Port of New York/New Jersey.

Both harbor departments claimed supremacy in their private contest for the regional title as well as leadership on the West Coast, where about 40 percent of all shipping crossing the docks came through one of the side-by-side harbors on San Pedro Bay. The Port of Long Beach was making brilliant use of every foot of wharfage and storage space on the many-sided, claw-shaped landfill that formed the modern port to build its container trade at a furious pace. Every addition or extension of that landfill gave Long Beach's skilled planners additional room for more containers and more dockage for new shippers, and a pattern began to emerge. Long Beach became much the busier of the two San Pedro Bay ports—in fact, the busiest on the West Coast—on the strength of large, low-value bulk shipments and lower-cost, long-term agreements with shipping lines moving high-value cargo. Los Angeles moved less cargo than Long Beach, but became the nation's most profitable port from higher freight charges, terminal rents, dock fees, and charges for harbor pilots.

Still, first-place honors are largely a matter of local pride, because there is more than enough traffic passing through the Bay of San Pedro to keep both ports fully occupied and their facilities taxed to capacity in the foreseeable future. Both are critically short of land to accommodate the rising tide of maritime commerce in Southern California. Long Beach's original master plan was programmed to handle the highest projected volume until the mid-1980s, but unprecedented growth caught harbor officials completely off guard and the port was rapidly running out of room by the mid-1970s. The paucity of space is almost as critical on the Los Angeles side, where slips have been filled in to provide more container facilities and the only place for expansion is by adding landfill to Terminal Island.

All indications are that this upward spiral of seagoing trade through the bay should continue well into the next century. Only a catastrophic national disaster or a complete collapse of the world economy could alter the trend, in the view of industry experts. As before, the San Pedro Bay ports are perfectly situated to exploit important new trends in international commerce. For some years now the emphasis on trade through the two ports has been shifting from the industrial nations to the more immediate and accessible markets of the Pacific Rim, where rapidly developing countries like South Korea, Taiwan, Indonesia, Malaysia, and Hong Kong—as well as that region's industrial leaders: Japan, Australia, and New Zealand—have been the biggest trading partners for both ports.

Pacific Rim trade potential was enhanced still further by the emergence of the People's Republic of China after years of self-induced seclusion from the western world. Now intent on becoming an active participant in international business and modernizing its industry, Mainland China needs vast quantities of industrial equipment and machinery. Long Beach was the first to send a trade mission to Mainland China after the normalization of relations, Los Angeles followed very shortly afterward, and maritime activity with China has been on the rise ever since. It appears to be only a matter of time before China rivals Japan as the foremost revenue-producer for both ports.

The nation's unfavorable balance of payments had long been a thorny situation and a political football of major proportions. The United States had offered generous tariff terms in an effort to help many foreign nations, including Japan, to recover from the ruin of World War II. Now that they had regained economic good health, some were not responding with the same generosity toward American goods entering their countries. Both ports responded when the government launched a vigorous drive to correct that one-way flow of commerce. In 1978 the Port of Long Beach became the first West Coast port to win the coveted Presidential "E" award for continued contributions to the national export expansion program. The Port of Los Angeles received the "E" award five years later.

Another significant source of additional harbor traffic was the increasing diversion of cargo from the Panama Canal to a faster and less expensive landbridge system, which involves unloading on the West Coast and shipping overland to all parts of the country and East Coast ports, where some cargoes are reloaded for the final ocean run to Europe. The landbridge system evolved as a ready solution to difficulties with the canal, where rising rates and political unrest, as well as the restrictive width of the famed waterway, caused growing concern among international shipping companies. Graphic evidence of the canal's limitations appeared when some of the largest of the new tankers and jumbo container ships began arriving in the harbor with long scrapes along their sides after barely squeezing through the canal. Delays in passage through the canal were equally serious.

Water-rail transportation became so popular within a few years that more than one-third of all containerized cargo was soon using the ocean-overland system. As the major port closest to the Panama Canal, the Bay of San Pedro has been processing millions of tons of this diverted cargo annually. A port study predicts that more than 90 percent of all cargo from the Orient to East and Gulf Coast ports will eventually be shipped via the landbridge route.

Seventeen years of snail-like progress through the bureaucratic morass to secure the necessary permits and approvals for the long-awaited deepening of Los Angeles Harbor finally came to fruition with final approval by the Coastal Commission in 1980 and award of the sixty-one-million-dollar dredging contract to a Missouri-based international construction firm. Congressman Glenn M. Anderson, a tireless champion of the harbor-dredging campaign, and Mayor Tom Bradley threw a symbolic switch on March 16, 1981, activating one of the largest electric dredges in the world. The giant dredge, with a cutter head resembling a sea monster, then began its 500-foot sweeps of the harbor floor to lower the main channel bottom from minus thirty-five feet to minus forty-five feet in the first major Los Angeles channel dredging in fifty-three years. The two-year dredging provided a depth for hundreds more of the huge new container ships that could not use the harbor before, including the latest supersize C-9 carriers that American President Lines put into service soon afterward and the towering, six-level, city block-sized car carriers in use today. A close-up view of these modern maritime giants cruising slowly along the main channel in San Pedro is an arresting sight.

The period of unprecedented growth in San Pedro Bay continued. By early 1984 the harbor was experiencing such a dramatic upswing in cargo traffic that ships were lined up outside the breakwater because of a shortage of dockworkers to unload them. The big surge in arrivals caught the Pacific Maritime Association and the International Longshoremen and Warehousemen's Union, which provide the stevedore crews, completely by surprise. Both sought to ease the crunch by advertising locally for help and bringing in dozens of dockworkers from San Francisco and other West Coast ports where business was slow—an ironic turn of events for local stevedores who were lucky to get a couple of days' work each week in 1981 and now were offered seven days per week if they wanted it.

No other ports in the country enjoyed such a spectacular climb in cargo volume as the Los Angeles-Long Beach duo, second in size only to the giant New York-New Jersey combine. That surge in cargo activity did not surprise industry experts, who have long considered the Bay of San Pedro among the fastest growing commercial harbors in the world, where most of West Coast shipping eventually will be concentrated. The unfortunate victims of the dockworker shortage were the shipping firms, whose vessels that cost upwards of $25,000 per day to operate could only sit and await their turn to be serviced.

Fiscal 1984 was another banner year for both ports, with Long Beach reestablishing its claim as the West Coast leader in revenue tonnage by topping fifty million tons for the first time that year. In that single twelve-month period Long Beach's containerized cargo rose an amazing 44 percent, while Los Angeles' increased by slightly less than half that. Los Angeles led in the category of general cargo increase—12.5 percent to 11.3 percent for Long Beach. Together the two ports made the Los Angeles Customs District the leading maritime customs collection center in the nation, after years of placing second to the New York/New Jersey Customs District. Long Beach also remained much the busier port; 4,670 ships stopped there in fiscal 1984, compared with 3,146 at the Port of Los Angeles.

Of all the unsung specialists who work be-

TOPSail '84 had a variety of impressive vessels on parade. Courtesy, Long Beach Harbor Department

hind the scenes but are absolutely essential to the orderly operation of a modern seaport, perhaps the least visible of all is the harbor pilot—member of an elite group of master mariners who know the depths and intricacies of their harbors from years of experience and unerringly guide arriving and departing vessels safely and securely to their assigned berths. The bay's first known harbor pilot was an iron man named Captain C.N. Crog, who was on call day and night for two straight years during World War II, with no vacation or even a day off. Times have changed since then. Today maneuvering the huge ships through the busy harbor are nineteen pilots at the Port of Long Beach and sixteen pilots at the Port of Los Angeles, each with an "unlimited ticket" authorizing them to command any ship of any tonnage on any ocean in the world.

One of the most colorful and successful special events in San Pedro Bay in recent years was TOPSail '84, which was conceived and directed by Long Beach Harbor Department Public Information Officer Elmar Baxter as a prelude to the 1984 Los Angeles Olympics. Sponsored by the Port of Long Beach and sanctioned as an official Olympic Arts Festival event, the tall ships' salute to sail on the Fourth of July was a fitting introduction to the four Olympic venues, including yachting, which were held a few weeks later in Long Beach.

A Welcome Ashore Party on the eve of the tall ships parade for the more than 600 officers, cadets, and crew members from the thirty-two sail and motor vessels taking part in the event was held in the *Spruce Goose* Dome for the benefit of the Service Organization for Seafarers (SOS), which operates the international Seafarers Center in Long Beach. The entire maritime community mobilized to support the event. Long Beach Harbor Department and shipping officials headed key committees. The city's hotels, restaurants, and business firms contributed everything from cutlery to canapes. More than 2,000 attended the gala party and over $25,000 was raised for the Seamen's Center.

TOPSail '84 eventually mushroomed into the largest single event of the Olympic Arts Festival. In a roundup of nationwide activities on that July 4, *Time* magazine reported the details of that memorable spectacle:

One of the most splendid of the Fourth's events was a parade of 32 tall ships down the California coast from Manhattan Beach to Long Beach Harbor. Some 5,000 private boats escorted the ships, which included Producer Dino De Laurentis' replica of the HMS Bounty. *The flotilla was a mile long. More than one million people lined the coast to watch it pass, and as it did, an eerie, reverential hush settled upon the crowds.*

James H. McJunkin, executive director of the Port of Long Beach since 1977, first joined the Long Beach Harbor Department in 1963 as traffic analyst and port traffic manager. He became director of trade development in 1967 and assistant general manager three years later. Courtesy, Long Beach Harbor Department

With the cornucopia of profits and good fortune already overflowing for both ports, the recent reemergence of, and demand for, coal as a primary energy source could elevate the Bay of San Pedro to an even more commanding position in the Pacific maritime picture. Coal imports ranked second only to lumber in harbor traffic during earlier times. Then American miners began producing their own coal, and oil became the lifeblood of commerce as industry mechanized. The demand for coal gradually diminished until it virtually disappeared from the harbor scene.

Many years passed before the oil crises of the 1970s spread fear throughout the world business community, and particularly in the nonproducing nations of the Pacific Rim. The most highly industrialized among them, Japan, faced certain economic ruin if the oil supply should run dry. The other fuel source, coal, was not as easily handled as oil, but at least it was always available from friendly sources. Many of the Pacific nations decided to play it safe and began converting their industries from oil to coal, which created an increasing demand for the variety of steam coal found in vast quantities in Colorado, Wyoming, Utah, and New Mexico.

Again the geographical luck of the draw played heavily in the Bay of San Pedro's favor. As the closest ocean exit to that huge supply of coal for the Far East, the harbor would almost certainly become the principal exporter of that commodity. The Port of Los Angeles' bulk loader was already approaching its capacity in the early 1980s with the shipment of three million tons of coal annually, and industry experts were predicting that demand could run as high as 140 or 150 million metric tons by the end of this century. The Los Angeles Harbor Department promptly drafted plans for a new, much larger coal-loading facility on the 190 acres of new landfill on Terminal Island, with the capability of processing fifteen million tons annually.

The Long Beach Harbor Department reacted just as eagerly to this new opportunity. Long Beach developed plans for an even bigger coal exporting facility than Los Angeles, and earned much more space in the local media with its aggressive, full-speed-ahead approach. Even though it shaped up as another round of competition between the ports for that special market, all indications were that if the anticipated demand came even close to materializing, both ports would have all the coal business they could possibly handle.

Then the world oil picture began to change and the demand lessened. Those Middle Eastern countries began to lose their absolute control over oil production and the ability to make life-and-death decisions on petroleum production. Dissension over pricing and quotas within their ranks and increased oil production elsewhere assured adequate reserves. The threatened nations slowed their rate of conversion from oil to coal. The urgency of the ports' coal-loading projects diminished accordingly and were finally put on hold. The experts now predict that the high-volume need for steam coal by the Pacific Rim countries is at least another decade away, at which time both ports could reactivate their original expansion plans on extremely short notice.

Never in the history of the Bay of San Pedro have so many major development projects of such magnitude been in progress in both ports as those begun during this decade. Following is a summary of those projects, concluding with the climactic 2020 Plan for the future expansion of the bay to the year 2020.

LONG BEACH WORLD TRADE CENTER

"Like a lighthouse beacon, viewable from the harbor and the surrounding city as the gateway to the Port of Long Beach," was one harbor official's apt description of the $550-million Long Beach World Trade Center now under

Above
This aerial of Long Beach shows the claw-like landfill that forms Long Beach outer harbor and the tall buildings of downtown Long Beach. The open section in the center is Long Beach Airport. The San Gabriel Mountains are in the background. Courtesy, Long Beach Harbor Department

Opposite page
The days may be numbered for the present Port of Long Beach administration building, which was opened in 1960. The Harbor Department might move into the new Long Beach World Trade Center and use this valuable land for additional container terminal development. Courtesy, Long Beach Harbor Department

construction in the downtown section of the city overlooking the port.

A joint venture between IDM Corporation of Long Beach and Kajima International Inc., the American subsidiary of Kajima Corporation of Japan, and sponsored by the Port of Long Beach, the trade center will provide over two million square feet of office space and will be the city's largest commercial development ever when it is completed in 1992. It will serve the entire Los Angeles area as one of thirty-three world trade centers around the globe, and the largest west of New York.

The complex will be located on a 13.5-acre site acquired by the Long Beach Harbor Department, bordered by the Long Beach Freeway, Ocean Avenue, Broadway, and Magnolia. Phase I will be a thirty-story tower that will contain 620,000 square feet of floor space, including a 400-room hotel and a 20,000-square-foot private World Trade Club on its penthouse floors. The club will offer private dining facilities, banquet rooms, and suites for the convenience of individuals and companies involved in international business. The first phase is due for completion and to be ready for occupancy by the end of 1988.

The twenty-five-story second tower will contain approximately 560,000 square feet of predominantly office space, with a 10,000-square-foot health club and tennis courts on an adjacent parking structure. A third tower will offer another 470,000 square feet for commercial use, with retail and other business accommodations available in a 95,000-square-foot low-rise complex connecting two of the two tallest towers.

A separate 260,000-square-foot federal building will be built within the trade center complex to house various federal agencies currently headquartered at several locations throughout Southern California. Land is so valuable in the modern harbor that the Long Beach Harbor Department may move its administrative offices to the new trade center and use its present site to accommodate new container business.

In addition to creating more than 5,000 new jobs, the complex will generate some $2.7 million annually in property taxes and make substantial contributions to the community in its dedication to promoting increased trade, communications, information, and cultural and educational exchange among nations in the interests of international commerce and world peace. "The World Trade Center will be the cornerstone of our city," one city official said. "It will make Long Beach the international city we claim to be."

In accommodating the local and international maritime industry, the center will offer such services as marketing, research data processing, telecommunications, seminars, meeting and conference facilities, and office, travel, and promotional services. Port officials believe the center will attract new business and revenues from other regional, national, and international sources that might not otherwise come to Long Beach, thereby bringing increased trade and tourism to the city as a whole.

INTERMODAL CONTAINER TRANSFER FACILITY

The steadily rising volume of minibridge traffic through the harbor, and particularly predictions of much greater numbers in the future, placed even sharper focus on a long-standing problem shared by the ports of Long Beach and Los Angeles—the lack of an onsite railyard and the need to truck cargo twenty-five miles to the nearest rail terminals in downtown Los Angeles. Nearly every other West Coast port, even those a mere fraction of the size of the Los Angeles-Long Beach complex, have rail terminals to the docks of the harborside cities they serve. Yet San Pedro Bay has historically serviced a city twenty-five miles away that has grown into an enormous population center, and the transcontinental railroad lines always ended there.

It was one of the few glitches in the bay's otherwise splendid geographical location, but competition for container business has made it a serious one, especially with the increasing popularity of ocean-overland transportation. Inflation has tripled the cost of trucking cargo from the harbor to the city. Shippers were paying from $75 to $125 to move each container

The $550 million Long Beach World Trade Center, shown as a cluster of light-colored buildings overlooking the harbor in this artist's rendering, will offer over two million square feet of office space. The first phase will be ready for occupancy by the end of 1997. At the upper left is the Queen Mary. *Courtesy, Long Beach Harbor Department*

to downtown railyards, and some found it less expensive to unload at other ports that had their own adjacent terminals. Environmentalists were also blaming the steady stream of container trucks for adding to the area's mounting traffic and pollution woes.

Obviously, it was foolhardy to permit this bottleneck to continue, and the two harbor departments finally got together to eliminate their mutual handicap. In the first large-scale construction project ever undertaken together, the ports of Los Angeles and Long Beach signed an agreement in 1981 for the joint construction of a new 150-acre Intermodal Container Transfer Facility (ICTF) on land owned by the Los Angeles Harbor Department 4.4 miles from the geographic center of the combined ports, with the Southern Pacific Transportation Company as a third partner and operator of the fifty-million-dollar facility.

Ground was broken in January 1985, and construction has begun on the first and largest phase of the project, which is due for completion in 1986. Phase I will consist of five loading and unloading tracks capable of handling up to 250 intermodal rail container cars. Parking space will be available for over 1,600 wheeled containers or trailers. Annual throughput capacity will be in excess of 360,000 loads, and an additional seven tracks are planned for installation as traffic increases.

Whatever the cost, the new ICTF stands to

return that investment many times over in the years to come. Every shipper in the Orient is aware that using the overland system and intermodal rail services saves a container ship more than 5,000 miles and eight days of sailing time that it takes for the Panama Canal route to the East Coast. In 1984 the two ports together handled more than two million twenty-foot containers, more than all other West Coast ports combined. Fully 57 percent of all West Coast minibridge traffic already moves through the Bay of San Pedro, and port officials in Long Beach and Los Angeles are confident that the convenience of the new railyard will enable them to lure away a large share of business from the two other major West Coast container centers, Oakland and Seattle. Both northern ports have ready rail access and were originally chosen by some shippers who would have preferred Los Angeles-Long Beach all things being equal, but balked at paying those annoying harbor-to-city drayage charges. Eliminating them should outweigh whatever advantage Oakland derived from being the main coastal stop for many steamship lines and the shorter sailing time to Seattle from some points in the Orient.

CABRILLO COMPLEX

The new Cabrillo Beach Recreational Complex represents the culmination of years of planning, negotiation, and prolonged diplomacy of the most sensitive nature. The biggest impediment to make the Cabrillo plan a reality was public acceptance—agreement by the citizens of San Pedro to have a major recreational installation on the ocean side of their city.

There was valid reason for communal apprehension over the projected recreational center. Even though it would create dozens of jobs and bolster the local economy, residents were understandably concerned about a commercial operation that would have waves of strangers congesting the narrow streets and overrunning the town. Besides, they had had their fill of what could be inflicted on San Pedro's reputation after years of trying to live down the stigma of Beacon Street, which lingered for years after that notorious sector had been razed to make way for redevelopment.

The city and the Los Angeles Harbor Department could have forced the issue but wisely chose to take a more conciliatory approach. Port officials explained the Cabrillo plan at dozens of community meetings. The project was discussed in detail at public hearings and in the local press. Applying an enlightened development concept, the Los Angeles Harbor Commission formed a broad-based citizens advisory committee and asked it to prepare a plan that would be acceptable to the community as well as to the harbor administration. The committee's recommendations were accepted in full as the basic structure of the final Cabrillo complex plan.

The only physical impediment to the project was forty-five acres of Fort MacArthur property that sat squarely in the middle of the area needed for the project. Mayor Bradley officially accepted title to that unused real estate early in 1981, and the big earth movers were soon rumbling in to rearrange the land for the first phase of the 370-acre complex.

The main feature of the Cabrillo facility will be three new marina basins containing approximately 1,400 boat slips, side ties, and moorings, which will bring the total of small-boat berths in the complex to over 3,000. Landside facilities will include a three-story, 260-room hotel, three major restaurants, various marina-related businesses, a 3.5-acre salt marsh and bird sanctuary, a 12.5-acre youth camp to be managed by the Boy Scouts of America and available to other youth groups, a community building, an operations building, a small-boat fuel depot, two large park areas, a pedestrian walkway along the waterfront, and a picnic area.

Once the project was in the works, the only contentious subject to surface involved the question of who should operate the marina part of the complex—private enterprise, as is usually the case, or the harbor department itself. All agreed that the hotel, restaurants, shops, and other businesses should be contracted out, but port management claimed it could operate the boating activity more efficiently and fairly—especially in view of the critical shortage of available slips in the Los Angeles area.

Those favoring city operation argued that the demand for slips had created a situation that encouraged inflated rates and under-the-table payments, and made slip tenants afraid to complain of lax marina management for fear they would lose coveted berth space. The city view ran into stiff opposition from a varied faction that included Councilwoman Joan Milke Flores of the 15th (Harbor) District, local unions, business leaders, the Chamber of Commerce, a number of marina operators, and many San Pedro residents.

The issue was resolved when Mayor Bradley, in an uncharacteristic departure from his usual modus operandi, intervened directly and requested that his appointed five-member Board of Harbor Commissioners approve port administration of the Cabrillo marinas. Three commissioners initially favored private operation and two were opposed. One commissioner acceded to Bradley's request and changed his vote to make the final tally three-to-two in favor of port administration. The two commissioners who refused to change their votes were replaced on the board as soon as their terms expired.

LOS ANGELES WORLD CRUISE CENTER

The passenger ship business is one of the very few areas of maritime commerce where the Port of Long Beach has never attempted to compete with the Port of Los Angeles. The older port's romance with the cruise trade dates back almost to the actual founding of the Port of Long Beach, when waterfront land in San Pedro was plentiful and, except for huge quantities of arriving lumber and outgoing petroleum, there was not a great deal of other activity in the harbor. In those days it was a simple matter to assign large sections of choice channel footage to the big operators like American President Lines and Matson when the cruise business was in full flower.

Conversely, by the time Long Beach became a serious contender for harbor traffic shipping had become big business and every square foot of landfill that Long Beach added to its expanding port had to be carefully budgeted. It could not afford the luxury of squandering valuable space on an activity that required large facilities and was only used on a part-time basis. Los Angeles already had adequate cruise ship capabilities for both ports, and Long Beach harbor officials were satisfied to let it remain that way.

As fate would have it those two cruise giants—APL and Matson—eventually withdrew completely from passenger service and converted to cargo. Their big, sprawling passenger installations were used only periodically until the mid-1970s, when the cruise business enjoyed a dramatic upsurge in popularity in Los Angeles Harbor. Regular callers included P&O Orient and Princess Cruises, Carnival Cruise Lines, Royal Viking Lines, Cunard Lines Ltd., Sitmar Cruises, Western Cruise Lines, and Sundance Cruises. Destinations ranged from weekend trips to Ensenada to longer voyages to the "Mexican Riviera," the Caribbean, Alaska, and round-the-world ports-of-call.

One passenger liner that calls Los Angeles its home port has been seen by more people than any other ship in history and is partly responsible for the recent upswing in the cruise trade—Pacific Cruises' *Pacific Princess,* the "Love Boat" of the highly-rated television series that is syndicated around the world. The opening aerial shots used as lead-ins were filmed in the harbor and segments for episodes are regularly shot at the old American President Lines passenger terminal in San Pedro, giving the Port of Los Angeles millions of dollars worth of international exposure.

APL had been using part of its original passenger property for container traffic, and when the Los Angeles Harbor Department and the shipping company signed a twenty-year agreement to build a new forty-seven-million-dollar container terminal for APL in the West Basin, harbor authorities decided to expand the old APL facility into a new world cruise center that would have the capacity for berthing five large passenger liners simultaneously. When completed in 1987 it will be the largest and finest passenger terminal on the West Coast.

In addition to the existing two-berth terminal off the main channel, the new thirty-five-million-dollar complex will again make use of the two berths directly on the channel, which have been used more recently to berth cargo ships. The existing passenger terminal will be expanded to include a large restaurant, two United States Customs stations, and car rental and limousine services. The transit shed on the main channel will offer the same services.

The World Cruise Center complex will also extend around the slip to include the parking lot of the Princess Louise restaurant and as far north as the Catalina Cruises Terminal. Another new wharf and passenger facility to accommodate a fifth ship is being built on what is now the Princess Louise parking lot, directly across the slip from the present terminal. A seven-story, 240-room hotel will be built beside the new passenger facility. An unused helicopter hangar behind the Catalina terminal is due for conversion into a banquet hall seating 500 persons.

A tram system will carry passengers to all parts of the complex. A tram transit station will be located outside the center on Harbor Boulevard for rental car pickup, city buses, and shuttles down the boulevard to Ports O' Call Village and the new Cabrillo Beach Recreational Complex. In a precedent-setting management policy, a consortium of the seven cruise lines that will use the center regularly will also administer the new wharves and buildings, rather than the Los Angeles Harbor Department, as has always been the case previously.

2020 PLAN

Speculation and preparation for the long haul—the ultimate, future expansion of the Bay of San Pedro—have cast rivalries aside and brought the two ports together in the biggest and most important project they have ever collaborated in. That is a master plan formulated in 1980, based on predictions that by the year 2020 the number of containers passing through the bay will rise by more than 500 percent and the amount of dry bulk cargo like coal and other commodities will increase by 800 percent.

Studies upon which the plan is based call for a rise in container cargo from 10.7 million tons in 1980 to 62.5 million tons in 2020, dry bulk volume excluding grain to skyrocket from 7.6 million tons to 57.3 million tons during that thirty-five-year period, and petroleum shipments to increase from 57.2 million tons in 1980 to 83.9 million tons in 2020.

To handle this gigantic growth, two ports working with the Army Corps of Engineers devised a plan of such proportions that it will change the geography and appearance of the bay forever. It will require enormous increments of manmade land, and the only place such quantities of new land can be created is by filling in part of the bay. The basic proposal is to fill in a total of 2,600 acres—almost a quarter of the open water that now surrounds the two ports—and deepen navigation channels to seventy-five feet, at an overall cost of six billion dollars. If carried out the massive landfills would add eighty billion dollars to the region's economy, almost half of that from new business diverted from other Pacific Coast ports.

The proposed development of 1,104 acres of landfill in Los Angeles Harbor and 1,496 acres in Long Beach Harbor offered two alternatives. The plan that has since been approved by both harbor departments is to add most of the land-

Above
E.L. "Roy" Perry, a career Corps of Engineers officer and former general manager of the Port of Tacoma, served as executive director of the Port of Los Angeles from 1979 until his retirement in 1985. Courtesy, Los Angeles Harbor Department

Top, right
Ezunial Burts, executive assistant to Mayor Tom Bradley, succeeded E.L. "Roy" Perry as the executive director of the Port of Los Angeles in 1985. Courtesy, Los Angeles Harbor Department

fill inside the breakwater to form a new 1,265-acre landfill section in what is now open water between Terminal Island and the middle breakwater at a cost of $1.1 billion. A causeway would connect the island to Terminal Island.

The alternate plan, which would be twice as expensive at an estimated $2.6 billion, provides for all 2,600 acres of landfill to be added outside the breakwater to form a large island that would be joined to the two ports by a bridge. In addition to the cost, the alternate plan had a built-in functional weakness that would have disqualified it from the beginning. Ships cannot safely load and unload without the protection of a breakwater, and any facility built outside it would be at the mercy of the open sea.

Under the approved plan some of the most remote sites on the new island might be suitable for handling dangerous cargo such as chemical shipments. However, the preferred site for the handling of such cargo would be on the only small fill—485 acres—outside the breakwater that would be farthest from homes and other populated areas around the harbor. Of that 485 acres, Los Angeles would own 185 acres and the Port of Long Beach 300 acres.

Of course, such massive rearrangement of the land-water ratio in the bay means something will have to give, and there is no question that wildlife and recreation will be most directly affected in a negative way. The plan will eliminate 2,150 acres of fish and marine habitant inside the harbors and 745 acres outside the breakwater, which will also be lost to recreational boaters. A shallow-water habitat would be eliminated, as would the present seaplane anchorage. Nine harbor sites of cultural or historical importance would be affected, the current habitat for migratory birds would be reduced, and tidal flushing would be decreased. But progress moves remorselessly onward with scant regard for sentiment or preference. Perhaps to ameliorate somewhat the harsh realities of that philosophy, the plan projects that the new business the project will generate by the time it is completed will create up to 40,000 new jobs by the year 2020.

Although it is generally agreed that large-scale expansion of the harbor is inevitable, the 2020 Plan has its detractors. Analysts from the Coastal Commission claim the landfills proposed in the plan are much larger than they need be, and they question the estimated volumes in the Army studies. They point out that the 2020 Plan is based on the premise that only a certain number of containers can utilize an acre of land, while highly computerized handling systems such as that at the Matson Navigation Company's facility on Terminal Island stack containers in less space than is usually considered necessary. Nevertheless, veteran harbor executives are confident that the demand for additional space by new business will utilize all of the landfill productively as it is added via a three-phased program.

The mid-1980s finds both ports at the pinnacle of prosperity and success. The Port of Los Angeles set new records in every significant category during fiscal 1985. General cargo tonnage through the port reached 22.2 million metric revenue tons—a 24 percent increase over the previous year. Total metric revenue tonnage rose to 45.1 million tons. Net income increased by 16.9 percent to $48.7 million. Vessel arrivals were up to 3,444 from 3,146 in fiscal 1984. Los Angeles passed the million mark in the number of containers processed for the first time. The volume of dry bulk cargo showed a 40 percent increase as well, and Los Angeles became the leading import auto port in the United States in fiscal 1985.

The Port of Long Beach's numbers were just as impressive and, in some cases, even more so. Its volume of general cargo tonnage topped Los Angeles by a slim margin with 22.6 million tons, but Long Beach handily outdistanced its rival in total metric revenue tonnage with 53.3 million tons, and in ship arrivals with 4,652. Net income rose to $31.3 million in fiscal 1985 from $21 million the previous year. Long Beach continued to reaffirm its leadership as the busiest container port on the West Coast with the further expansion of seven container terminals in the inner and outer harbors, which will bring the total space devoted to container cargo to 525 acres, with twenty-five container cranes to service them.

The Port of Los Angeles observed its seventy-fifth anniversary in 1982, and now, with its record of exceptional achievements and a future bright with promise, there could scarcely be a more appropriate or timely occasion than the year 1986 for the Port of Long Beach to celebrate its own diamond anniversary.

From that historic day—June 2, 1911—when an obscure coastal steamer unloaded a cargo of redwood lumber at the city's single wooden dock and marked the beginning of a second port in the Bay of San Pedro, the growth of the Port of Long Beach to its present world-class stature is one of the most colorful and improbable success stories in maritime history.

TOPSail '84 was enjoyed by a variety of boating enthusiasts. Courtesy, Long Beach Harbor Department

CHAPTER XI

PARTNERS IN PROGRESS

The San Pedro Bay—America's gateway to the Pacific, and, if we are to believe the projections of so many experts and economic forecasters, America's gateway to the future. Today San Pedro Bay is America's most important harbor complex and an international leader in commerce and trade. With nearly one-half of all West Coast foreign commerce moving across its berths, the port complex of Los Angeles/Long Beach has transformed Southern California into one of the world's vital trade and financial centers, servicing not only America and the Pacific Rim, but also the entire globe.

How did this transformation of two small ports at the ocean's edge of Southern California into the mammoth, modern cargo complex occur in less than eighty years? Surely, the vision and business acumen of the founders and subsequent administrators of both ports were instrumental to the ports' ascendancy in international trade. But, as any maritime veteran will attest, the interaction of many different, yet essential, companies and services is crucial to the success of a harbor.

As much as the ports of Los Angeles and Long Beach have afforded the base of operations for a billion-dollar industry, so also have the ancillary companies in the area offered services and products to the international shipping community that made San Pedro Bay the preferred port of call for the world's cargo fleets. As the ports grew, so did the need for businesses to service the needs of the harbor; as better services were made available, so also did they enhance the attractiveness of the ports to shippers and shipping lines from all parts of the world.

The organizations whose stories are detailed on the following pages have chosen to support this important literary and civic project. These are the stories of companies that have made the ports what they are today, and what they will be in the next century. They are tales of careful planning and fortuitous timing; they are histories of firms that grew with the ports and also helped the ports to grow.

More important, these are stories of people. They are recountings of human enterprise, be it by an individual or a host of individuals in multimillion-dollar corporations. They detail the triumph of hard work and dedication to a vision. This, then, is the history of the human element that has made San Pedro Bay the international trade center that it is today.

MARINE EXCHANGE OF LOS ANGELES/LONG BEACH

The lone sentinel cupped his hands to his lips, blowing hard to stave off the predawn chill that squeezed its way through the heavy coat to still clammy skin beneath his outergarments. The hike along the rocky coast from San Pedro's beaches to the height of Point Fermin was not a long one, but the lookout still built up a sweat along the way to his position on the rocky coast.

Straining to see through the morning mist, his eyes latched onto his waited-for charge. Slowly steaming into the southern tip of San Pedro Bay, the ship cautiously lowered her speed, as if looking for the final okay to enter the safety of the harbor. After the long ocean voyage the captain was not about to endanger his vessel with a rash course change spurred by the sight and smell of solid land after so many weeks at sea.

Finally identifying the ship as the waited-for vessel, the lookout hurried over the slippery rocks, timing his steps with the breaking of the waves on the rocks to keep from getting doused by an unexpected breaker. Now his job was done; he would notify the ship's agent that the vessel had arrived and then wait again for the next ship's arrival.

Yet, from such simple and expedient means grew what eventually became the Marine Exchange of Los Angeles/Long Beach. Serving the vast San Pedro Bay harbor complex, the Marine Exchange has become an integral part of the fabric that comprises the United States' largest and busiest port complex. For over sixty-five years it has been the eyes and ears of the ports of Los Angeles and Long Beach, monitoring the movements of the many ships that call into Southern California from all points on the globe.

Formed in 1920 by W.H. Wickersham, a local steamship agent and customhouse broker, as an aid to the many companies that depended on the accurate and timely information that was needed to service the ships that called into San Pedro Bay, the Marine Exchange provided a needed service not only to agents and owners, but also to ship chandlers, fuel brokers, hotels, and many other businesses that cater to the ships and their crews.

Wickersham recognized the need for a central location for the service and decided that the top of Warehouse Number 1 in the Port of Los Angeles would be the ideal spot for the lookout activities needed for the expanding harbors. Warehouse Number 1 still houses the lookout tower of the Marine Exchange, manned twenty-four hours a day, seven days a week.

By 1923 the Los Angeles Chamber of Commerce saw the need and value of the Marine Exchange's service to the economy of a growing Southern California. With financial problems threatening the continued operation of the nonprofit organization, the chamber stepped in and established the Exchange as a Marine division within the chamber.

Marine Exchange leaders soon realized that the information that was being garnered on ship arrivals and departures had a commercial value to many businesses in the harbor area. From this came the Three-Day Advance Arrival Report, containing the date, time, ship's name, call sign, nationality, rig, last port of call, local agent, and berth at which she is expected to tie up. Today this service is subscribed to by 250 firms that require the latest information on ship movement in the ports.

Following a nonfatal collision of two tankers just outside the breakwater of San Pedro Bay, a vessel traffic information service was inaugurated in January 1983. This strictly voluntary program was initiated to assist ships that are entering or leaving the two highly congested areas of the major approaches of both ports. As vessels enter the zones, they voluntarily report their position to the Marine Exchange; the lookout personnel then relay pertinent information regarding positions of other vessels in the area.

From the top of the Marine Exchange Tower at the entrance to Los Angeles Harbor, two Marine Exchange employees signal to the S.S. Catalina, *a passenger steamer that, until the early 1960s, ferried visitors between Catalina Island and San Pedro Bay.*

The Marine Exchange of Los Angeles/Long Beach will continue to service the needs of the shipping industry of Southern California. As it nurtures the growth of the ports of Long Beach and Los Angeles to international prominence, it will continue to serve as the "eyes and ears of the harbor" well into the twenty-first century.

YAMAMOTO BROS., INC./SHIP CHANDLERS

Ships and men of foreign nations have always been a part of the fabric of the life and flavor of port towns. San Pedro in the early part of this century was no different, with the possible exception being that it was natural for West Coast ports to see more ships and crews from Japan than other American seaports. Japan, eager to sample the life and cultures beyond its island empire, plied the seas in her ships to bring the fruits of these cultures to her shores.

San Pedro was an ideal spot to drop anchor because nearby Terminal Island was the site of one of Southern California's largest Japanese communities. The Terminal Islanders provided a friendly port for the Japanese crews who had spent many weeks on board their ships in their journeys across the Pacific. Here in San Pedro and Terminal Island Japanese foods and stores could be purchased and stocked for the trip back to Japan.

It was about that time, 1932 to be exact, that a young entrepreneur who had emigrated from Japan a number of years earlier saw an opportunity for himself and his young family. If the crews wanted these types of foods and supplies, why not provide them—directly to their berths? Out of this simple premise John Sohei Yamamoto started his business, a business that grew from a mom-and-pop grocery store to an important and efficient full-service ship chandlery service located in Wilmington and Vallejo, California.

World War II was to be a trying time for all Japanese on the West Coast. The federal government made no distinction between citizen and alien, and soon John and his family found themselves relocated to Arizona. The family's store, on Harbor Department land, was razed during the war, and the future appeared dark indeed.

Following the war, without any capital available, John started off as a food peddler. The government made a partial reimbursement to John for the property confiscated during the war. With these funds John started a small grocery store in San Pedro. By that time more and more ships from the Far East were calling into Southern California's ports, and more and more time was being spent servicing the growing number of ships that required the special service that only the Yamamotos could supply. Finally, during the mid-1950s, John decided to enter the ship chandlery business on a full-time basis. He closed the store in San Pedro and moved to a warehouse and office in Wilmington, which was a more centralized location to service the ports of Los Angeles and Long Beach.

Today's operation, managed by John's son, James, handles ninety ships per month primarily from Japan and other Pacific Rim nations. His staff of nineteen works to meet the needs and requests of the many ships that call in the Southern California ports of Los Angeles, Long Beach, Port Hueneme, and San Diego. A new office and warehouse, recently opened in Vallejo, will service the ships that call in the San Francisco Bay area, Sacramento, and Stockton.

The company has grown to become a vital stores and food supplier to the many Japanese ship lines that call into Southern California and the San Francisco Bay area. In fact, more than fifty years after John Yamamoto first provided stores to his first ship in Los Angeles Harbor, Yamamoto Bros., Inc./Ship Chandlers remains as the only ship chandler serving the major Japanese shipping companies on the California Coast. With the arrival and departure of every Japanese ship at San Pedro Bay, the dream and vision of John Yamamoto and his family remains to this day—a living legacy to one of San Pedro's early Japanese pioneers.

John Yamamoto and his young family in their Terminal Island grocery store in 1938. Young James, seated on the countertop, today leads the only ship chandlery service on the California Coast that services Japanese shipping lines exclusively.

GENERAL TELEPHONE

The Long Beach main switching office on the corner of Elm and Sixth streets in 1935. Extensively remodeled, the building is still in use.

It was only fitting that the first major project of Long Beach's redevelopment was the 1969 opening of the new headquarters building of General Telephone on Ocean Boulevard. For as the city of Long Beach has grown and experienced tragedy and setbacks, so also has General Telephone experienced triumphs as well as disappointments in its development in Long Beach.

The history of General Telephone began in 1929 with the Associated Telephone Company. Previously known as Union Home Telephone Company, Associated merged with five other Southern California telephone firms that year to form Associated Telephone Company, Ltd. The firm was to retain this name until 1953, when it was renamed General Telephone of California.

Soon after the new corporation was formed, the discovery of oil in Long Beach Harbor, the popularity of Long Beach as a vacation site, and the increase in port activities caused the company to build a new facility on Elm Street to handle the increase in local calls and to house the engineering and administration offices.

Future growth for the firm seemed assured even though Long Beach was suffering through the depths of the Depression like the rest of the nation. Then, on March 10, 1933, the city suffered a major earthquake that destroyed many structures, including one of the company's buildings. However, Associated employees, realizing the importance of communications, worked tirelessly to repair the lines and damaged facilities to restore phone service in record time. By the end of the 1930s Associated Telephone Company was fully recovered and again growing with Long Beach.

However, the onset of World War II called for all communications equipment and supplies to be diverted for the war effort, and many of Associated's employees joined the Armed Forces. But the phone company was not to be denied its role in the war effort. With the strategic Long Beach Naval Station directly across the waters, Associated provided vital communications services for the facility.

By the war's end the demand for telephone service, like many other items that were rationed or curtailed during the war years, skyrocketed. The firm took several years to fill all of the 18,000 orders that were received for new phones, and by 1946 the Long Beach exchange could boast of being the largest in Associated's nationwide system.

By 1955 the postwar prosperity was in full bloom, and the phone system experienced dramatic changes and progress. The seven-digit dialing system was necessitated by the rapid growth in phone subscribers, and Long Beach residents could finally dial their own phone calls within the 213 area code. In addition, in 1963 direct distance dialing (DDD) made its debut in Long Beach, allowing residents to call most areas in the country without operator assistance.

By the late 1970s the impact of electronics was making spectacular headway into the telecommunications field, and a new electronic switching system was installed in the market switching center on North Atlantic Boulevard. Over the next five years five more electronic switching systems were added by General Telephone throughout the area.

Today General Telephone's new building overlooks the bustling international port that it was so instrumental in developing over the years. The company's 500 local employees can rest assured that from their vantage point in the heart of Long Beach, General Telephone has played, and will continue to play, a vital and indispensable role in the city's rebirth and future success.

Associated Telephone Company's installation and repair trucks in 1929, when they served about 28,000 telephone customers in the greater Long Beach area.

DAILY COMMERCIAL NEWS

"A harbor, even if it is a little harbor, is a good thing, since adventures come into it as well as go out, and the life in it grows strong, because it takes something from the world and has something to give in turn."

—Sarah Orne Jewett in *Country Byways, River Driftwood.*

For the past seventy-five years, dating back to when the Port of Long Beach was just getting its feet wet in the international trade waters, the Los Angeles-based *Commercial News* has been there to document the "adventures" of the companies and organizations that have contributed so extensively to the growth and viability of the industry in Southern California.

It is no coincidence that the development of the *Commercial News* and the port run parallel. Since the founding of the paper back in 1911 by Charles A. Page, grandfather of one of the company's current publishers, the *Commercial News* has focused on the movement of goods from one point to another.

Commercial News

Business — Commerce — Industry — Transportation

TRinity 0567 LOS ANGELES, CALIFORNIA, THURSDAY, JULY 13, 1933 5c Per Copy

CKS, ALLIED DUSTRIES ARE RAFTING CODES

Rail Lines Announce Cut in Harbor Rates

HARBOR AUDIT COMPLETED; LOSSES REPORTED; ECONOMIES SUGGESTE

Cooperative Cotton Association Leases Port Storage Space

SHIPPING AND PORT NEWS BRIEFS

Tentative Code for Van, Storage Group Is Formulated Here

One of the early editions of the Commercial News.

Throughout its history the *Commercial News* has championed the importance of transportation and trade to the area's economy.

The history of the *Commercial News* is a microcosm of the history of the steamship industry as well—when business has been good for the steamship lines it has been good for the *Commercial News.*

The *Commercial News* has been a barometer of the trends in the industry: Over the years it has been one of the first publications to record such developments as containerization, LASH, roll-on/roll-off, and the changes in the economy that have necessitated those developments.

Fortunately, the firm's efforts have not gone unnoticed over the years. Recipients of various honors have ranged from former publishers Charles A. Page, Sr., and Charles A. Page, Jr., and former editor Brad Daniel to current staff members.

Executives throughout the industry have also recognized the value of the publication: "The *Daily Commercial News* has been a standard for the shipping and transportation industry for many years. It is one of the primary sources of information that we rely on on a daily basis," commented James H. McJunkin, executive director of the Port of Long Beach.

Echoing his comments was Joseph J. Zaninovich, president of the Los Angeles Board of Harbor Commissioners, who said that "the *Daily Commercial News* is required reading for all of us in the Southern California maritime industry."

Until the summer of 1985 the *Commercial News* had always been under the total direction and guidance of the founder's family. Then, in mid-1985, Raymond Page and Bill Irwin took over the helm of the organization as publishers.

Since then the *Commercial News* has been undergoing a revolution of its own. People have been added in all departments: editorial, advertising, circulation, and production.

Modernization efforts are ongoing throughout the entire operation: a new telephone system, a direct telephone line for the San Francisco Bay Area, representatives in both the Bay Area and on the East Coast, subscriber to a news wire service providing updates from around the world on a continuous basis, and computerization to improve the overall production and appearance of the publications.

Today the Los Angeles Commercial News Group publishes three major transportation and trade publications: the *Daily Commercial News & Shipping Guide,* the *Weekly Commercial News,* and *Cargo* magazine.

The goal has always been clear and remains the same today: to be *the* source of information.

For the past seventy-five years the Los Angeles-based Daily Commercial News *has been reporting international trade news. The new look shown below carries on the tradition.*

DAILY COMMERCIAL NEWS AND SHIPPING GUIDE

LXVI 66TH YEAR NO. 19 LOS ANGELES, CALIFORNIA WEDNESDAY, JANUARY 29, 1986 50 CENTS PER COPY

charter firm in HK must restructure debt

ITC speaker discusses the future of NVOCCs

INDEX

Port of LB says DOE must file documents

Nakasone promises continued liberalization of Japan

Danish Parliament votes for EC referendum soon

PORT OF LONG BEACH

As the Port of Long Beach celebrates its seventy-fifth anniversary of service to maritime commerce and the Southern California community, it can look back with pride at the accomplishments that have shaped not only the face of the maritime industry, but of the regional, national, and international economies as well.

Ideally situated at the hub of trade between the Pacific Rim nations and the United States, Long Beach is continuing to expand on its role as the gateway to the Pacific. As cargo movement trends have dramatically shifted from the Atlantic Ocean to the Pacific in the last decade, the "century of the Pacific" may very well also be the "century of the Port of Long Beach."

The multitowered Long Beach World Trade Center, to be located in the heart of the city, is destined to become the home for a multitude of international businesses trading in the Pacific Rim.

Long Beach's ascendency to its position as the leading port on the West Coast began nearly a quarter-century ago with the advent of the containerization of cargo. Prior to that time cargoes were laboriously hand loaded by pallets, slings, and hoists onto or off of waiting ships. Equally time consuming was the fact that many of the cargoes had to be first taken out of the trucks or loaded into them once the cargoes were on the face of the dock.

The initial concept of containerization was one of those brilliant leaps of imagination that owes its subsequent success to the beauty of its simplicity. Since all of the cargoes that were trucked into or out of the ports were carried on huge tractor trailers or vans, why not simply load the entire trailer directly onto the ship and then off-load it onto a waiting truck at the other end of the journey?

As with many new ideas, there were some who were skeptical of whether the idea would work. Not so at the Port of Long Beach. Being a modern port that physically had grown by dredging and landfilling over the years, harbor officials realized a winner when they saw it—and containerization seemed like the wave of the future. Plans were made to create hundreds of acres of additional land to accommodate the new terminals that would be required. New traffic patterns within the terminals themselves would have to be implemented to allow for the technology that would accompany the new method of transporting cargoes across the oceans.

Once the facilities were completed, shipping lines from all across the globe made Long Beach a port of call because of the ultramodern equipment to be found there. Today that trend continues. As the leading West Coast port in the United States, Long Beach moved over 53.2 million metric revenue tons across its berths in 1985; of that, 19.1 million mrts and 1.14 million TEUs (20-foot-equivalent units) were containerized cargoes, the most ever recorded on the Pacific Coast.

But moving containers on and off ships is just the beginning of the story of international transportation. With the tremendous amounts of cargoes moving between Pacific Rim countries and the United States, coupled with the arrival of deregulation of the trucking and rail industries, it soon became evident that movement of shipments by a combination of modes of transportation to inland or other port destinations was becoming an efficient and economic alternative to the traditional all-water routes of transportation through the Panama Canal. This fact was not lost on other ports up and down the West Coast, and soon the race for intermodal traffic movements heated up among the major ports in California, Oregon, and Washington.

In early 1985 Long Beach, together with the Port of Los Angeles and the Southern Pacific Transportation Company, launched an ambitious project to capture the lion's share of this intermodal business. Realizing that a twelve-million consumer population base made the Southern California region an ideal port of entry for many international shippers, officials from the three entities decided to further capitalize on the fact that the region also boasts a rail shipping time to the Gulf states and the rest of the Sunbelt that is one day less than ports in the Pacific Northwest or the San Francisco Bay area. Further, year-round mild climates eliminate shipper's concerns over delays caused by snow, ice, or other inclement weather situations.

The result of this joint effort is the Intermodal Container Transfer Facility (ICTF) now under construction on property owned by the Port of Los Angeles and adjacent to Long Beach. The 150-acre site, with sixteen gates and twelve rail tracks, represents a commitment of fifty-four million dollars. Completion of the first phase is scheduled for the fall of 1986.

Located only four miles from each port, the ICTF will facilitate the movement of containers from ship to rail in the shortest time possible. With eight of the gates reversible, the ICTF will also be an ideal facility to handle export cargoes bound for Pacific Rim markets. An important side benefit for the community will be the reduction of truck traffic on local freeways.

While the Port of Long Beach looks to the entire nation as a market for its transportation networks, concern for the local business person also remains high on the list of the varied interests of the harbor.

Since its opening in 1982 Long Beach's Foreign Trade Zone No. 50, the only such facility in the region, has developed a stature and reputation that is truly remarkable considering its short existence. Offering duty-free manufacturing, manipulation, distribution, and warehousing facilities for a variety of businesses, FTZ No. 50 has rapidly become the standard for innovation and the concept

High-speed gantry cranes load and unload container vessels in record time. Fully containerized ships are usually in port for a single eight-hour longshoreman shift.

The 950-foot American California, *one of twelve U.S. Lines' vessels, represents the latest generation of containerships. These new vessels can carry 4,486 TEUs (twenty-foot-equivalent units) on deck and below deck.*

Coffee beans from China await further distribution from Foreign Trade Zone No. 50 in Long Beach.

of a regional trade zone.

From its original 11.5-acre site in north Long Beach, Foreign Trade Zone No. 50 has mushroomed to encompass two expansion zones, the first in Ontario, some sixty miles from Long Beach, and the second site in nearby Santa Ana. The Ontario operation encompasses 1,350 acres of land adjacent to the Ontario International Airport in the booming Inland Empire area of Riverside and San Bernardino counties. The area, once the agricultural outback of Los Angeles, is now one of the most dynamic economic areas in California. The new Santa Ana site, located in the heart of Orange County, is a 43-acre zone that will specialize in high-technology enterprises.

In addition to the general-purpose expansion zones, FTZ No. 50 also includes two specific-use subzones. The first is the Toyota Motor Manufacturing, U.S.A., truck bed facility in north Long Beach. This 18.7-acre site is involved in all aspects of truck bed assembly from the initial stamping of raw materials to the final painting and shipping of the units.

The second subzone is National Steel and Shipbuilding Company of San Diego. Consisting of 74 acres of land area and 54 acres of water area, the company is a major vessel construction and repair facility that employs 5,426 full-time workers.

In 1985, 362 commodities from thirty countries, valued at approximately $79.2 million, passed through FTZ No. 50; 225 firms took advantage of the benefits of the zone, and 5,823 full-time jobs were involved in its activities. If these figures are not impressive enough, consider the fact that four additional sites may soon join the growing regional family of Foreign Trade Zone No. 50.

As the future of the Port of Long Beach's Foreign Trade Zone reflects the unlimited growth potential of the entire region, so also do other spectacular projects that will carry the port to the threshold of the twenty-first century.

Initiated in response to the federal government's request for a comprehensive plan for the future development of the San Pedro Bay, the 2020 Plan, so named for the year in which the final phase of the project will be completed, is, in essence, the future of the port itself. Conceived by planners at both San Pedro Bay ports,

The newest construction project at the Port of Long Beach, the Pier A expansion, will house the Long Beach Container Terminal upon its completion.

the 2020 Plan represents the land-use needs for both ports from now through the year 2020. The grand scope of the plan entails the creation of nearly 2,600 acres of new land through dredge and landfill, at a cost of four billion dollars. The economic benefits in terms of jobs and revenue are equally staggering. By the year 2020 planners estimate that the entire project will have generated nearly 800,000 jobs annually. The impact in terms of spending for construction and retail items will be as huge as the project itself.

The development of the project is, of course, necessitated by the projected increase in cargo movements that will occur in the San Pedro Bay in the next thirty-five years. At the present rate of growth it is estimated that 223 million tons of cargo will be passing through the port complexes by the year 2020. However, even with improvements to existing facilities, there would be a 100-million-ton shortfall in cargo-handling capability. Should such a situation occur, it is feared that much of this cargo would be diverted to other ports or even other nations. Hence, the 2020 Plan is viewed as the vital link to the future of the ports.

Heavy-lift and unusual cargoes are still an important part of the port's business. Here, a piece of equipment for a generating plant is off-loaded and awaiting placement on board a rail car.

As officials at the Port of Long Beach are preparing their terminals for the anticipated cargo increases on their berths, so also are they preparing for the increase in financial, shipping, maritime-related, and governmental activities that will surely follow. Toward this end, the Port of Long Beach, together with the international joint venture of IDM Corporation of Long Beach and Kajima International, one of Japan's largest construction firms, has proposed what will be one of the most exciting new construction projects in Southern California: the Long Beach World Trade Center.

The $550-million, multitowered complex will attract companies involved in all facets of international trade, while at the same time offering a center for world class restaurants, hotels, retail shopping, and entertainment and recreation facilities. Located in the heart of the Los Angeles/Orange County business region, the 2.2-million-square-foot World Trade Center will be headquarters for international trade and commerce for the western United States, and will also stand as the embodiment of the dynamism of both the City and the Port of Long Beach.

While many of the plans of the Port of Long Beach reflect projects that will see their completion years in the future, progress also occurs in the present. A new 88-acre container facility has just been completed on Pier A for Long Beach Container Terminal. It features the latest in computer technology and utilizes the newest generation of container cranes designed for third-generation containerships. Also in the immediate future is the expansion of the port's major container complex on Pier J. Envisioned to add 135 acres to the area, the new land will afford expansion opportunities for the container terminals that call Pier J home.

While the multimillion-dollar complex of the Port of Long Beach stands as a remarkable example of planning and foresight filled with technological and engineering wonders, the port also takes pride in the benefits that it has provided to the people of the area and especially to the citizens of Long Beach. It plays a major role in the creation of more than 187,000 jobs in Southern California and generates in excess of $4.4 billion throughout the regional economy in the form of private business revenue, wages and salaries, business purchases, and tax revenue. In these and other areas of activity, the port will continue to be a good neighbor to the surrounding region.

This concern with people and the human element of international business will continue to play a vital role in the operation of the port. As international trade assumes an increasingly complex posture, worldwide competition will focus on the ability of workers in the maritime industry to increase productivity and maintain or increase their positions in the global market. New associations and alliances between all elements of the shipping and transportation fields will be necessary to remain competitive globally. As the Port of Long Beach was built in the spirit of partnership, so also will its future successes be attributable to person-to-person communications and a commitment to international cooperation.

UNOCAL

The year was 1874 and the Pennsylvania oil fields were awash in the production of the lifeblood of America's engines of industry. As the nation's thirst for the fuel that powered her growth grew by each passing month, two young businessmen decided that their futures lay in the black Pennsylvania crude.

That same year Lyman Stewart and Wallace Hardison formed their partnership and entered the oil production business. For nearly ten years the partners labored in Pennsylvania, but when word of new oil finds in the West reached them, they began to contemplate a move to California. In 1883 Stewart and Hardison moved to Santa Paula and began anew. They merged with two smaller companies and incorporated as Union Oil Company of California in 1890.

In the next few years the company acquired many producing properties in Los Angeles. It established its corporate headquarters in the city in 1900.

The company's long association with the Port of Los Angeles predates the port. Union Oil partially funded a 1909 plan to dredge the then-shallow San Pedro Harbor in order to turn it into a deep-water basin capable of handling seagoing vessels. When the project ran into financial difficulties, the firm took on the entire project, building sea walls and wharves and creating industrial sites. The City of Los Angeles annexed the area in 1922.

Because of the new tanker access, Union Oil built its Los Angeles refinery on a 200-acre site adjoining the harbor in 1916. Today that site spans more than 400 acres, with the refinery's rated capacity at 108,000 barrels of crude per day.

Today the company is one of the nation's most successful corporations and its 27th-largest industrial firm. In April 1983 a reorganization resulted in Union Oil becoming the principal operating arm of Unocal Corporation. Unocal is the nation's thirteenth-largest oil company and ranks ninth in net earnings of all U.S. oil firms and twenty-first among the country's industrial firms.

In 1933, when this photograph was taken, Union Oil Company of California was already well established at the Port of Los Angeles.

To ascend to such a position is the result of the talents and foresight of many people throughout the years. Unocal engineers and researchers have always stood at the cutting edge of new technology for the entire industry. In the areas of petroleum production and refining, geothermal projects, and enhanced recovery processes, Unocal has always maintained its dedication to research and development.

It was Union Oil's vision and determination that saw the possibilities of using oil for propelling steamships on their ocean journeys as early as 1888. Six years later the firm's engineers conducted the first conversion in the West of a railroad locomotive to an oil-burning engine.

Realizing that the uses of petroleum products had only minimally been tapped, the company took a bold step to ensure its future success by establishing the West's first petroleum laboratory at Santa Paula in 1891. Nine years later Union established the West's first petroleum department that specialized in the geological aspects of oil exploration and production. In 1920 Union was already looking to oil enhancement techniques by acquiring its first oil shale properties in western Colorado. Research and development was now recognized as a major key to the success of the company, and in 1922 Union Oil's Research Department was formally launched. By year's end seventy-four researchers were em-

Workmen begin grading for the railroad spur tracks on Union Oil Company of California property in 1919.

ployed in the department, and today 1,000 scientists, engineers, and support personnel work at Unocal's Fred L. Hartley Research Center in Brea, California.

The early 1970s saw a dramatic reevaluation of operations as America and the industry were rocked by the Arab oil embargo. However, with a tradition for innovation and risk taking, Union Oil saw the crisis as an opportunity to seek out new ways of increasing production from existing fields and to explore the feasibility of alternative sources of energy.

Today Unocal is the world leader in geothermal energy production. The Geysers field in Northern California is the world's largest geothermal-electric operation. There 1.1 million kilowatts of energy are produced by clean, natural steam. Permitting procedures are now under way for what will be the world's largest geothermal power plant, a 147,000-kilowatt facility that is scheduled to begin operation in 1988. In addition to its efforts in California, Unocal geothermal operations are in place in the Philippines. The company has drilled exploratory wells in Indonesia and has done geophysical work in Japan and Italy.

In addition to its alternative energy projects, Unocal is also involved in coal mining in Canada through its wholly owned subsidiary, Unocal Canada Limited.

Internationally, Unocal continues to make impressive gains through its exploration and production activities in Indonesia, Thailand, Canada, and the Netherlands. In the North Sea, gross oil production at the firm's offshore fields is averaging 22,900 barrels of crude per day—nearly one-half of the Netherlands' total oil production. In addition, exploration properties have been obtained in Madagascar, Egypt, Togo, and Zaire.

The Unocal Chemicals Division is another step forward for the corporation. While providing fertilizers and agricultural chemicals for more efficient crop production, the firm's Poco Graphite, Inc., subsidiary has emerged as a world leader in providing premium-grade graphite to the semiconductor industry and for biomedical and aerospace applications.

Along with its petrochemical activities, Unocal is also involved in several real estate developments. A 54-acre industrial site in Simi Valley, California, and a 101-acre site in Schaumburg, Illinois, are among the firm's holdings. On the residential side, a 372-unit condominium complex is under way in Southern California, and the planned fifty-acre shoreline development at Lake Arrowhead is proceeding.

Together with all of its accomplishments in the oil and chemicals fields, Unocal remains committed to the quality of life of the entire community. Environmental concerns are as important to the company as economic ones; in a single year over 700 Unocal facilities are routinely inspected to assure compliance with environmental and health and safety regulations.

Further, the Unocal Foundation provides financial support to various educational, cultural, and civic programs that enhance the life of Unocal's employees and neighbors.

Union Oil Company of California (Unocal) at the Port of Los Angeles, 1985.

HARBOR SHIP SUPPLY

C.F. Crouthamel, founder.

Like many of the early pioneers in the San Pedro area, C.F. "Charlie" Crouthamel was a transplant from another state. But without Charlie's move to the city, San Pedro would have been denied what Harbor Ship Supply is today—the largest ship chandler on the West Coast.

It was in the early 1930s that young Crouthamel, recently discharged from the U.S. Navy, returned to his home state of Pennsylvania. His stay was to be short-lived, however, as he soon received word from an acquaintance in San Pedro of an offer of employment in the ship chandlery business. Having been assigned to San Pedro during his active duty, Crouthamel was already familiar with the city; further, having worked in the quartermaster section of his unit, he was experienced in working with ships' provisions and equipment.

By the time 1932 rolled around, Crouthamel was ready to stride out on his own. Moving into an old warehouse in Wilmington, he started his company with the barest of equipment and staff. From that humble beginning, Harbor Ship Supply has grown to become one of the largest and most respected ship provisioners in the nation.

Crew requirements were vastly different in the firm's early days. Refrigerated provisions were still years away, and a great portion of a ship's order in those days consisted of ice and live animals. Since the steamers of the day utilized coal for fuel, many a wagon load of coal also was delivered to shipside by Crouthamel's growing company.

In those days provisions made up 99 percent of a ship's needs; today that figure is about 30 percent. The remainder of a ship's needs is for deck and engine parts, fitting, tools, and safety equipment. A good sale in those days averaged $1,000; today a full stores delivery ranges in the $60,000 area and is the key element in the firm's present business.

Currently Harbor Ship Supply has offices in the San Francisco and Los Angeles area, with over 71,000 square feet of warehouse space and 76,000 cubic feet of freezer and cooler space. Produce is picked up daily from the L.A. markets and meats are prepared at the firm's own federally supervised plant under strict government approval.

Over the years Harbor Ship Supply has acquired distributorships for many of the most-needed items required to operate a vessel. That—coupled with an inventory of some 15,000 line items valued at over two million dollars—allows the company to compete with any chandler anywhere in the world.

Harbor Ship Supply, one of the most respected ship provisioners in the nation, keeps a fleet of trucks on call twenty-four hours a day, seven days a week. All are radio-dispatched to any port on the West Coast.

With the help of modern computers to regulate stock, a large fleet of trucks to transport goods, and years of experience to locate and purchase competitively, Harbor Ship Supply has become the dominant force on the West Coast.

Presently the firm is under the direction of Harold Crouthamel with his son, Jeff, assisting him in this unique 24-hour-a-day, 7-day-a-week business. With three generations of experience and dedication to the founding principles of dependability, quality, and service, Harbor Ship Supply will surely continue another half-century of service to the marine industry.

TRW INFORMATION SYSTEMS GROUP

For a company such as TRW that has been a world leader in advanced electronics, electronic systems, and software, it is natural that the latest addition to the existing major business entities of Electronics and Defense, Automotive, and Industrial and Energy should be the Information Systems Group.

With full-fledged group status, this new organization has the dual task of integrating and coordinating TRW's commercial information businesses, while concurrently utilizing the company's vast technical expertise to enhance products and services for new markets and customers. The group is aggressively developing a unique merging of entrepreneurship with proven experience and common sense.

TRW has become one of the world's largest software companies. Evolving from that strength and expertise, it was a natural development for the company to move aggressively into the commercial application of its past experiences. The process began more than twenty years ago with the entry into the consumer credit information arena. The Information Services Division is today the national leader in its industry, maintaining information on 120 million consumers, providing 50 million credit reports annually, and updating its record systems with over 3 billion entries per year. Today the division also provides high-quality business credit reports and services as well as target marketing services.

In a bold step, the group is offering the TRW CREDENTIALS (SM) Service. This unique package of direct-to-the-consumer credit services enables an individual to have access to his credit report at any time, to be notified whenever his records are accessed, and permits him to electronically apply for credit. It eliminates the burden and confusion of filling out applications. On the horizon is the possibility of an integrated system of credit applications, evaluations, loan decisions, and disbursements that can be done through automatic teller machines—all in a matter of minutes.

TRW also has a highly regarded, nationwide computer systems and peripheral equipment service and maintenance organization. Focused within the Customer Service Division, this business activity is a prime example of the successful practical application of experience and technological expertise.

As an outgrowth of the tremendous volume of electronic information services that have become the company's trademark, it was an equally logical progression into the systems services and maintenance arena. Today TRW is the largest independent, third-party provider of service, maintenance, and repair for computers and peripheral equipment in the United States. The division's technicians will set up any system that a customer requests; recondition, customize, and redocument a new or used system; and provide equipment storage services as well. To support its customers the organization maintains thirty-six million parts and assemblies in its inventory.

A relatively new area of activity for the Customer Service Division involves the maintenance and servicing of sophisticated medical diagnostic equipment. These services are provided nationally, involving very highly trained personnel. An example of the company's expertise in scientific instruments and equipment is the Mars lander satellite which contained, within a one-meter cube, a TRW-built, fully equipped robotic chemical and organic analysis laboratory that was used to determine if life existed on the planet. It performed flawlessly.

However, these are not the only spheres in which the group operates. The Real Estate Information Division is a more recent addition specializing in providing a broad range of information products and services to a variety of customers. Fundamentally, the division provides, on a nationwide basis, title insurance, appraisal, and escrow/closing services, as well as maintaining computerized property tax and title filing data bases. Daily, these businesses provide responses to some quarter-million inquiries. TRW expects its real estate information services to become a significant and basic element of the group. That process is clearly under way as the division already has become the nation's leading provider of these services to the secondary mortgage industry.

But in addition to the tremendous capabilities of the company are the very human interests that are reflected in the decision to locate the Information Systems Group headquarters in Long Beach. With a spirit of entrepreneurship as its engine, the organization found a welcome environment in the upbeat business renaissance of the city. With sparkling new buildings in easy access to the entire Los Angeles basin, fine neighborhoods for its employees, and room to expand, the TRW Information Systems Group believes that it has found a home that will allow it to pursue its goal of fully participating in the mainstream of the information age.

ARCO TRANSPORTATION COMPANY

A barrel of crude oil, which cost twenty dollars in 1860, could be had for ten *cents* one year later. There simply weren't enough refineries to handle the unrestrained output of the newly discovered Pennsylvania fields, so the Atlantic Petroleum Storage Company adapted.

Founded in 1865 with "large and commodious warehouses and docks the tidewater, for the storage and shipment of Petroleum and its products," Atlantic Richfield reincorporated in 1870 as the Atlantic Refining Company, then did well enough at refining to attract the attention of a young cost accountant named John D. Rockefeller.

Rockefeller believed that competition itself was wasteful and inefficient and so set about gathering fully 95 percent of the entire American oil business under the wings of his Standard Oil Trust. Atlantic operated as Standard Oil's Refining Division from 1874 until 1911, when the U.S. Supreme Court decided that things were getting out of hand and ordered the trust dissolved. Suddenly Atlantic Refining found itself on its own again by Supreme Court decree, but it had no oil to refine, no way to market its products, and no pipelines or tankers to transport it anyway! J.W. Van Dyke, who had been the refinery manager under Standard Oil, ordered five new tankers and told his people to "go find the company some crude oil."

General Pershing's troops loading supplies at Columbus, New Mexico, for the expedition into Mexico in pursuit of Pancho Villa. Courtesy, Columbus Development Board, Inc.

Meanwhile, new strikes were attracting the oil gamblers to Kansas. A twenty-year-old druggist from Independence got so excited that he bet—and lost—his family's drugstore in speculation, then "accidentally" blew his big toe off in a hunting mishap and bought backyard leases with the insurance settlement. His bent for gambling paid off in 1904, and within three years the flamboyant Harry Sinclair had become the richest man in Kansas.

Sinclair Oil and Refining Corporation was founded in 1916 and began busily suturing a system of pipelines and refineries into the heart of America. "The Sinclair Oil and Gas Company made oil history the past thirty days that has never been equaled or even approached in the history of industry," said the May issue of the National Petroleum News.

In retrospect, 1916 was a big year for the forerunners of today's Atlantic Richfield Company. Sinclair was off and running; Atlantic accepted delivery of its first "huge" tanker; opened the nation's first modern service station; and Pancho Villa was burning Columbus, New Mexico, to the ground.

With the help of President Woodrow Wilson, Mexican forces had defeated the rebel leader Pancho Villa in 1915. Wilson had allowed the Mexican Army to bring reinforcements across U.S. territory, and after his defeat, Villa swore that he would get even with the gringos. Shooting across the border became so common that hotelkeepers in El Paso proudly advertised their establishments as bulletproof!

Villa made good on his promise in 1916. He overran the 13th Cavalry Regiment at Columbus, New Mexico, shot all the men he could find, and burned the town—using kerosene stolen from the fledgling Rio Grande Oil Company. President Wilson immediately sent a punitive expedition into Mexico to teach Villa a lesson, but Mexico forbade the Americans to use their railroads or to enter their towns. Six hundred trucks were used to supply the army of General John J. "Blackjack" Pershing, and the Rio Grande Oil Company got the contract to gas them up. Twenty years later Rio Grande's properties would become the backbone of the Richfield Oil Corporation.

ARCO Juneau *accepts the first load of Alaskan crude at Valdez in 1977.*

And so the years passed. Atlantic Refining has responded to its president's "find oil" order with a vengeance, then revolutionized the shipping industry in order to haul its product to America's East Coast.

Atlantic changed tankers forever in 1939 at the launching of the SS *J.W. Van Dyke.* Besides being one of the world's largest ships (a strapping 19,000 DWT), the *Van Dyke* was welded together. She was stronger than traditionally riveted ships, faster, easier to build, easier to clean, and leakproof. She also had turboelectrics instead of the conventional geared drive, which again cut costs and provided power for her cargo pumps, allowing her to be off-loaded *twice* as fast as her competitors. The *Van Dyke* was the first modern tanker, and she became the model for the famous T-2 tankers that enabled the Allies to win World War II. Without her it would have simply been impossible to build the T-2s in time, and therefore impossible to fuel our forces abroad. Of course, Hitler's submarines were only too quick to realize that. The logs of the *Van Dyke* and her unsung progeny tell a story more unbelievable than the *wildest* fiction to come out of World War II.

In 1963—still looking for oil—Atlantic acquired the Hondo Oil and Gas Company. Hondo's owner, a young entrepreneur named Robert O. Anderson, took a seat on Atlantic's board of directors and soon proved the significance of the Hondo acquisition. Anderson was elected chairman of the board two years later, and under his guidance Atlantic merged with the Richfield Oil Corporation (descendant of the old Rio Grande Oil Company) in 1966. Richfield brought its strong West Coast operation to the merger, as well as its exploration program on Alaska's North Slope. Without knowing it at the time he signed the merger, Anderson had a bonanza containing approximately 47 percent of the *entire* U.S. oil reserves right under his feet!

On March 13, 1968, Atlantic Richfield announced its discovery of Alaska's Prudhoe Bay Field, and it became apparent that the just-completed merger wasn't going to be enough. Atlantic was East Coast, and Richfield was West Coast; now they needed nationwide refineries, pipelines, marketing facilities, and tanker routes to handle the volume of crude oil that was expected to flow from Alaska. Harry Sinclair's mid-continental system provided the answer, and Sinclair Oil Corporation merged with Atlantic Richfield in 1969, thereby creating one of America's largest corporations.

ARCO Transportation was given the job of transporting the oil from the wellhead to the refinery, and then to the customer.

Sounds easy? Here's this customer in California, named Joe. Joe drives into his gas station and says: "Fill her up." In goes gasoline, check the oil and get the windshield, drive away—a piece of cake—but let's see what really happened:

First, after twenty years of unsuccessful Alaskan exploration, some frozen Atlantic Richfield engineers find oil on the North Slope (1968). Unfortunately, their bonanza is above the Arctic Circle, thousands of rugged miles from Joe. The sun doesn't even rise there during the winter, and the wind-chill factor may fall to 115 degrees below zero! They've got to build the pipeline that couldn't be built across 800 miles of country that can't be described, and they've got to do it *without* making an impact on nature. When, in 1977, the 120,000 DWT tanker *ARCO Juneau* finally accepted the first load of North Slope crude at Valdez, TAPS (the Trans Alaskan Pipeline) was the largest privately financed construction project *ever* undertaken.

Well, that gets Joe's gasoline 800 miles closer. Only 3,000 miles to go—next comes ARCO Marine, America's largest-tonnage tanker fleet.

With nearly eleven million barrels of cargo capacity, this transportation subsidiary works year-round hauling crude oil south from the TAPS terminal at Valdez. Let's assume, for Joe's sake, that designing, building, maintaining, and safely operating the largest fleet of American tankers in the mountainous waters of the North Pacific is no big deal—and that the mammoth descendants of the *Van Dyke* just happened to be there when the oil showed up. Let's just say that ARCO Marine off-loads Joe's oil at one of the nation's largest and most modern tanker facilities: ARCO's state-of-the-art facility at Berth 121, Long Beach.

Here, tankers big enough to carry four *Van Dykes* on their main decks—with loads of over 1.5 million barrels—pump Alaskan crude ashore at rates of 65,000 barrels an hour; and here it passes into the care of the Four Corners Pipe Line Company, another Transportation subsidiary that oversees an interlocking pipeline network connecting fifteen oil fields, six marine terminals, four products terminals, and twenty refineries.

Of course, it's impossible to say where Joe is bound with a full tank of gasoline, but it's very likely that when he gets there he'll see the effects of ARCO Transportation. As a subsidiary of one of Southern California's largest corporations, ATC employees help support aid to education, community programs, health and medical services, humanities and the arts, public information, and environmental programs with the help of the Atlantic Richfield Foundation, whose annual grants (largely given to back up the individual ARCO employees who volunteer their own time and money) exceed $35 million.

ARCO Alaska *at ARCO's Berth 121, Long Beach.*

THE JANKOVICH COMPANIES

San Pedro was a strange place indeed in 1921—half a world away from his native Yugoslavia, but a new world nevertheless, especially for an inquisitive young Thomas Jankovich. Thomas' father had immigrated to America eight years earlier, and, after working in Alaska, Montana, and Washington, mainly as a fisherman, the senior Jankovich decided that the time was right to call for his family from the old country.

Young Jankovich saturated himself with the new sights, smells, and sounds that abounded in his new home. Language, as it was for all newcomers to America, was a problem for Thomas; he found himself in kindergarten at the age of seven, but within months he had made up the difference and was in his proper grade. At the time San Pedro was home to nearly 10,000 Japanese-Americans living on Terminal Island, and young Jankovich became friends with many of the Japanese students in his school. To this day he still remembers those days with great fondness.

Thomas B. Jankovich, Sr. (seated), and Tom J. Jankovich, Jr.

Though Jankovich struggled with the language, little did he realize that in less than twenty years, he would be the owner of his own company and would be laying the foundation for the fulfillment of the American Dream.

By the time 1934 rolled around, San Pedro was already well on its way to becoming a major international port. Ships from all nations of the world dropped their anchors there, and the demand for fuel and lubricants steadily rose with every passing year.

That year Jankovich was employed by a Shell Oil Company agent who supplied fuel to ships from a facility in the Port of Los Angeles on one of the harbor's earliest piers. The nation was in the depths of the Depression and the hours were long and unpredictable, but young Jankovich threw himself into the job, displaying tenacity and hard work. He worked for the firm for another five years before opportunity came knocking at his door.

In 1939 Clarence Dillon, the Shell Oil agent for whom Jankovich was working, decided to retire and move to Oregon, and Shell Oil allowed Jankovich to take over the distributorship. Curiously enough, after a year of retirement Dillon moved back to San Pedro and ended up working for his former employee. The nature of the company was such that Dillon worked with Jankovich for another twenty-one years before again taking his retirement.

The war years were tough sledding for Jankovich. The commercial fishing fleet based in San Pedro was the backbone of Tom's business, but, with the outbreak of World War II, the federal government utilized the boats for patrol purposes. However, the Navy did award some contracts to Jankovich for supplying fuel and petroleum products to naval vessels in the area, which helped the company make it through the war years.

It was inevitable that Jankovich's son, Tom Jr., would eventually find his way into the business. Immediately after his high school graduation, Tom Jr. began to work for his father on a full-time basis. However, he also saw the need to finish his education, and soon found himself attending college in the evenings, eventually earning his diploma.

The Jankovich Companies operate from Berth 74 at the Port of Los Angeles, as they have since Tom Jankovich, Sr., began his one-man fuel distributorship in 1933.

In the mid-1970s Jankovich bought all of the equipment and facilities from Shell and became a jobber of fuels and lubricating oils. While handling Shell products still made up the bulk of the business, the firm was now able to work with all oil companies, thus laying the groundwork for the other Jankovich companies that were soon to follow.

In 1977 Tom Jr., having learned the business well, assumed the reins of the corporation as its president. It was at this point that the firm began a period of dramatic growth and expansion.

The nations of the Pacific Rim were rapidly emerging as America's leading trading partners, and ships from Japan, Korea, Taiwan, Hong Kong, and Australia were calling at the ports of Long Beach and Los Angeles at an astonishingly increasing pace. With the commercial fishing fleets rapidly decreasing in size, Tom Jr. realized that the future of the firm lay in servicing the many ships that were now calling in San Pedro Bay.

The new international shipping companies that were springing up in the ports also demanded new facilities to handle the boom in transpacific trade. With new terminals and more efficient equipment, there was also a need for faster and more efficient delivery of fuel and supplies to the waiting ships.

As the maritime scene changed, so also did Jankovich and Son, and the waterside facility at Berth 74 would soon become the corporate headquarters for the rapid expansion that was just around the corner.

Only two years prior to Tom Jr. assuming the presidency of Jankovich and Son, the second of the family-owned businesses came into existence. San Pedro Marine began the delivery of lube oils to all ports from Port Hueneme in Oxnard to San Diego. The timing must have been right since that company is today the largest single provider in the industry. San Pedro Marine's ten-truck fleet of tank vehicles delivers nearly five million gallons of product annually, directly to waiting ships. It is also the only firm that supplies bulk lube oils to ships at anchor. A specially built motorized barge, the *Vickie Ann,* allows San Pedro Marine to service large supertankers whose drafts are too deep to enter the inner channels of the ports.

Bulk lube oils are provided to ships at anchor in the Los Angeles/Long Beach Harbor by San Pedro Marine, Inc.

In 1982 another Jankovich enterprise was established in response to the growing ship traffic in San Pedro Bay. J&S Water Taxi, now the largest such operation serving both the ports of Los Angeles and Long Beach, utilizes a fleet of five vessels. With speeds of up to eighteen knots, J&S craft carry pilots, customs officers, crew members, supplies, and maintenance crews to and from ships and oil-drilling platforms.

The youngest of the Jankovich companies is Petro America, Inc. Formed to market and transport petroleum products to an even larger market, Petro America works hand in hand with San Pedro Marine to deliver products to railroads, airlines, trucking lines, and petroleum exploration and production consortiums. The firm also acts as the brokering arm of the Jankovich companies, interacting with all of the major independent petroleum refiners and wholesalers.

J&S Water Taxi, with the fastest boats in the harbor, carries customs officials, pilots, crew members, technicians, supplies, and specialized cargo between Los Angeles and Long Beach.

In the face of all this growth, Tom Jr. has made sure that the parent company, Jankovich and Son, continues as the flagship of the family of businesses. Today the firm still sells fuel to waiting ships at berth and at anchor, only considerably more than Thomas Sr. did in 1934—twelve million gallons more. A good sale in the 1930s would have been 5,000 to 6,000 gallons of fuel and 500 gallons of lube oil; today's vessels take on 250,000 gallons of fuel at a time and an additional 5,000 gallons of lubricating oil.

Thomas Sr. is still a daily presence at the business he founded in 1933. However, his one-man firm has grown to four companies, employing sixty people and maintaining a fleet of nine vessels and ten petroleum delivery trucks—certainly no small achievement for a wide-eyed seven-year-old who set foot in America sixty-five years ago.

Though the firm has grown to a multimillion-dollar operation, Thomas Sr.'s basic principles still stand as the philosophy of the Jankovich companies: Getting larger for the sake of growth is not the issue—getting better at serving your customers is. If a job is well done, then growth comes about naturally.

METROPOLITAN STEVEDORE COMPANY

It was a time of unbounded energy and optimism; the sprawling metropolis of Los Angeles was still decades away, but its foundation was being laid by the hustle and bustle that was to be found at the area's two ports, Los Angeles and Long Beach. As the many ships from all parts of the globe dropped anchor in San Pedro Bay, burly men of the stevedore gangs labored for weeks at a time unloading the lumber for first homes of the early pioneers of Southern California and exotic foodstuffs from equally exotic ports halfway across the world.

That was the 1920s, a time when the strong backs of laborers like the stevedores were the necessary ingredients of the future growth. It was also during that time that the Metropolitan Stevedore Company was incorporated by seven men who, early on, saw the growing need for an organized system of providing stevedore gangs for the increasing number of ships that were calling at the ports of Los Angeles and Long Beach.

Utilizing the traditional rope slings and two-wheel handcarts, stevedores worked long and unpredictable hours unloading building materials, fruits from the tropics, and rubber from the East Indies. But unloading a ship was only half of the stevedore's job. The empty holds of the ships were soon loaded with outbound cargoes that required the same long hours and strong muscles of these early dockworkers. Borax from the floors of the California deserts, ores from the Southwest, produce from the Central Valley, and seafood from the local waters were all carefully arranged on the cargo slings and hoisted on board by block and tackle.

Sixty years later the cargoes remain the same, but the look of the operations is significantly changed. Today women as well as men are employed by Metropolitan Stevedore and can be seen operating forklifts and driving trailer rigs as readily as their male counterparts. In addition, Metropolitan Stevedore has grown from seven employees to over 600 working at twenty-three berths at various terminals and piers in the ports of Los Angeles and Long Beach. Specialized machinery and cranes have replaced the ropes and slings of the past, and huge metal container "boxes" now

Metropolitan Stevedore is also responsible for dispatching all foodstuff supplies, as well as baggage and passengers, for the various cruise ships that dock at Berth 93 in the Port of Los Angeles.

New automobiles, bound for showrooms in Southern California and the Southwest, are off-loaded from huge auto carriers by experienced Metro stevedores.

dot the piers like oversize parcels waiting to be routed around the globe, being directed by electronic manifests flowing from the latest computer terminal.

Today Metropolitan Stevedore Company is one of Southern California's largest cargo-handling services businesses. With a philosophy of providing professional services for the movement of any type of cargo, Metropolitan offers customized service and equipment to all of its customers.

Using an automated ship-to-dock conveyor system, Metropolitan Stevedore unloads thousands of cartons of bananas daily from incoming ships—transferring them to trucks en route to area markets.

As the innovations of the 1960s and 1970s resulted in specialized ships to carry specialized cargoes, the stevedore's job changed as well. With the advent of the container, the dockworker became the operator of a high-speed, $2.5-million gantry crane capable of moving thirty 40-foot containers in an hour. Twenty years ago a ship laid over in a port for several weeks awaiting her holds to be emptied; today a fully containerized vessel remains in port for a single eight-hour stevedore shift. When automobiles were first imported into this country, each vehicle was lifted over the side in the conventional sling. Today specialized auto carriers, shaped like huge floating shoe boxes, carry 4,500 cars on each voyage, and Metropolitan's stevedores now board the ships in continuous gangs to drive the vehicles off on specially designed ramps built directly into the sides of the ships.

While efficiency and service remain the hallmarks of the company's functions, Metropolitan has also scored significant achievements in the areas of employee safety and environmental concerns. The firm has been the recipient of several safety awards from the Pacific Maritime Association. It was the first Southern California company to be awarded the top honor in the coastwide Class A stevedore safety division.

Along with its concern for safety is an equal concern for the coastal environment in which it operates. At the Metropolitan operated dry-bulk handling facility at the Port of Long Beach in 1962, three large dust-collecting units were also part of the design. At the same pier settling tanks were added to maintain the water quality at the facility. The tanks are designed to trap any surface and rain runoff water from flowing directly into the sea. Only after the water is sufficiently treated is it allowed to be discharged.

As innovation and adaptation have marked the rise and continuing success of Metropolitan Stevedore Company since its inception in 1923, so will they guide the firm into the challenges of the twenty-first century. As the company has grown and changed with the maritime industry, so will it continue to serve the primary needs of the industry—to move cargoes in the swiftest and safest manner possible.

One of the most sophisticated dual-loader dry-bulk facilities in the country is operated by Metropolitan Stevedore on Pier G at the Port of Long Beach.

AL LARSON BOAT SHOP

San Pedro, a city steeped in the traditions of ocean commerce, is also known for its rich ethnic diversity that has added a unique history to this port community. Nowhere is the marriage of these two institutions more evident than in the histories of the Rados and Wall families and in the company that bears the stamp of these San Pedro pioneers to this day—the Al Larson Boat Shop.

It was in 1919 that Romolo Rados and his son, John, recent immigrants from a section of Austria-Hungary that is today Yugoslavia, arrived in San Pedro after a short stay in Canada. Boat builders in their native country, the family opened its boat works, Harbor Boat Building Company, shortly after arriving in the city.

Harbor Boat Building soon began to grow and prosper with the development of the city. By the time World War II arrived the company had already designed and built seventeen yachts, thirty-two fishing vessels, and twenty Navy ships, including 80-foot patrol craft and 64-foot mine layers. On the commercial side, the firm built the prototype of the great tuna clippers that transformed San Pedro into one of America's largest fish-processing areas.

In the 1960s ownership of the company was transferred to the LTV Corporation; several other transfers of ownership followed, but always with a member of the Rados family at the helm. In 1968 John passed away, and seven years later the business finally closed its doors after nearly fifty years of operation.

Nearly twenty-five years before the Rados family moved to San Pedro, another immigrant visited the city in search of his older brother. Reynold Anderson Wall, a Danish sea captain, arrived in San Pedro after spending several years in the British Merchant Marine. Captain Wall learned through a seaman's union in San Francisco that his brother might be in the San Pedro area, and upon his arrival, soon located his brother.

The Al Larson Boat Shop is the oldest privately operated shipyard in Los Angeles.

After obtaining his master's license, Wall moved to San Pedro permanently in 1913. Captain Wall's first job was as master of the Banning family yacht, *Cricket*. In 1924 he joined the Los Angeles Harbor Department as a tug operator and later as the port pilot.

Wall and his wife, Louise, had two sons, George and Andrew. George graduated from medical school in 1939, and Andrew went to sea as a cadet on several merchant ships following graduation from high school. After passing his ensign's exam for the Coast Guard Reserve, Andrew entered active duty in 1942. He earned his aviator's wings the following year and flew until the end of the war.

By that time Andrew had married a fellow San Pedroan, the former Gloria Rados, daughter of John Rados. Following service in the Korean War, Andrew began working for his father-in-law's firm, Harbor Boat Building Company. In 1959 he purchased the Al Larson Boat Shop.

Today the Al Larson Boat Shop is the oldest privately operated shipyard in the Los Angeles area. At two sites in the Port of Los Angeles, Andy's sons continue in the finest traditions of the Rados and Wall families.

The shipyards are completely self-contained operations with fully equipped machine, carpenter, welding, paint, electrical, and pipe-fitting shops. Today 60 percent of the company's business is for the U.S. Navy, both at the Larson shipyards and at the U.S. Naval Shipyard in Long Beach. Additionally, work is done for the Coast Guard and on California's oil and offshore supply boat industry.

In the mid-1960s the firm took a step in the direction of servicing private pleasure craft with the construction of the Al Larson Marina at the Port of Los Angeles. The 125-slip facility services craft of twenty to fifty feet in length. In 1980 a restaurant, The Oyster Wharf, was built and a 100-slip marina was added on the main channel at Los Angeles Harbor, which the firm now operates.

With the third generation of the Rados/Wall family continuing in the maritime service industry, the history and accomplishments of John Rados and Reynold Wall will certainly be maintained well into the next century.

A Coast Guard buoy tender, a Navy tug, a commercial supply boat, and an offshore geophysical boat are waiting at the Berth 214 facility for repairs.

CONTAINERFREIGHT CORPORATION

High density, high-volume commodities are handled efficiently at Los Angeles' 272,000-square-foot, rail-served building.

Although a relative newcomer in the long history of successful transportation companies, ContainerFreight Corporation may truly be said to be a pioneer in the specialized field of containerized cargo handling.

Conceived in 1968 after founder Richard A. Elms attended a Port of Los Angeles seminar on containerization, ContainerFreight commenced operations in November of that year with the acquisition of two small California trucking companies. As ambitiously stated in the original prospectus, the firm's objective was "to provide a variety of integrated services in the distribution of containerized and conventional general commodity freight." To that end, it had been the hope of management to be in business in time to participate in the intense competition for contracts being awarded by the six Japanese steamship companies that were beginning full containership operations in the fall of 1968. Delays in raising capital and acquiring appropriate facilities, however, precluded that objective, and the contracts were awarded to the competition.

Less than a year later, however, ContainerFreight was selected by Kawasaki Kisen Kaisha (K Line) to operate a 50,000-square-foot container freight station in Oakland, California. In addition, local containerized cargo trucking contracts with American President Lines and the U.S. Post Office were the beginning of a container trucking operation that was to grow to more than 300 power units in 1986.

Publication in 1970 of an innovative FAK container-load rate tariff, which is an industry standard today, established ContainerFreight as a major local motor carrier in the Los Angeles and San Francisco Bay areas. Prior to that time containerized cargo was still moved on time-honored commodity trucking rates, which resulted in widely varying prices for container movements, depending on the type and weight of the cargo.

A new dimension to ContainerFreight's transportation services was added in 1972 when Zim Container Service began West Coast operations and elected to call only at the Port of Long Beach, selecting ContainerFreight to provide substitute, over-the-road service to Northern California ports. Other major containership operators followed suit, and the new interport or "line-haul" aspect of the firm's service continued to assume ever-increasing importance.

The following year Raymond M. Veltman was elected chairman of ContainerFreight, and his leadership took the company into its first truly profitable period in the mid-1970s and established a steady growth pattern that continues to this day. From annual revenues of $2.2 million in 1972, the firm's sales rose continually to more than $20 million prior to the sale of ContainerFreight to Consolidated Freightways, Inc., in 1984.

Another major milestone in the corporation's development came in 1975 with the establishment of a full-service Container Freight Station in Los Angeles/Long Beach Harbor. Beginning with a small, 40,000-square-foot facility, the Los Angeles CFS operation has grown to a total of 272,000 square feet in 1986 to become the largest ContainerFreight operation, as well as the site of its corporate headquarters.

In 1981 ContainerFreight became one of the first motor carriers to be awarded nationwide, general commodity trucking authority under new Interstate Commerce Commission entry rules. Permitted to operate on a multistate basis for the first time, the firm was quick to open a terminal in Seattle, Washington, followed by additional terminals in Portland, Oregon, and Vancouver, British Columbia.

Today, with terminals in every major Pacific port area, ContainerFreight Corporation stands as the West Coast's largest motor carrier specializing in containerized cargo movements.

Containerized cargo and empty equipment move swiftly between major cities, ports, and international borders with ContainerFreight, an ICC-licensed carrier with operating authority in all fifty states.

CALIFORNIA COTTON FUMIGATING COMPANY

Of the many varied businesses in the ports area, one of the most interesting and important operations also happens to be one of the oldest in the San Pedro Bay. California Cotton Fumigating Company is now into its third generation of family ownership and operation—an enterprise that began when a young Texan, E.A. Hackett, started a business in Wilmington, the heart of the harbor, in 1939.

Prior to that time Hackett was employed by California Cotton Mills in its Los Angeles office's fumigation division, which was established in 1929. However, when the company decided to separate its Southern California plant from its San Francisco office in 1939, Hackett saw his opportunity and moved swiftly to acquire the plant with his partner, Maurice Buckhands. The two men changed the name of the firm to California Cotton Fumigating Company and continued as partners until Buckhands' death in 1953. Hackett then bought Buckhands' interest from his widow. Today the firm is run by Hackett's daughter, Linda, and her husband, Tom Jacobson.

While the name of the business may seem self-explanatory to the casual observer, the commodities that pass through its buildings are as varied and exotic as the cargoes that pass over the piers of the ports of Los Angeles and Long Beach. While cotton remains as a major product which requires fumigation, California Cotton has literally seen everything that has ever moved in or out of the ports. Because of stringent health and agricultural regulations imposed by federal, state, and county agencies on many incoming and outgoing products, virtually all fresh produce being imported into the country must be inspected as a condition of entry, and may require fumigation. Last year over three million lugs of grapes, peaches, apricots, and plums from Chile were fumigated at the Los Angeles terminals. And November and December of each year sees chestnuts from China entering the country in time for the holiday season.

In 1939 E.A. Hackett purchased the Southern California operation of California Cotton Mills with his partner, Maurice Buckhands. Today, three generations later, the Hackett family still owns the firm, now called California Cotton Fumigating Company.

Egypt, known throughout the world for its importation of cotton, requires that all exports of cotton to their country be fumigated prior to being loaded on board ships. In 1985 alone, 120,000 bales bound for Egypt were treated at California Cotton Fumigating's plant. And Egypt is not the only consignee that requests that its shipments be fumigated prior to being shipped. A Japanese food company requests that all pancake mix from Kansas be so treated; purchasers of animal hides in Germany and the Far East also have similar requirements for their purchases before being sent out of the country; and buyers of sunflower seed in Australia ask that their shipments of seed be fumigated to render them sterile to prevent germination.

While housing the largest vacuum fumigation chambers on the West Coast, California Cotton also has smaller units to handle the unique jobs that pass through its plant, such as the stuffed lion that was sent from Africa back to Los Angeles. The firm also possesses the capability to travel to a specific area on the piers to conduct a fumigation job. Its fleet of specially equipped trucks is capable of handling a complete fumigation task when called upon to do so.

Sometimes the company is called upon to service a product on its way out of the country and also on its way back in. After cotton bales are delivered to their final destinations, the cotton wastes and burlap baggings are shipped back to the United States. On their arrival in the ports, the wastes and baggings are fumigated prior to their reemergence as felt, car mats, and carpet matting.

The majority of these operations are in strict accordance with U.S. Department of Agriculture regulations and supervision. Even some varieties of fresh flowers arriving at the airports are trucked to the fumigation chambers to prevent unwanted pests from entering California. Roses, orchids, and tulips from Holland as well as exotic flowers and plants from Australia may undergo fumigation.

The advent of the container revolution has not made the products inside the boxes exempt from fumigation. Australia and New Zealand, fearing the introduction of wood-boring insects, require that all containers utilizing wood in any manner be fumigated and sterilized prior to being shipped to their countries. In those instances, the entire container is draped with huge tarps and fumigated with methyl bromide for several hours after which the gas is extracted by fans.

The ultimate job for California Cotton occurs when it is called upon to fumigate an entire ship. Banana ships and grain ships are usually the types of vessels that require such servicing. The largest ship ever to be so fumigated was a Japanese grain carrier of 63,400 tons, or 1,844,625 cubic feet. The assignment took three days and was the largest fumigation job of its kind ever completed on the West Coast.

As the nature of the cargoes has changed on the waterfront, so have the facilities and work of California Cotton changed to meet these new challenges. As long as cargo passes through our ports, California Cotton Fumigating Company will be there to serve the needs of shippers everywhere. As owners Linda and Tom Jacobson note, "We've seen everything that has come through the ports—whether it's chestnuts from China or even our latest product, F-15 parts bound for Australia, we've seen them all."

The early operations of California Cotton Fumigating Company took place on this site on Anacapa Street in Wilmington. Today the present location of the firm is only a few blocks away.

THUMS

Located several hundred yards from the white sand beaches of Long Beach near the entrance to the new Downtown Marina, are these pastel-colored, camouflaged, and soundproofed oil derricks. They were constructed by THUMS with respect for the natural environment, which was deemed of equal importance to the recovery of petroleum from the vast oil fields under the city.

It's a story often told among the natives of Long Beach. The story about the visitor to the city who inquired as to how he or she might reserve to stay in one of the exclusive condominiums or hotels on the man-made islands located a few hundred yards offshore—only to learn that their eyes were certainly not the first to be so fooled. For the beautiful high-rise "condos" or "hotels" are neither available for rent nor are they lodgings at all. In fact, the pastel-colored structures are camouflaged and soundproofed oil derricks.

Not any ordinary, run-of-the mill oil rigs, to be sure, but nevertheless they are oil rigs in the truest sense, located several hundred yards from the white sand beaches of Long Beach at the entrance to the new Downtown Marina. Even more remarkable is the fact that not only are oil drilling rigs situated on each island, but several hundred wells are to be found on any one of the four oil islands of Long Beach. The story of these man-made islands is truly a success story of the balancing of economic and environmental interests that results in overall benefits for all parties concerned.

The birth of the islands, which were built specifically for oil production, began in 1965 and 1966. The City of Long Beach, through the Department of Oil Properties and its contractor, THUMS (an acronym for the oil company consortium of Texaco, Humble (now Exxon), Union, Mobil, and Shell), accepted as a fact that the protection of the natural environment should be granted equal importance with the recovery of petroleum from the vast oil fields under the city and bay.

Even as the plans for the construction of the islands were being drawn, aesthetic and environmental protection issues were being included in the initial design concepts. Though some may have doubted the feasibility of such a balancing process, fears were allayed when the islands were recognized with two significant awards, one from the National Society of Professional Engineers as the outstanding engineering achievement of 1966 and the other from the Long Beach Beautiful Committee for an aesthetic contribution to the city.

Located in water depths of twenty-five to forty feet, the islands cost approximately two million dollars each to construct, plus an additional one million dollars for beautification, including trees, shrubs, drilling rig shrouds, and aesthetic structural forms of up to eighty feet. Each island is constructed of 160,000 tons of rock barged from Santa Catalina Island and 900,000 yards of sand fill.

Another remarkable aspect of the islands is the fact that the hundreds of wells on them are all operated by electrically powered submersible pumps or subsurface hydraulic pumps. These factors allow the wellheads to be situated below ground level, which accounts for the noise-free and visually appealing atmosphere of the islands. The islands are named after four American astronauts who lost their lives early in the U.S. space program—Grissom, White, Chaffee, and Freeman—and more than 613 million barrels of oil have been extracted from the islands and nearby Pier J since THUMS began its operations.

Because all the facilities and pumps are electrically powered, over 50,000 feet of communications cable and 50,000 feet of power distribution lines serve the islands from the mainland. The produced oil is piped directly to onshore facilities through 140,000 feet of steel pipelines. These lines are buried at depths of from ten to twelve feet below the ocean floor and are specially coated to prevent corrosion. To ensure environmental safety, the pipelines are continuously maintained and chemicals are internally applied to protect against corrosion. In addition, an internal electronic inspection is periodically conducted to detect potential areas of pipeline wave.

Such concern for the welfare of the area's natural beauty has proven beyond a doubt that progress and economic development can coexist with environmental protection. The THUMS oil islands of Long Beach have pioneered this marriage of interests and stand as a continuing reminder of the need for the sharing of ideas and of the potential success of such progressive cooperative attitudes.

SOUTHWEST MARINE

For any company to see its business mushroom approximately thirtyfold in less than ten years is truly an exciting phenomenon. Couple this with the fact that in 1977, when the firm was founded, the eldest of the four partners of Southwest Marine was only thirty years old, and the mind reels at the dedication, long hours, and expertise that was involved in creating a $100-million ship repair company.

The Engel brothers, Art, Herb, and David, had grown up in the ship repair business. Having worked with their father, Herbert Sr., since their youth at the Triple A shipyard in San Francisco, they were well-heeled in experience when they along with Bill Johnston pooled their savings in 1977 and formed Southwest Marine in Chula Vista, just south of San Diego.

The company's first contract was for the refurbishing of nine U.S. Navy landing craft, and the young men literally worked on their hands and knees to get the job done. Johnston remembers the "good old days" when they performed all work by themselves including scraping barnacles from the bottoms of the vessels—all without pay. Today Southwest Marine maintains yards in four locations and during its peak season employs 2,000 workers. Revenues annually exceed $100 million.

A year after the Chula Vista operation began, a second yard was purchased in San Francisco. The San Pedro facility in the Port of Los Angeles was obtained in 1981, and four years later a facility in American Samoa joined the Southwest Marine family. The firm is continually looking to the possibility of further expansion to service the ships of all nations.

From scraping ships' bottoms by hand, the company now services supertankers of up to 265,000 deadweight tons on 1,500 feet of berthing space at the San Pedro site. While a large portion of the work performed by the firm is for the U.S. Navy, a surprisingly large amount of business that passes through the facilities is for commercial foreign flag carrier repairs, as well as U.S. flag vessels.

The success of Southwest Marine may be based on the fact that the owners are basically people-oriented and realize the importance of maintaining harmonious labor relations with their employees. The company provides health and welfare benefits for its workers, and regular Employee Involvement Committee meetings are held with top management to discuss suggestions, changes of procedures, or other employee concerns.

Johnston, general manager of the forty-acre San Pedro yard, states, "Because we are a nonunion company, we can compete on an international level. We have less restraints on a job, and this results in a more efficient level of productivity." The track record of Southwest Marine seems to bear out the validity of the owners' philosophy in a truly dramatic fashion.

An offshore jack-up rig, representing the new technology under repair at the Terminal Island facility.

The early days of the shipyard.

SUNKIST GROWERS, INC.

A few letters—a few lines of ink on, of all places, an orange. And yet, those few lines of ink stamped on fresh citrus from Sunkist Growers, Inc., represent one of the most recognizable trademarks throughout the world. The name Sunkist, whether on fresh fruit, beverage cans, or citrus products, has come to signal assured quality for consumers in America, Europe, and the Far East.

However, the recognition and quality that Sunkist represents did not happen overnight. The trust that consumers feel when they see the Sunkist name got its start in 1893. At that time the fertile western agricultural regions were already providing a large portion of the nation's fresh produce. However, growers of citrus often suffered major financial setbacks because of a lack of marketing representation and expertise and well organized shipping procedures. Unsold fruit rotted in packinghouses or in the fields, and commission or auction dealers, sometimes utilizing questionable practices, raked off a large share of the profits before disbursing the proceeds to the growers.

Thus, in 1893 sixty Southern California orange growers banded together to save themselves and their orchards from looming economic crisis. Pooling their resources, they decided that their best chance for survival lay in marketing their products directly as a cooperative, bypassing the commissioned agents. This bold step required the growers to assume the expenses for packing, shipping, and marketing, and these pioneers were certainly willing to assume that risk. It was decided early on that the proceeds from their efforts would be distributed according to the amount and quality of the grower's crop, thus assuring that individual initiative would be maintained.

Those sixty growers called their organization the Southern California Fruit Exchange, and in 1905 incorporated as the California Fruit Growers Exchange. Now, nearly a century later, the original principles of that early organization continue to act as guidelines for the cooperative. Continuing to operate as primarily a membership cooperative marketing association, Sunkist Growers, Inc., maintains three basic objectives: to develop and maintain ready and reliable markets for members' fruit; to gain for member-owners the best possible return for their produce; and to supply the public with readily available, top-quality fresh citrus fruit and processed citrus products at reasonable prices.

A packinghouse in the early 1900s.

Consumers know from experience that they can depend on the quality of fresh citrus with the Sunkist stamp, and produce buyers know the selling value of that quality. But few realize the effort that goes into the standardization of grades and the uniformity of quality before the fruit is shipped. Sunkist-affiliated packinghouses follow very specific rules and regulations, and Sunkist staff inspectors work with packinghouse managers to make sure the grading standards are observed. This system of self-policing for quality control has been one of the most important elements in Sunkist's success.

Fruit that does not meet the standards for premium- or second-grade fresh fruit is used for a wide variety of processed products. Sunkist's member-growers own two processing facilities where fruit is converted into

Sunkist citrus destined for markets in the Far East is loaded at Long Beach Harbor.

juice and peel products. The manufacturing methods make such efficient use of the fruit that by the time it has been passed through one of these operations, every bit of juice, pulp, and oil has been extracted by squeezing, pressing, or distilling. Even the seeds and spent peel are used.

Through the years the organization has been identified with many "firsts" in agricultural marketing. The cooperative's members have endorsed and financed milestone programs in fruit-handling techniques, and new market development.

In the 1960s, when the western citrus industry expanded production far beyond the needs of traditional domestic markets, Sunkist pioneered the development of new outlets overseas. It was Sunkist that paved the way for the elimination of Japan's import quota on fresh lemons in 1964 and on grapefruit in 1970, and it was Sunkist that made breakthrough sales of lemons to East Bloc countries at the height of the Cold War. In recent years the company has exported 25 to 30 percent of its total fresh fruit shipments to some twenty-five overseas markets led by Japan, Hong Kong, Southeast Asia, and Western Europe.

A major leap forward for Sunkist occurred, interestingly enough, in Hong Kong in the mid-1950s. Hong Kong Bottlers was marketing a new product that represented a first for Sunkist. The new product was Sunkist Orange Drink, and it marked the first time that consumers had seen the name Sunkist on products other than fresh citrus. The immensely successful Sunkist Licensed Products Program was thus launched and remains as one of the most dramatic triumphs in food-marketing history. Today more than 400 different products in nearly forty countries boast the Sunkist trademark, generating nearly $800 million in annual retail sales. Soft drinks, juice products, candies, fruit jelly desserts, and vitamin C are only a few of the products that have been licensed by the firm.

The original association of sixty growers has become the largest fresh produce shipper in the United States and a world leader in agricultural marketing. Today nearly 6,000 California and Arizona citrus growers comprise the cooperative, with 60 packinghouses and a dozen district exchanges also included in the Sunkist family. With more than four billion pounds of fruit handled for its members annually, Sunkist Growers, Inc., is a true success story of the West. The organization's well-earned reputation for quality and its international marketing achievements are lasting testaments to the vision of its founders—and a tribute to the significance of a few lines of ink on an orange—the Sunkist trademark.

Packinghouse workers grade fruit according to Sunkist's strict quality standards.

Sunkist Growers, Inc., is headquartered in Sherman Oaks, California.

GRAHAM & JAMES/LONG BEACH

If the shipping lanes across the vast oceans bind the nations of the earth to one another, then it can be said that the laws of admiralty form the framework within which these connections operate. In the realm of international trade and shipping, the need for rational procedures and agreed-upon rights and obligations between parties is paramount for the orderly movement of commerce.

So it was that in 1934 Chalmers G. Graham, a San Francisco attorney, formed a law practice specializing in admiralty. Two partners followed in 1941 and in 1942, the latter being Clarence Morse, who went on to become the first general counsel and later chairman of the Federal Maritime Commission. In 1947 another partner, Leonard James, was added to the firm. Today Graham & James has expanded to encompass a general practice coupled with an emphasis on international business in twelve offices worldwide. However, with its roots in the maritime industry, it is natural for admiralty to remain as a major portion of the firm's practice.

With the rise of the importance of the ports of San Pedro Bay in the international business scene, it was fitting that a branch office dedicated exclusively to admiralty be opened in Long Beach. Thus, in 1955 attorney Reed M. Williams was sent to Long Beach to open the new office of Graham & James.

The Long Beach office was ideally situated to benefit from the good fortune that the ports of Los Angeles and Long Beach have enjoyed during the past three decades of growth and prosperity. As trade with the Pacific Rim exploded, the ports of San Pedro Bay grew to become the most important in America; as the ports became the gateway to the Pacific, so also did the Long Beach office of Graham & James gain in stature and international repute.

Today the office represents all segments of the maritime industry, including shipping companies, their underwriters, terminal operators, and shipping conferences and associations. Attorneys handle matters dealing with charters; vessel acquisitions; international financing; vessel casualties; cargo claims; personal injury claims by longshoremen, seamen, and cruise passengers; terminal and stevedore contracts; and maritime taxes and offshore operations. Representation of both domestic and foreign clients before federal and state courts, administrative and regulatory agencies, and international and maritime arbitrations are examples of the scope of activities of the Graham & James/Long Beach admiralty staff. The firm's attorneys regularly appear before the Federal Maritime Commission, the U.S. Coast Guard, the U.S. Customs Service, the Immigration and Naturalization Service, and the Maritime Administration.

As the nature of international trade changes, so must the requirements for a successful admiralty firm. The admiralty attorneys at Graham & James/Long Beach now find themselves to be experts on chemical and mineral exports, exotic fruits from foreign countries, and even the food served on cruise ships.

Drawing on the resources of the firm's branches located throughout the world, the Long Beach office provides a full range of admiralty expertise for all of its clients both here and abroad. Graham & James/Long Beach stands not only on the edge of the Pacific Rim, but indeed on the leading edge of the future of international maritime law.

This carved granite walrus, which greets visitors to Graham & James' San Francisco office, has been adopted as the firm's symbol.

INTERNATIONAL TRANSPORTATION SERVICE

Well before the current vogue of international investments in the United States burst upon the scene, one company in Long Beach was already laying the groundwork for one of the maritime industry's most successful businesses and Southern California's leading container terminal.

Founded in 1971 at the Port of Long Beach, International Transportation Service (ITS), has grown with the containerization revolution in the international shipping arena to become the port's largest tenant. Early on ITS' parent company, Kawasaki Kisen Kaisha (K Line) of Japan, foresaw the future of U.S.-Japan trade relations—and that future lay in containerized cargo movement.

Containerization, a concept both beautiful in its simplicity and grandly efficient in its operation, was the new and closely scrutinized method of cargo handling when K Line decided to take a chance and build its first subsidiary facility outside of Japan. The result was the ITS container terminal in Long Beach. Prior to the advent of containers, cargo had to be loaded in the conventional method, utilizing ropes, slings, and an assortment of pallets and boxes. This process required weeks to fully off-load a ship and hundreds of work hours to complete the job.

Containers, which are simply large twenty- or forty-foot-long metal boxes that can be stacked on board a vessel and lifted off onto a waiting truckbed, and vice-versa, make the job of cargo handling easier by standardizing the size of the boxes to streamline the stowing process on board the ships. Today ITS' terminal operation is strongly supported by its two in-house IBM System 38 computers. This allows full control of vessel and yard operations and immediate information for ITS' customers and managers. Most dramatically, cargo could be delivered literally from ship to receiving dock in one continuous operation.

ITS has grown from its original 50 acres to become one of the West Coast's largest container terminals; its 115 acres can accommodate three vessels at its 2,300 feet of wharf space simultaneously with four high-speed container cranes, each capable of lifting forty tons.

The firm's experienced professionals are also able to tailor the terminal's services for any customer's special needs, from chassis leasing to intermodal shipments. A container freight station is located near the terminal's entrance gates and adjacent to the on-site rail-loading facilities. ITS employs the most modern equipment and techniques.

With the coming of the mid-1980s transpacific shipping expanded at a breakneck speed; fully containerized vessels crossed the sea from the Far East to the West Coast with astonishing speed and regularity. With more and more containers crossing the wharves at ports from Southern California to Canada, ITS again took a dramatic step forward with the opening of another container terminal, this time inTacoma, Washington. The Husky Terminal, a joint effort between ITS and Cooper/T. Smith Stevedoring Company, opened in 1985. Once again ITS' commitment to the future of international business cooperation was dramatically demonstrated.

Though International Transportation Service has grown to become a leader in international trade, its officers and staff take equal pride in the fact that the firm has also become a good corporate neighbor in Long Beach. ITS' efficiency in container stevedoring is evidenced by its renowned high productivity and by its excellent safety record, first on the West Coast in accident prevention in 1985. ITS employs well over 300 people, with many longtime staffers on board. A genuine concern for employee well-being has made the company a highly desirable place to work. By supporting and participating in numerous civic and community functions, ITS and its employees have shown that the future of international relations may lie in successful business ventures that bind people and cultures across the oceans.

Founded in 1971 at the Port of Long Beach, International Transportation Service (ITS) has grown with the containerization revolution in the international shipping arena to become the port's largest tenant.

LONG BEACH CONTAINER TERMINAL, INC. (LBCTI)

The newest and most modern of Long Beach's container terminals is Long Beach Container Terminal, Inc., the home of the Orient Overseas Container Line as well as several other container shipping lines. The facility is one of an international network of container terminals that fall within the overall strategic management direction of Furness Withy (Terminals) of Felixstowe, England.

The roots of LBCTI lie halfway around the world in Hong Kong. There, in the mid-1930s, C.Y. Tung began his shipping empire with four old Yangtze River steamers. Tung constantly strove to increase his worldwide holdings, and in the succeeding years built his empire into one of the largest shipping and financial multinationals in the world. In 1980 the Furness Withy group of companies was acquired by the Tung Group, and, as a result, a new terminals division was created that has since become one of the world's leading forces in the area of development, management, and operation of container terminals.

The terminal was only a dream on the drawing boards just a few years ago. Conceptually designed in 1978, the facility officially was opened to the maritime industry in 1980 after extensive planning to afford shippers and trucking firms the most efficient manner of container movement into and out of the terminal area.

As the major port of call on America's West Coast, LBCTI is ideally situated to provide the fastest intermodal shipment of cargoes to inland points and beyond. Also, with an estimated twelve million people in the Southern California marketplace, the terminal serves as an important link between products for the American consumer and the manufacturing centers of the Pacific Rim.

From the ten-acre facility that opened in 1980, LBCTI now occupies fifty-five acres on the Pier J container complex at the Port of Long Beach. Because it was the latest container terminal to be built in the port, it incorporates the most sophisticated computer technology and was built with a commitment to utilizing the worldwide data-processing capabilities that are available to assist the company in its shipping activities. However, the present facility is only the first chapter of the terminal's ongoing progression into the twenty-first century.

In 1986 a brand new Long Beach terminal opened on literally new land at Pier A in Long Beach. Comprising 87 acres and 5 berths of 2,700 linear feet, LBCTI once again bears the honor of being the newest and most modern container terminal in the Port of Long Beach. The facility consists of twenty-four acres of new land that was created by dredging and landfilling and allows even more shipping lines to utilize the terminal.

This increase in land was accompanied by four high-speed container cranes of the latest design. These cranes are necessary to accommodate the new, larger container vessels that are now plying the oceans of the world. Additionally, on-line, real-time computer systems help speed containers through the facility on to their final destinations. Another innovation utilized at the new terminal is a system for weighing containers. The container and its cargo are weighed by an electronic scale mounted on each container yard transtainer. This fast, accurate process immediately provides a direct digital readout in metric tons indicating the correct weight of the container and cargo. This system greatly reduces the transaction time that a truck and driver spend in the terminal.

Innovation and growth are not merely terms for the management of LBCTI. Even with a new terminal in Long Beach, its sights are set on still further opportunities for expansion. Whether that expansion takes place on the North American continent or anywhere else in the world, the skills and experience of the LBCTI management team will play a vital role in the future development of the already highly successful Terminals Division of the international Tung Shipping Group.

Long Beach Container Terminal, Inc., with its state-of-the-art container terminal handling equipment, is the newest, most modern public container terminal in the Port of Long Beach.

J.M. COSTELLO SUPPLY COMPANY, INC.

The J.M. Costello Supply Company in Wilmington is already into its third generation at its original site on Avalon Boulevard in Wilmington, but its beginnings go all the way back to the early years of this century in San Francisco. Young Joseph Costello's family had recently moved to the Bay Area from Cambria Pines several hundred miles down the coast, and the youngster's playgrounds were now the streets near his home. Costello, always one who loved a good risk, along with his friends, took turns lying in front of the city's cable cars. However, young Joe sought still greater adventures, so in 1909 at the age of eleven, he followed the footsteps of his father and grandfather and shipped out to sea as a deckboy on the steamer *State of California,* a coastal passenger vessel.

Jobs on later ships included working in the engine room and working on mail ships to and from Panama with stops along the West Coast. Following a short stint on shore, Costello longed for the sea and finally signed on board the lightship *Blunts Reef* off the rugged Mendocino coast.

World War I rescued Costello from the isolation of the lightship, and he found himself running mail and troops throughout the Pacific. After the war Costello earned his first engineer's license in 1919 and signed on board the *Eastern Moon,* carrying cargo from New York to northern Europe. A maritime strike forced Costello to change ships, and he soon found himself on the Yangtze River in China, delivering oil to cities along the river's bank.

Joseph M. Costello, 1898-1982, founder.

Costello returned to the West Coast after that tour of duty and was soon sailing along the coast delivering lumber from Vancouver, British Columbia, to San Francisco and San Pedro. It was during that period of time that Costello found himself shipwrecked twice. The first occurred off the coast of Point Conception on a foggy day. The ship languished for two weeks on the rocks before she was set free by a combination of a salvage crew and a high tide. A few years later Costello was again on a ship that found itself stranded, this time on a sandbar off the coast of Ecuador.

After those experiences Costello was ready to try his hand at making his living on the shoreside. In 1939, along with two partners, he founded the heavy marine supply business that still operates from its original site in a building that was constructed in 1898.

Today the company is operated by Costello's children. The firm still specializes in heavy marine supplies, providing needed parts and safety equipment for tankers, cruise ships, and all types of cargo vessels. The company has filled many strange requests over the years, one of the more unusual being a request for two live goats to be delivered to an Indian crew on board a cruise vessel for use in a religious festival. In the 1930s the firm even operated a water taxi that ferried passengers to the infamous gambling ships that anchored in international waters off the San Pedro coast.

As long as ships cross the seas, parts and supplies will be needed for the swift journeys from port to port. For more than forty-five years J.M. Costello Supply Company has provided this important service to the shipping industry. With the coming of a new generation of ships, the future of the industry will make another step forward, and Costello Supply will continue to be a part of that future.

Richard Costello, vice-president.

Don Costello, president.

Kathleen Costello, secretary/treasurer.

HUGO NEU-PROLER CO.

Hugo Neu-Proler Co. commenced operations in Los Angeles in 1962. It emerged as a result of the combining of two specialty businesses. The principal operation of Hugo Neu & Sons, Inc., was, and still is, steel scrap exporting. In 1948 the firm began importing scrap from Japan to the United States. Later, as the Japanese steel industry had a demand for scrap, America became a scrap export nation, and the Japanese called on the company to help supply its needs. As other countries developed steel industries, they too required scrap, and the United States became a scrap-selling nation.

Today Richard Neu serves as chairman and John Neu serves as president of Hugo Neu & Sons, Inc. Houston-based Proler International, a New York Stock Exchange company, was a family-owned business in 1962. Herman Proler currently serves as its chairman and president.

During the Korean War Proler International was called upon by the U.S. government to be a supplier of shredded tin cans for the American copper industry. At the time tin cans were used for leaching copper in a hydrochloric acid solution. By 1959 Proler had enlarged the tin can shredder to such an extent that it started to shred whole automobiles. The product was then homogeneously shredded into fist-size pieces of steel, which were later patented and called Prolerized scrap.

In 1962, when the Prolerizer was installed in the Port of Los Angeles, it became one of the solutions to the problem of cleaning up America's landscapes. With the installation of the Prolerizer, old automobile hulks were no longer littering the roadsides. Today the shredder is commonplace throughout the world; 220 exist in the United States alone.

The original Prolerizer was updated and automated in 1985 so that it alone can service almost all the automobiles that are abandoned and dismantled in California. The production capability of the updated Prolerizer, utilizing solid-state controls and high-speed feed, is now at 2,500 cars per day.

Prior to 1962, scrap had been loaded aboard ships with cranes and magnets. Through mechanization and modernization, Hugo Neu-Proler designed and built the apron conveyor for bulk loading the scrap onto ships. Updated with solid-state computer controls, the bulk loader now is able to load in excess of 12,000 tons of scrap per day. The scrap, which was once stowed under the decks of ships and pulled under by hand to utilize space, is now automatically conveyed and shot into spaces underneath decks or tanks.

In 1986 a 2,000-ton shear will be installed, capable of increasing the firm's scrap-handling capability an additional 1,000 tons per 24-hour day. Today the company's facility at Terminal Island stands as the largest scrap exporter on the West Coast, and probably the world.

Old hulks, which were once a problem for this country, are recycled to aid in the balance of payments. The steel mills of the world are now able to utilize the waste products of California consumers. Southern California dumps, in turn, have more space because material that was once thrown away is recycled.

By 1986 Hugo Neu-Proler Co. had become the funnel for a majority portion of the recycled steel scrap generated in Southern California. This represents approximately 10 percent of the United States' scrap exports.

Aerial photograph of Hugo Neu-Proler Co., the West Coast's largest scrap export facility.

WRATHER PORT PROPERTIES, LTD.

The Queen Mary *arrived at the Port of Long Beach in 1967 and was opened to the public in 1971. Since then it has become a California landmark.*

Adjacent to the Queen Mary *is the world's largest airplane, Howard Hughes' 200-ton* Spruce Goose.

Who would expect to find a multifaceted entertainment complex nestled in a corner of one of the world's busiest ports? Consisting of the Hotel Queen Mary, the *Queen Mary* and *Spruce Goose* attractions, extensive meeting facilities and a multitude of shopping and dining opportunities, Wrather Port Properties, Ltd., is an internationally renowned entertainment destination.

Since her arrival at the Port of Long Beach in 1967, the *Queen Mary* has stood as one of Southern California's most popular landmarks. First opened to the public in 1971, millions of visitors have taken the opportunity to relive the elegance and luxury of the *Queen Mary*'s sailing days.

Wrather Corporation, which also owns the Disneyland Hotel, took over the management of the *Queen Mary* in 1980. After a $20-million renovation program in 1981, the *Queen Mary* once again sparkles as the pride of British shipbuilding.

Today at the *Queen Mary* attraction specially designed exhibits feature replicas of original staterooms, crew's quarters, the children's playroom, and the first-class Drawing Room. Special engine room and wheelhouse displays actually allow visitors to experience what might have occurred aboard ship during a near-collision at sea. Other exciting highlights include one of the ship's giant propellers, the anchor and whistle, the emergency steering station, and lifeboat and nautical demonstrations.

Adjacent to the *Queen Mary,* housed in the world's largest clear-span aluminum dome, sits Howard Hughes' 200-ton *Spruce Goose.* The legendary *Spruce Goose* is the world's largest and most controversial plane.

The gargantuan flying boat was originally designed to transport World War II troops across the Atlantic safely above menacing enemy U-Boats. Hughes labored five years over the plane, fighting Senate criticism of his "folly," nicknamed the *Spruce Goose.* The mammoth airplane took its solitary flight above the choppy Long Beach Harbor waters on November 2, 1947.

Today a special viewing platform built adjacent to the plane allows visitors to view the seaplane's entire flight deck, cockpit, and huge cargo hold. Surrounding the plane are a variety of unique display modules which show close-up details of fascinating areas of the plane and audio-visual presentations of the *Spruce Goose's* construction, its one-and-only flight, plus Hughes' aviation and movie careers.

Another highlight of Wrather Port Properties, the Hotel Queen Mary, offers the romance and excitement of an ocean cruise without ever leaving port. Refurbished to its original splendor, every aspect of the ship allows guests to "relive" the personalized hospitality of the *Queen Mary's* 1,001 transatlantic voyages.

The 390 unique staterooms are the largest ever built for a ship and feature all the amenities of a first-class hotel. Wood-paneled walls, porthole windows, and nostalgic furnishings preserve the quality traditions established by the *Queen Mary* on her 1936 maiden voyage.

Wrather Port Properties, Ltd., also offers a variety of dining experiences and a multitude of shopping opportunities. Additionally, the Hotel Queen Mary features meeting rooms accommodating from 10 to 1,200 guests plus extensive catering facilities.

The future holds great excitement for Wrather Port Properties. A bevy of new developments are scheduled over the next twenty years, the first of which includes a new hotel to be built adjacent to the Hotel Queen Mary. Other plans include an extensive merchandise and entertainment center, office buildings, restaurants, and exhibit area.

MIDWAY FISHING TOOL COMPANY

The petroleum-rich oil fields of western Kern County near Bakersfield, California, can ofttimes frustrate even the most patient drilling operator who relentlessly challenges the stifling summer heat and the chilling winter fog in the quest to discover and produce greater quantities of oil.

As if the rugged hilly terrain and harsh elements of nature weren't enough to contend with, the task of drilling for oil is further compounded when underground formations and conditions bring about drilling system breakdowns.

On a day in 1909 representatives of the Standard Oil Company found themselves faced with a serious drilling system breakdown and were concerned over the delays and cost caused by a damaged drilling string. The technology and tooling necessary to solve problems of this kind were not readily available to the oil men. However, their desire to overcome production delays sent the Standard Oil representatives in search of a solution to their problem.

Several miles away in the area known as Midway, halfway between the towns of McKittrick and Sunset (now Maricopa), Elmore D. Jones operated his blacksmith shop. It was to this shop the Standard Oil representatives came and asked Jones to design a tool that would help them "fish" out the damaged drilling string. Jones obliged the oil men, and soon was producing more handmade fishing tools to help them pull the broken strings up to the surface. From this incident, Midway Fishing Tool Company was launched. Today the heart of the firm's business is still the fishing tool rental operation, but the company has also grown into an international supplier and designer of a myriad of petroleum tools and equipment.

Elmore D. Jones founded Midway Fishing Tool Company in 1909 along with J.W. Squires and B.N. Youngken. He served as president from 1917 until his death in 1956 at which time his son, E. Delwin Jones, took over the post.

After the 1909 incident Jones joined with J.W. Squires, a local oil lessor, and B.N. Youngken to form a partnership to continue servicing the growing needs of the oil industry in the area. The following year the firm was formally incorporated with Squires as president, Youngken as vice-president, and Jones as secretary. By 1917 Jones had bought out Squires' stock and assumed the helm of the company as its president.

As the years progressed Jones saw his business continue to prosper, and in 1922 the first of Midway's branch offices opened in Brea, California. That office was subsequently moved to Long Beach in 1925 and soon became the company's headquarters. As the oil industry continued to boom in California, more branch offices made their appearance. They included Bakersfield in 1935, Ventura in 1951, and subsequent shops in Woodland; Santa Rosa; Santa Maria; Brawley; Coalinga; Roosevelt, Utah; and Ely, Nevada. The corporate headquarters was moved to

A bull wheel, used in the early days of oil drilling and a reminder to passersby of a bygone era, greets visitors to the corporate headquarters in Long Beach.

Roseville, California (twenty miles east of the California state capitol in Sacramento), in 1986 to ensure a more central location to encompass all of its locations.

By the 1960s it became apparent that, in some ways, Midway could best serve its customers by assuring a constant supply of parts and equipment. To this end, the Superior Tool Company of Santa Fe Springs was acquired in 1966. Seven years later the California rental tool division of the Baash-Ross Company was purchased and integrated into Midway's existing tool operations. Superior Tool continues to produce a variety of equipment for the oil industry including pumps, crankshafts, and manifolds.

While maintaining a respected reputation for providing tools and equipment to the industry, Midway has also developed into an important contributor in the design and manufacture of tools. The Bakersfield facility houses a large computerized manufacturing operation that produces a wide variety of equipment and oil tools. Midway also has been a leader in the development of a fully unitized wellhead for offshore applications. This line includes all conventional wellheads that are adaptable to various electric submersible pumps. These electrical wellheads are utilized in enhanced recovery projects and are perfect complements to the oil and geothermal wellheads that Midway manufactures and has put into operation in the United States, Indonesia, and Central America.

Electric wellheads were developed because of a crisis that the oil industry faced a number of years ago. As natural gas and water pressure in the fields began to decline, a new method was needed to extract the remaining underground oil. The use of a submersible electric pump that could generate enough pressure to deliver the oil to the surface was decided upon as the best method to enhance the recovery of oil in the older fields. These pumps are now widely used throughout the industry, and Midway is proud to have been a leader in their development.

Robert P. Jones, chairman of the board and son of the company founder, served as president from 1966 to 1984.

Since the days of Elmore Jones, Midway has remained under the guidance of the Jones family. Del Jones succeeded his father as president, and following his retirement, brother Robert continued the family tradition as chairman of the board. In 1984 Elmore's granddaughter, F. Desta Jones, was named president and chief executive officer of the company.

After more than seventy-five years of service to the oil industry, Midway Fishing Tool Company has also exhibited a peculiar tenacity and innovative spirit that characterizes the oil industry. As the firm looks to an increasing international presence through additional branch offices, it is certain to continue as a leader in the oil tool and energy equipment industries.

A view of Midway's corporate headquarters in Long Beach with (inset) an artist's rendering of Midway's first office in Taft, California, in 1910. Although the original clapboard structure no longer remains, Midway still has an active office and shop in Taft. Illustration by M. Crook

LILLICK McHOSE & CHARLES

Ira S. Lillick, one of the earliest Stanford University graduates, began practicing law in San Francisco in 1897. He became internationally known in admiralty or maritime law, representing ship owners and agents, underwriters, and other maritime clients. He employed young lawyers, and in 1928 the firm, now known as Lillick McHose & Charles, was formed. Legal work involving ship operations developed in Southern California, and, as a result, in 1929 a Los Angeles office was opened.

The firm has also expanded elsewhere and now has an office in Washington, D.C., largely to handle maritime regulatory work with the Maritime Administration and Maritime Commission. In addition, the firm has opened California offices in San Diego and Sacramento.

Prior to World War II the Los Angeles practice was primarily concerned with maritime law, radio, and later television. During the past forty years the practice has expanded greatly, and the firm is now active in banking, business organizations, general litigation, real estate, creditor's rights, labor, products liability, taxes, trusts, and estates.

Law of the sea continues to be important, and Lillick lawyers in Southern California have been active in the ports of Los Angeles and Long Beach as well as San Diego. Problems involve the construction and operation of ships and watercraft of all kinds. Many major maritime cases arising in Southern California have been handled including explosions such as the *Sansinena;* collisions like the *Chicago/Silverpalm* and *Catalina/Arbutus;* allisions such as the *President Van Buren* and *W.S. Miller;* and fires including the loss of the *Sandanger.* Maritime legal work also involves a variety of injury and death cases involving seamen, longshoremen, passengers, divers, and other "casualties of th sea."

John C. McHose opened the Lillick Los Angeles office in 1929. He is a past president of the Maritime Law Association of the United States and the Propeller Club, Port of Los Angeles/Long Beach, and a titular member of the Comite Maritime Internationale. During World War II he served as assistant regional director and legal representative for the United States War Shipping Administration for the South and Southwest Pacific areas.

The firm has served as counsel in maritime cases occurring in various parts of the world such as the *Torrey Canyon* stranding in Southwest England, the *Esso Seattle/Guam Bear* collision in Guam, the *Glomar III* incident in Australia, and the loss of the yacht *Goodwill* with all aboard off Baja, California.

Lillick attorneys are active in various maritime organizations including the Propeller Club, the Maritime Law Association of the United States (MLA), and the Comite Maritime Internationale (CMI). Two partners have been president of the MLA and titular members of the CMI, the international association of some forty-one maritime countries which, since 1896, has drafted and sponsored many international conventions that have helped to establish worldwide uniformity in maritime law.

PATRONS

The following individuals, companies, and organizations have made a valuable commitment to the quality of this publication. Windsor Publications and the Marine Exchange of Los Angeles/Long Beach gratefully acknowledge their participation in *Long Beach and Los Angeles: A Tale of Two Ports.*

ARCO Transportation Company*
Bank of San Pedro
Budget Steamship Agencies, Inc.
California Cotton Fumigating Company*
California Shipping Lines
California United Terminals
Carmichael International Service
Connolly Pacific
ContainerFreight Corporation*
J.M. Costello Supply Company, Inc.*
Daily Commercial News*
Eaton Tugboat Company
Ernst & Whinney-Long Beach
Evergreen Marine Corp.
General Telephone*
Graham & James/Long Beach*
Harbor Ship Supply*
Harbor Weighers Inc.
Hugo Neu-Proler Co.*
Robert W. Hunt, M.D.
International Transportation Service*
Jacobsen Pilot Service, Inc.
The Jankovich Companies*
Jones Industrial Hardware Co.
Julian Ship Supplies
Kai R. Kuhl Company, Inc.
Al Larson Boat Shop*
Lillick McHose & Charles*
Long Beach Container Terminal, Inc. (LBCTI)*
McCutchen, Black, Verleger & Shea
Metropolitan Stevedore Company*
Midway Fishing Tool Company*
Kenneth and Elisabeth Norquist
Office Systems of California, Inc.
The Pasha Group
Port of Long Beach*
Southwest Marine*
Starboard Group, Inc.
Stevedoring Services of America
Sunkist Growers, Inc.*
THUMS*
Travel and Trade Career Institute
TRW Information Systems Group*
Unitor Ships Service Inc.
Unocal*
Westcoast Shipping Company
Williams, Dimond & Co.
Worldport LA
Wrather Port Properties, Ltd.*
Yamamoto Bros., Inc./Ship Chandlers*

*Partners in Progress of *Long Beach and Los Angeles: A Tale of Two Ports.* The histories of these companies and organizations appear in Chapter XI, beginning on page 162.

BIBLIOGRAPHY

Berner, Loretta. *Rancho Los Cerritos.* Ramona, CA: Acoma Books, 1975.

Bowman, Lynn. *Los Angeles: Epic of a City.* Berkeley, CA: Howell-North Books, 1974.

Case, Walter H. *History of Long Beach.* Long Beach: The Press Telegram Publishing Co., 1935.

Dana, Richard Henry. *Two Years Before the Mast.* New York: Harper & Bros., 1840.

Dumke, Glenn S. *The Boom of the Eighties in Southern California.* San Marino, CA: Huntington Library, 1944.

Epley, Malcolm. *Long Beach's 75 Years; Highlights and Anecdotes.* Long Beach, CA: Long Beach Diamond Jubilee, 1963.

Fink, Augusta. *Time and the Terraced Land.* Berkeley, CA: Howell-North Books, 1966.

Gleason, Duncan. *The Islands and Ports of California.* New York: Devin-Adair Co., 1958.

Graves, Jackson Alpheus. *My Seventy Years in California.* Los Angeles: Times-Mirror Co., 1929.

Hager, Anna Marie and Everett G. Hager. *San Pedro Harbor Highlights.* Glendale, CA: La Siesta Press, 1968.

Hillinger, Charles. *The California Islands.* Los Angeles, CA: Academy Publishers, 1958.

Historical Society of Long Beach. *The Pike on the Silverstand.* Edited by Loretta Berner. Long Beach, CA: Historical Society, 1982.

Krythe, Mamie. *Port Admiral: Phineas Banning, 1830-1885.* Menlo Park, CA: Lane Book Co., 1957.

Ludwig, Ella A. *A History of the Harbor District of Los Angeles.* Los Angeles: L.A. Historic Record Co. Inc., 1927.

McWilliams, Carey. *Southern California Country.* New York: Duell, Sloan and Pearce, 1946.

Marquez, Ernest. *Port of Los Angeles: A Phenomenon of the Railroad Era.* San Marino, CA: Golden West Books, 1975.

Matson, Clarence H. *Port of Los Angeles.* Los Angeles: Los Angeles Chamber of Commerce, 1914.

______________. *Building a World Gateway.* Los Angeles: Los Angeles Chamber of Commerce, 1945.

Meyer, Larry L. and Patricia L. Kalayjian. *Fortune's Harbor.* Tulsa: Continental Heritage Press, 1983.

Miller, Ray. *History and Growth of Port of Long Beach.* Long Beach, CA: Long Beach Harbor Department, 1940.

Nadeau, Remi. *Los Angeles: From Mission to Modern City.* London and New York: Longmans, Green & Co., 1960.

Port Admiral Society. *Miracle of a Muddy Tide Flat.* Los Angeles, 1980.

Queenan, Charles F. *The Port of Los Angeles: From Wilderness to World Port.* Los Angeles: Los Angeles Harbor Department, 1983.

Smith, J. Spencer and Paul A. Amundsen. *Ports of the Americas.* New York: American Association of Port Authorities, 1961.

Smith, Sarah Bixby. *Adobe Days.* Fresno, CA: Valley Publishers, 1974.

Talbert, T.B. *Sixty Years in California: Memoirs of Pioneer Days of Long Beach and Huntington Beach.* Huntington Beach, CA: Huntington Beach News, 1952.

Thompson, Thomas H. and Augustus West. *History of Los Angeles County, California.* Oakland, CA: Thompson & West, 1880. Republished in Berkeley, CA: Howell & North, 1959.

United States Army Corps of Engineers Los Angeles-Long Beach Areas Cultural Resource Survey. Washington, D.C. Printing Office, 1978.

Weaver, John D. *Los Angeles: The Enormous Village, 1781-1981.* Santa Barbara, CA: Capra Press, 1980.

Willard, Charles Dwight. *The Free Harbor Contest at Los Angeles.* Los Angeles: Kingsley-Barnes & Neuner Co., 1899.

Other Sources

Historical Society of Long Beach

Historical Society of San Pedro

Interviews with Raymond F. Berbower

John E. Marriner Address to Propeller Club (February 27, 1959)

Long Beach Harbor Department Annual Reports

Long Beach Harbor Department publications

Long Beach *Independent*

Long Beach Library

Long Beach *Press-Telegram*

Long Beach *Sun*

Los Angeles Chamber of Commerce publications

Los Angeles City Archives

Los Angeles County Archives

Los Angeles Harbor Department Annual Reports

Los Angeles Harbor Department publications

Los Angeles Municipal Directory (1922)

Los Angeles Times

Oliver Vickery columns, San Pedro *News-Pilot*

Panama Canal Record

San Pedro *News-Pilot*

Title Guarantee and Trust Company. San Pedro and Wilmington. Los Angeles, 1937.

William Oleson columns, San Pedro *News-Pilot*

INDEX